Israel

The Inheritance of God

Israel

THE INHERITANCE OF GOD

By Paul R. Wilkinson

ARIEL
MINISTRIES

Israel – The Inheritance of God
(Author: Paul R. Wilkinson)
© 2020 by Ariel Ministries

ISBN: 978-1-951059-71-2
Library of Congress Control Number: 2020921933
REL101000 RELIGION / Theology / Dispensationalism / Jesus / Replacement Theology / Church History

Editor: Christiane K. Jurik
Cover design by Jesse and Josh Gonzales

All rights reserved. No part of this publication may be reproduced, distributed, or transmitted in any form or by any means, including photocopying, recording, or other electronic or mechanical methods, without the prior written permission of the publisher, except in the case of brief quotations embodied in critical reviews and certain other noncommercial uses permitted by copyright law. For permission requests, write to the publisher at the address below.

Unless otherwise noted, all Scripture quotations are from the English Standard Version (ESV). However, the personal pronouns referring to the Triune God have been capitalized in order to distinguish them from those referring to mankind.

Printed in the United States of America

Published by Ariel Ministries
P.O. Box 792507
San Antonio, TX 78279-2507
www.ariel.org

Dedication

I dedicate this book to
"the God and Father of our Lord Jesus the Messiah,
the Father of mercies and God of all comfort,
who comforts us in all our affliction" (2 Cor. 1:3-4)
and who will yet comfort His beloved Israel.

Endorsements

Those of us who are Jewish believers in Messiah Jesus sometimes experience "pushback" from other evangelicals when we point out the continuing role of the people of Israel in Bible prophecy. We are told things like "Your statement is self-serving" or "You are biased." Yet for the honest, careful student of Scripture, there is no other conclusion than to recognize the fact that the God of creation has entered into a special relationship with the people of Israel, not because we are better than anyone else, but rather to demonstrate His faithfulness. As a Gentile believer, Paul Wilkinson simply takes that honest view of God's Word and has shared with us a masterful study on such a central topic of Scripture. Very encouraging and refreshing!

Mottel Baleston
Messianic Jewish teacher, Messengers Messianic Outreach, New Jersey.

~

Paul Wilkinson's newest book, *Israel: The Inheritance of God*, is saturated with scriptural support and his contextual explanation of how these passages lay out God's stated biblical plan for His elect nation, Israel. While traversing from Genesis to Revelation, Wilkinson masterfully lays out and expounds upon God's plan for the world and how it is being implemented through Israel, His chosen nation. This book focuses on God! Wilkinson provides the divine perspective on God's plan for history and the fact that Israel, along with the church, is at the center of the outworking of His purpose for history. In the outworking of His plan, God's loyal love is put on display by His purpose for and treatment of Israel.

This book sheds welcome light on one of the most important topics in the Bible: God's dealings with His chosen people Israel. For too long, many within the church have improperly merged Israel and the church. Unless one spiritualizes future Israel, there is no way around the fact that the modern state of Israel has to exist in order for hundreds of prophecies to be fulfilled in the future, as noted throughout Wilkinson's book. *Israel: The Inheritance of God* helps to restore Israel's role in biblical history and also brings into focus her immense role in the future. God's millennial kingdom will be brought in by a believing remnant.

Wilkinson has written a book that is thorough and scholarly yet also devotional in tone. This is a work that will be satisfying to both scholars and interested laymen since it rightly divides the Word of God and interacts with issues relating to Israel in our day. I could not recommend this book more highly.

Dr. Thomas Ice
Professor of Bible & Theology, Calvary University, Kansas City, Missouri; Executive Director, Pre-Trib Research Center, Kansas City, Missouri

~

Rarely do editors endorse a book they have worked on—and maybe rightly so! There is a bit of a danger that they might approach the review with a bias. However, *Israel: The Inheritance of God* is worthy of an exception. This book has made me fall in love with my God to an extent that surprised me. The depth of the author's passion for the Word is palpable on every page. Without falling into the "trap" of sentimentality, Wilkinson was able to "do the splits" between making scholarly and devotional points unlike any other author I have had the pleasure to work with.

The author's love for the God of Israel permeates every page and touches the deepest layers of the heart. His writing style can best be described as a battle cry. Editing this book energized my walk with the Lord and brought to memory personal convictions that had gotten somewhat muddied by life's trials. The preciseness of Paul's exegesis reminded me of Dr. Fruchtenbaum's approach to teaching the Scriptures. It is a preciseness that resonates with my soul.

Christiane K. Jurik, M.A.
Editor-in-Chief, Ariel Ministries

Contents

List of Abbreviations	xiii
Foreword	xv
Introduction	1
Occupied with Israel	2
The Creator Inherits	4
Why Should We Care?	7
Chapter 1: *Nachalah*	9
Tribal Inheritance	14
Brought Out, Brought In	17
A Valuable Inheritance	20
A Treasured People	22
Conclusion	23
Chapter 2: The Irrevocable Blessing, Part 1	25
Blessed Beginnings	26
A Tale of Two Brothers	27
A Divine Eulogy	29
A State of Blessing	31
The Divine Right to Curse	34
Fickle Man, Faithful God	39
What God Has Done	41
Irrevocable Blessing, Irreversible Decree	44
Conclusion	45
Chapter 3: The Irrevocable Blessing, Part 2	47
In Satan's Service	49
What a Question!	50
Back to Balak	53
A Star out of Jacob, a Scepter out of Israel	56
The *Aaronic* Blessing?	58
The Blessed One	60
Conclusion	62

Chapter 4: For His Name's Sake — 65

In the Sight of the Nations — 66
The Prophetic Panorama — 68
Introducing God — 70
Resurrection — 75
God's ZIP Code — 78
Conclusion — 79

Chapter 5: The Loyal Love of the Lord — 83

The Loyalty of God — 84
The Superabundance of God's Mercy — 86
A Bridge into the New Covenant — 89
The Loyal Love of the Church? — 89
God is our *Chesed* — 92
Israel's Future Secured — 94
Conclusion — 96

Chapter 6: "How long, O Lord?" — 99

Commissioning the Prophet — 100
The Pastoral Prophet — 101
A Good and Godly Question — 104
The Prophetic Eye — 106
He Was Pierced! — 108
Conclusion — 110

Chapter 7: When No One Else Cares — 113

The Lord Is Israel's Shepherd — 113
A Peculiar "Prophet" — 115
A People Sought Out — 118
The Good Shepherd — 124
Conclusion — 126

Chapter 8: Pleading Israel's Cause — 129

The Heart of the Matter — 130
Ministers of the Altar — 133
The Advocate of Advocates — 138
A Remnant Will Be Saved — 140
Foreknown, but not Predestined — 141
Conclusion — 145

Chapter 9: The Golden Gateway of God — 147

Parables and Prodigals — 147
A Word of Consolation — 149
The Movement of God's Heart — 150
Forerunner of the Messiah — 152
The Unchanging God — 154
The Golden Gate — 156
Conclusion — 161

Chapter 10: Comfort God's People! — 165

A Human Touch from Heaven — 166
Miserable Comforters — 167
A Priestly Responsibility — 169
Waiting for Consolation — 172
Comforting the Mourners — 174
The Paraclete — 176
Hallmark of the Messiah — 177
Conclusion — 181

Chapter 11: Speak to the Heart — 185

The Heart of the Matter — 185
Balm, not Blame — 187
God's Workmanship — 188
The Whole Truth, and Nothing but the Truth, to Israel! — 192
For Zion's Sake — 193
A Vow of Non-Silence . . . and Praise — 198
Conclusion — 201

Chapter 12: Jealous for Zion — 205

Revelation at Sinai — 205
Burning with Jealousy — 208
Great is Thy Faithfulness — 212
Idolatrous and Adulterous Israel — 213
A Cup of Fury . . . and of Comfort — 216
The Brokenness of God — 217
God's Honor Killing — 221
The Jealousy of Jesus — 222
Conclusion — 225

Chapter 13: The King of Israel — 229

- God is King! — 230
- The King is Coming! — 232
- Palm Sunday — 234
- The King Is Crucified! — 236
- Who Killed Jesus? — 239
- "Thy Kingdom Come!" — 243
- One King, Two Thrones — 244
- Conclusion — 247

Conclusion — 251

Bibliography — 257

List of Abbreviations

General Abbreviations

c.	circa
cf.	confer, compare
d.	died
e.g.	for example
etc.	and so on
LXX	Septuagint
NT	New Testament
OT	Old Testament
p., pp.	page(s)
v., vv.	verse(s)
vs.	versus

Bible Translations

ASV	American Standard Version
DBY	John Nelson Darby's New Testament ("The Darby Bible")
ESV	English Standard Version
KJV	King James Version
LXX	Septuagint
NASB	New American Standard Bible
NET	New English Translation
NIV	New International Version
NKJV	New King James Version
NLT	New Living Translation
RSV	Revised Standard Version
YLT	Robert Young's Literal Translation

Books of the Bible

Gen.	Genesis
Ex.	Exodus
Lev.	Leviticus
Num.	Numbers
Deut.	Deuteronomy
Josh.	Joshua
Judg.	Judges
Ruth	Ruth
1 Sam.	1 Samuel
2 Sam.	2 Samuel
1 Kgs.	1 Kings
2 Kgs.	2 Kings
1 Chron.	1 Chronicles
2 Chron.	2 Chronicles
Ezra	Ezra
Neh.	Nehemiah
Est.	Esther

Job	Job	Jn.	John
Ps.	Psalms	Acts	Acts
Prov.	Proverbs	Rom.	Romans
Eccles.	Ecclesiastes	1 Cor.	1 Corinthians
Song	Song of Solomon	2 Cor.	2 Corinthians
Isa.	Isaiah	Gal.	Galatians
Jer.	Jeremiah	Eph.	Ephesians
Lam.	Lamentations	Phil.	Philippians
Ezek.	Ezekiel	Col.	Colossians
Dan.	Daniel	1 Thess.	1 Thessalonians
Hos.	Hosea	2 Thess.	2 Thessalonians
Joel	Joel	1 Tim.	1 Timothy
Am.	Amos	2 Tim.	2 Timothy
Obad.	Obadiah	Titus	Titus
Jonah	Jonah	Philem.	Philemon
Mic.	Micah	Heb.	Hebrews
Nah.	Nahum	James	James
Hab.	Habakkuk	1 Pet.	1 Peter
Zeph.	Zephaniah	2 Pet.	2 Peter
Hag.	Haggai	1 Jn.	1 John
Zech.	Zechariah	2 Jn.	2 John
Mal.	Malachi	3 Jn.	3 John
Mt.	Matthew	Jude	Jude
Mk.	Mark	Rev.	Revelation
Lk.	Luke		

Foreword

In 2019, Ariel Ministries published *Israel Betrayed*, a book series that addresses the history of replacement theology and the rise of Christian Palestinianism. The two volumes of this series were written by Andrew Robinson and Paul Wilkinson. I was sure that we had covered all that I felt strongly about in regard to replacement theology. Then we received another manuscript by Dr. Wilkinson, one he titled *Israel: The Inheritance of God*. As soon as I started reading it, I realized that the author was able to shed light on an aspect of biblical Israelology that the previous books had only touched upon: the reasons behind God's choice of Israel as His people.

When studying these reasons, one has to dig deep into the Scriptures. The picture that emerges is that of a God whose connection to Israel is unbroken because of His own nature and character. Since He put His name on Israel and thus made the people His possession, He must fulfill the promises He made to Israel. The focus shifts from Israel to the God of Israel, and the reader cannot help but walk away with a deeper adoration for this God.

Ariel Ministries is devoted to discipling Jewish and Gentile believers alike. *Israel: The Inheritance of God* is a powerful tool to fulfill this goal of ours, which is why we decided to publish it. Our hope is that every believer who reads this book will find himself or herself more aware of the completeness of God's love (Eph. 3:17-19). We also hope that this awareness will lead to an understanding of the believer's responsibility to carry God's consolation to Israel "in their hearts, convey it with their lips, and confirm it through their actions."

Dr. Arnold G. Fruchtenbaum
October 2020, San Antonio, Texas

Introduction

> I am persuaded that God never revealed anything without a sanctifying purpose; for His nature is holy, His purpose holiness; and I believe the sober and holy study of the Word of God . . . will concentrate the affections upon Him . . . and give enlarged views of His kingdom, wisdom, and glory, peculiarly calculated to sink in our estimation this world . . . and to fix our minds on the Lamb's glory.[1]

These words were penned in 1829 by a young Anglo-Irish clergyman who was just beginning to publish his studies on Bible prophecy. His name was John Nelson Darby (1800-1882), the principal founder of the Plymouth Brethren. What Darby had to say about the national restoration of Israel, the imminent rapture of the church, and the second coming of Jesus continues to inspire many Christians around the world. It has been said of his writings that "they form a mine of wealth, only it is he who digs deepest who obtains most of its riches."[2] High praise indeed, but this book is not about John Nelson Darby,[3] a mere man who devoted his own life to digging deep into the wealthiest mine of all—the Bible. It is about the one, true, living God of Abraham, Isaac, and Jacob, who moved other men at divinely-appointed times in history to proclaim a message that will endure longer than that of any man or movement.

In particular, this book seeks to address the reason why God inspired the human authors of the Bible to write what they did about "Israel," a

---

[1] John Nelson Darby, "Reflections upon the Prophetic Inquiry and the Views advanced in it (1829)," in *The Collected Writings of J. N. Darby*, ed. William Kelly, Vol. 2 (Kingston-on-Thames, London: Stow Hill Bible & Tract Depot, n.d.), p. 3.

[2] *Pilgrim Portions: Meditations for the Day of Rest, Selected from the Writings, Hymns, Letters, etc., of J.N.D.* (London: G. Morrish, n.d.), preface.

[3] See Paul R. Wilkinson, *For Zion's Sake: Christian Zionism and the Role of John Nelson Darby* (Milton Keynes, UK: Paternoster, 2007), which is an edited version of my doctoral thesis. The book was later republished under the new title *Understanding Christian Zionism: Israel's Place in the Purposes of God*, ed. Andrew D. Robinson (Bend, OR: Berean Call, 2013).

name that occurs 2,569 times in the English Standard Version (ESV). I believe this is especially important at a time when a disturbing number of Christians are precariously misguided about the modern State of Israel. Even within the true church, many believers are either indifferent to Bible prophecy, confused by the range of interpretations, or led astray by those who distort the Word of God. There are even those who mistranslate the Scriptures to suit their own political and theological agendas. A case in point is the Danish Bible Society, which has published *The Contemporary Danish Bible 2020*. This translation omits all but one of the references to Israel in the New Testament "to avoid confusing the Land of Israel with the State of Israel."[4] Shame on them!

Occupied with Israel

The Bible is clear: *Every* believer is called by God to "work out [their] own salvation with fear and trembling" (Phil. 2:12), and to "contend for the faith that was once for all delivered to the saints" (Jude 3). But without a biblical understanding of the Jewish roots of the Christian faith, any such endeavor will be deficient! As the Lord Jesus declared, "salvation is of the Jews" (Jn. 4:22, KJV). The starting point, therefore, has to be a full recognition of the Jewish identity of Yeshua/Jesus, "the pioneer and perfecter of our faith" (Heb. 12:2). Without this, a believer's growth "in the grace and knowledge of our Lord and Savior Jesus the Messiah" (2 Pet. 3:18) will be severely stunted and his or her personal witness greatly hindered.

Likewise, *every* believer is called by God to study His Word and "live according to Scripture" (1 Cor. 4:6, RSV). Integral to the Bible is the history (both past and prophetic future) of God's relationship with Israel. Remove or reinterpret the meaning of "Israel," and the Bible either falls apart or is rendered incomprehensible. Over time, believers may become further oc-

---

[4] Cnaan Liphshiz, "Danish Bible Society's translation omits dozens of references to Israel," *Times of Israel*, April 21, 2020, www.timesofisrael.com.

cupied with Israel by engaging in the multifaceted and often deeply disturbing study of church history as it relates to the Jewish people.[5] Others may focus on the momentous events that preceded the establishment of the modern State of Israel in 1948, such as the gathering of the Allied Supreme Council in San Remo, Italy, in 1920, when the Balfour Declaration was made "a binding [and irrevocable] act of international law."[6] Others, myself included, may be concerned with the hydra-headed movement I have previously labeled "Christian Palestinianism,"[7] which vehemently opposes the Jewish State and all who stand with Israel. Still others may be involved in political advocacy on Israel's behalf or in providing economic support to Jewish believers in the land. Whatever believers may individually devote their time, energy, and resources to, the church as a whole has been commissioned to proclaim the gospel "to the Jew first" (Rom. 1:16) and to bear faithful witness to God's Son and Israel's King (Acts 1:8; 2 Cor. 5:20).

All this was anything but clear to me in February 1990, when I was born again on the campus of York University in the north of England. That night, as I sat in a special meeting arranged by the Christian Union, I believed everything the preacher said about Jesus and the way of salvation. I had believed in God from an early age, largely thanks to my late grandfather's witness, but there was no reality of God in my life. As I sat in my seat that night hearing what Jesus had accomplished through His life, death, and resurrection, I was convicted of my sin and my need of the Savior. Though my understanding was limited, I at least recognized the problem, acknowledged the solution, and knew what I had to do to be saved. By repenting of my sin and confessing Jesus to be my Lord, God, and Savior, I

---

[5] Including my late pastor, Andrew Robinson (1951-2016), author of *Israel Betrayed, Volume 1: The History of Replacement Theology* (San Antonio, TX: Ariel Ministries, 2018).

[6] Howard Grief, *The Legal Foundation and Borders of Israel under International Law: A Treatise on Jewish Sovereignty over the Land of Israel* (Jerusalem: Mazo, 2013), 18, 34.

[7] Paul R. Wilkinson, *Israel Betrayed, Volume 2: The Rise of Christian Palestinianism* (San Antonio, TX: Ariel Ministries, 2018).

was born again and became a child of God that instant.[8] However, my *relationship* with Jesus was only just beginning.

Did I fully comprehend in that life-changing moment *who* my Savior was and *why* He had died in my place? I knew enough to be saved, enough to become a believer, but not enough to be a faithful disciple and ambassador of God's Son. I can look back and say, with regret, that it took several years before I acquired a proper understanding of the Jewishness of Jesus and the place of Israel in the purposes of God. This deficiency was due, in large measure, to the churches I attended and their adherence to some form of replacement theology. By God's grace, my understanding developed over time, and yet thirty years on, I am still left wondering whether I have fully grasped the significance of Israel.

The Creator Inherits

From Genesis to Revelation, the Bible is clear: The universe belongs to God, the Creator of all things. This truth has been under relentless attack ever since Charles Darwin conceived and propagated his blasphemous and utterly preposterous theory of evolution—a theory that has bewitched many in the church. With this in mind, let us consider the following sample of statements upon which the Word of God and the *true* Christian faith stand:

> In the beginning, God created the heavens and the earth. (Gen. 1:1)
>
> Behold, to the LORD your God belong heaven and the heaven of heavens, the earth with all that is in it. (Deut. 10:14; cf. Neh. 9:6)
>
> For the pillars of the earth are the LORD's, and on them He has set the world. (1 Sam. 2:8)
>
> "Whatever is under the whole heaven is mine." (Job 41:11; cf. Ex. 19:5; Ps. 50:10-12; 1 Chron. 29:14)
>
> The earth is the LORD's and the fullness thereof, the world and those who dwell therein. (Ps. 24:1; cf. 50:12, 89:11; Ex. 9:29; 1 Cor. 10:26)

---

[8] See, for example, Jn. 1:12-13; 3:3-16; Rom. 10:9-13; Eph. 1:13-14; 1 Pet. 1:3-5; 1 Jn. 5:1,11-13.

> Of old you laid the foundation of the earth, and the heavens are the work of your hands. (Ps. 102:25; cf. 104:5)
>
> Thus says the LORD: "Heaven is my throne, and the earth is my footstool ... All these things my hand has made, and so all these things came to be," declares the LORD. (Isa. 66:1,2)
>
> Have we not all one Father? Has not one God created us? (Mal. 2:10)
>
> "For in those days there will be such tribulation as has not been from the beginning of the creation that God created until now, and never will be." (Mk. 13:19)
>
> In the beginning was the Word, and the Word was with God, and the Word was God. He was in the beginning with God. All things were made through Him, and without Him was not any thing made that was made. (Jn. 1:1-3)
>
> The God who made the world and everything in it, being Lord of heaven and earth, does not live in temples made by man. (Acts 17:24; cf. 14:15)
>
> Yet for us there is one God, the Father, from whom are all things and for whom we exist, and one Lord, Jesus the Messiah, through whom are all things and through whom we exist. (1 Cor. 8:6)
>
> For by Him [Jesus] all things were created, in heaven and on earth, visible and invisible, whether thrones or dominions or rulers or authorities — all things were created through Him and for Him. (Col. 1:16; cf. Rom. 11:36; 1 Cor. 8:6)
>
> Long ago, at many times and in many ways, God spoke to our fathers by the prophets, but in these last days He has spoken to us by His Son, whom He appointed the heir of all things, through whom also He created the world. (Heb. 1:1,2)
>
> Worthy are you, our Lord and God, to receive glory and honor and power, for you created all things, and by your will they existed and were created. (Rev. 4:11; cf. 10:6, 14:7)

As the Creator, God was entitled to apportion any part of the earth as He determined and for His own praise, purpose, and pleasure. Through the Prophet Jeremiah, He announced: "I give it to whomever it seems right to me" (Jer. 27:5-6). This foundational truth is affirmed in both Testaments:

> When the Most High gave the nations their inheritance, when He separated the sons of man, He set the boundaries of the peoples according to the number of the sons of Israel. (Deut. 32:8, NASB)

> And He made from one man every nation of mankind to live on all the face of the earth, having determined allotted periods and the boundaries of their dwelling place. (Acts 17:26)

Not only did God apportion specific territories to the peoples of the earth, but He also singled out one seemingly insignificant piece of land before claiming it as His own. It was of Canaan that the Creator declared, "The land is mine" (Lev. 25:23).[9] Before we look at why He did this, let us look at the verse in Deuteronomy 32 highlighted above. According to most English Bible translations, the boundaries that God set for the peoples of the earth were fixed according to "the number of the children [or sons] of Israel."[10] Although the meaning of the verse is not entirely clear, it seems that when God apportioned the earth in the beginning, He did so in direct reference to the one nation He had determined to create and set apart for Himself. This is in keeping with what we read elsewhere in Scripture about Israel's centrality in the geopolitical and prophetic purposes of God for this earth. In the book of Ezekiel, for example, we are told that God placed Jerusalem "in the center of the nations, with countries all around her" (Ezek. 5:5), and that the Jews are a people who "dwell at the center of the earth" (Ezek. 38:12). In this way, then, human history was inextricably tied from the very beginning to the land and people that were to become known as "Israel."

For the purpose of this book, the very next verse in Moses' Deuteronomic song is particularly noteworthy: "For the LORD's portion is His people; Jacob is the lot of His inheritance" (32:9, KJV). The Hebrew word translated "portion" is *chêleq* and is used elsewhere in connection with the tribe of Levi. The Levites were to receive no inheritance in Canaan because "God Himself" was to be their portion (Num. 18:20; Deut. 10:9). The word is used in a similar context by the psalmists (Ps. 16:5; 73:26; 119:57; 142:5).

---

[9] See also 2 Chron. 7:20; Jer. 2:7; Ezek. 38:16; Joel 3:2.

[10] So reads the KJV, NKJV, ASV, NASB, DBY, and NIV, which are in accord with the Masoretic Text (MT). The rendering in the Dead Sea Scrolls is "sons of God," which appears in the RSV and ESV. The Greek translation of the Old Testament, known as the Septuagint (LXX), rendered the text "angels of God." In the NET and NLT versions, the boundaries of the peoples are said to have been fixed "according to the number of the heavenly assembly/in His heavenly court" (NET/NLT).

In Deuteronomy 32:9, however, the subject and object are reversed: The people are the portion, and that portion belongs to God. Furthermore, we are told that God allotted "Jacob" (a personal name for the nation of Israel) to be His "inheritance," or as other translations read, His "heritage" or "possession." The Hebrew word is *nachălâh*. What we have here is breathtaking humility on the Creator's part. Without any hint of favoritism, bias, or prejudice, the Most High stooped to honor "the least of all peoples" (Deut. 7:7) by setting them apart to be His earthly inheritance. Why and how God did this will be the focus of the book.

Why Should We Care?

For those who acknowledge Israel's central and enduring place in the purposes of God, it has become almost second nature to speak of the Jewish nation as being God's *elect* or *chosen* people. Israel, in that sense, is theologically and prophetically cut-and-dried for believers who handle the Word of God correctly, but therein lies a danger: overfamiliarity. This is why John Nelson Darby's statement is so important, for to study Israel should not be an end in itself, but a means to concentrate the affections upon God.

Let us recall the following indictment that Messiah Jesus brought against many of the Jewish religious leaders of His day: "You search the Scriptures because you think that in them you have eternal life; and it is they that bear witness about me, yet you refuse to come to me that you may have life" (Jn. 5:39-40). Those He spoke to had knowledge, but they did not know. They had chapter and verse *about* God but no relationship *with* God. Their minds were open to learning, but their hearts were closed to the Teacher. In his book *Prophecy Made Plain*, Cyrus Ingerson Scofield (1843-1921), who is perhaps best known for his *Scofield Reference Bible*, made a telling statement:

> I confess with shame that there was a time in my Christian life when I thought lightly of prophecy; when I said to myself, if not in words, at least in fact, "What has that to do with me? What I wish to know is how I may be saved; how I may get blessings; how I may get to Heaven. Never mind what God intends to do with the Jewish people; never mind what His purposes are

toward the world; He will in due time fulfil all these things. Why should I care particularly what He is going to do with Israel? I'm not an Israelite." I say there was a time when that was my attitude toward the prophecies. Do you not see that I was actually refusing the most intimate fellowship with the Lord?[11]

Scofield warned his fellow prophecy students of the dangers of a lifeless study of God's Word that fails to bring them closer to Jesus. I believe the illustration he used serves both as a timely reminder to every believer who stands with Israel and as a solemn warning to those who care little, if at all, about God's chosen nation:

Suppose that in one of our families a father should say to his son or daughter: "Come with me apart, I wish to tell you what my great plan of life is . . . and I wish to bring you into fellowship with me in these things." And suppose that child should say: "I don't care anything about that; it is not a matter that concerns me; all I care about is to know you in your character of a provider; I like to sit at your table and eat the good things which you have provided, and to know that you will continue to provide me with all the things of which I stand in need. As to these purposes you talk about, I don't care anything about them; they don't concern me." If that child thus shut out all the larger part of the father's mind, the father's purpose, and the father's thought from his life, how formative upon the character of that child could that father be?[12]

---

[11] C. I. Scofield, *Prophecy Made Plain: Addresses on Prophecy* (London: Alfred Holness, n.d.), p. 13.

[12] Ibid., pp. 13-14.

Chapter 1:

Nachalah

So Paul stood up, and motioning with his hand said: "Men of Israel and you who fear God, listen. The God of this people Israel chose our fathers and made the people great during their stay in the land of Egypt, and with uplifted arm He led them out of it. And for about forty years He put up with them in the wilderness. And after destroying seven nations in the land of Canaan, He gave them their land as an inheritance." (Acts 13:16-19)

The above extract is from the Apostle Paul's exhortation to the synagogue at Antioch in Pisidia. Many were convicted that day and were urged by Paul and Barnabas "to continue in the grace of God" (Acts 13:43). I offer the following précis to highlight a great truth that ran through Paul's message and also runs through this book. In the wider context of the above passage (Acts 13:16-32), the apostle declared how God:

1. "Chose" the fathers of Israel
2. "Made great" the people of Israel while they were in Egypt
3. "Led them out" of Egypt
4. "Put up with them" for forty years in the wilderness
5. "After destroying seven nations in the land of Canaan . . . gave them their land as an inheritance"
6. "Gave" judges to Israel
7. "Gave" Saul as king to Israel
8. "Removed" Saul
9. "Raised up David to be their king"
10. "Brought to Israel a Savior, Jesus, as He promised"
11. "Raised Him from the dead"
12. "Fulfilled" what He had promised the patriarchs

I believe the great truth running through Paul's message was this: God *was* the prime mover, He *is* the sovereign overseer, and He will *yet be* the finisher and perfecter of Israel's history.

I doubt if any believer would take issue with eleven of the twelve sovereign acts of God summarized above. I say eleven because number five has been and sadly remains a stumbling block to many. But there is no getting away from the historical record: *God Himself* cleansed Canaan of its indigenous peoples and gave the land they occupied to His people Israel. To take issue with this is to take issue not with Israel but with God and the authority of His Word. In his Antiochian address, Paul merely reaffirmed the consistent testimony of Scripture, that Canaan was dispossessed according to *God's* intention and *God's* implementation. Consider the following:

> "I will give to you and to your offspring after you the land of your sojournings, all the land of Canaan, for an everlasting possession, and I will be their God." (Gen. 17:7-8)

> When the LORD your God brings you into the land that you are entering to take possession of it, and clears away many nations before you . . . and when the LORD your God gives them over to you, and you defeat them, then you must devote them to complete destruction . . . The LORD your God Himself will go over before you. He will destroy these nations before you, so that you shall dispossess them. (Deut. 7:1-2; 31:3)

> Now Joshua was old and advanced in years, and the LORD said to him . . . "I myself will drive them out from before the people of Israel. Only allot the land to Israel for an inheritance [*nachălâh*], as I have commanded you. Now therefore divide this land for an inheritance [*nachălâh*] to the nine tribes and half the tribe of Manasseh." (Josh. 13:1-7)

> And you have seen all that the LORD your God has done to all these nations for your sake, for it is the LORD your God who has fought for you . . . The LORD your God will push them back before you and drive them out of your sight . . . For the LORD has driven out before you great and strong nations . . . One man of you puts to flight a thousand, since it is the LORD your God who fights for you, just as He promised you. (Josh. 23:3-10)

> Whatever the LORD pleases, He does . . . He it was who struck down the firstborn of Egypt . . . who struck down many nations and killed mighty

kings, Sihon, king of the Amorites, and Og, king of Bashan, and all the kingdoms of Canaan, and gave their land as a heritage [*nachălâh*], a heritage [*nachălâh*] to His people Israel. (Ps. 135:6-12)

O God, we have heard with our ears, our fathers have told us, what deeds you performed in their days, in the days of old: you with your own hand drove out the nations, but them [the children of Israel] you planted; you afflicted the peoples, but them you set free; for not by their own sword did they win the land, nor did their own arm save them, but your right hand and your arm, and the light of your face, for you delighted in them. (Ps. 44:1-3)

In his devotional commentary on Psalm 44, the renowned English Baptist pastor and preacher, Charles Haddon Spurgeon (1834-1892), offered the following insight: "Canaan was not conquered without the armies of Israel, but equally true is it that it was not conquered by them; the Lord was the conqueror, and the people were but instruments in his hands."[1] This is critically important in light of the fallacious charges of "occupation" and "land theft" that have been relentlessly leveled against the modern State of Israel. Consider the biblical account of Jephthah, to whom the elders of Gilead turned when the Ammonites attacked Israel. Jephthah sent messengers to the Ammonite king to ask why he was warring against his people. As we read in the book of Judges, "the king of the Ammonites answered the messengers of Jephthah, 'Because Israel on coming up from Egypt took away my land, from the Arnon to the Jabbok and to the Jordan; now therefore restore it peaceably'" (Judg. 11:13). This charge ran contrary to the historical record, as Jephthah made clear in his detailed refutation:

> Israel *did not take away* the land of Moab or the land of the Ammonites, but when they came up from Egypt, Israel went through the wilderness to the Red Sea and came to Kadesh. Israel then sent messengers to the king of Edom, saying, 'Please let us pass through your land,' but the king of Edom *would not listen*. And they sent also to the king of Moab, but he *would not consent* . . . Israel then sent messengers to Sihon king of the Amorites, king of Heshbon, and Israel said to him, 'Please let us pass through your land to our country,' but Sihon *did not trust* Israel to pass through his territory, so Sihon gathered all his people together and encamped at Jahaz and fought with Israel. And *the* LORD, *the God of Israel, gave* Sihon and all his people

---

[1] C. H. Spurgeon, *The Treasury of David, Volume One: Psalm I to LVII* (Peabody, MA: Hendrickson, 2005), p. 300.

into the hand of Israel, and they defeated them. So *Israel took possession* of all the land of the Amorites, who inhabited that country. And *they took possession* of all the territory of the Amorites from the Arnon to the Jabbok and from the wilderness to the Jordan. So then *the LORD, the God of Israel, dispossessed* the Amorites from before His people Israel; and are you to take possession of them? Will you not possess what Chemosh your god gives you to possess? And all that *the LORD our God has dispossessed* before us, we will possess. (Judg. 11:15-24)

The charge that was leveled against Israel by the Ammonites was completely groundless, yet it was used by the king to justify war. The same lying spirit that compelled the Ammonite king to act the way he did has been driving the Palestinian Arabs, the Arab-Muslim world in general, non-Arab countries (e.g., Turkey, Iran, and Russia), the United Nations General Assembly, and many church denominations and NGOs, in their multifaceted "wars" with the Jewish State. But Israel is *not* an occupying power, and Israel did *not* steal land belonging to another people. Israel has only ever sought peace with her Arab neighbors, including the ever-belligerent Palestinian Arabs.[2] In the words of the psalmist, "Too long have I had my dwelling among those who hate peace. I am for peace, but when I speak, they are for war!" (Ps. 120:6-7).[3] I believe the final message that was sent by Jephthah to the Ammonite king—which, had it been heeded, could have averted the "very great slaughter" that subsequently befell the Ammonites—is pertinent to today's conflict:

---

[2] At the time of writing (September 2020), Israel has just signed agreements with two Arab Gulf states, the United Arab Emirates and Bahrain, to normalize diplomatic relations. These "peace agreements" were brokered by U.S. President Donald Trump and his administration. Agreements with other Arab nations may follow. I believe these are simply stage-setting for the Ezekiel 38 war. According to Ezekiel's prophecy, Israel will be attacked by a confederacy of nations while she is "dwelling securely" (Ezek. 38:14). It seems that some of Israel's neighbors will protest against the invasion and the taking of spoil by that confederacy, but will do nothing to help (Ezek. 38:13).

[3] I have dealt with this issue at considerable length in my previous book, *Israel Betrayed, Volume 2: The Rise of Christian Palestinianism* (2018). See also: Paul R. Wilkinson, "What Should We Think About Israel's 'Occupation'?," in *What Should We Think About Israel? Separating Fact from Fiction in the Middle East Conflict*, ed. J. Randall Price (Eugene, OR: Harvest House Publishers, 2019), pp. 123-132.

"I therefore have not sinned against you, and you do me wrong by making war on me. The LORD, the Judge, decide this day between the people of Israel and the people of Ammon" (Judg. 11:27).

Furthermore, Scripture clearly tells us *why* the holy, just, and righteous God of all the earth dispossessed Canaan and settled His people there. As Moses explained to the Israelites before they crossed into Canaan,

> Not because of your righteousness or the uprightness of your heart are you going in to possess their land, but because of the wickedness of these nations the LORD your God is driving them out from before you, and that He may confirm the word that the LORD swore to your fathers, to Abraham, to Isaac, and to Jacob . . . When you come into the land that the LORD your God is giving you, you shall not learn to follow the abominable practices of those nations. There shall not be found among you anyone who burns his son or his daughter as an offering, anyone who practices divination or tells fortunes or interprets omens, or a sorcerer or a charmer or a medium or a necromancer or one who inquires of the dead, for whoever does these things is an abomination to the LORD. And because of these abominations the LORD your God is driving them out before you. (Deut. 9:5, 18:9-12; cf. Lev. 18:24-30)

In this way, then, God gave the land of Canaan to the Israelites as an inheritance (*nachălâh*), but not before something even more profound had taken place. Here is Moses again, addressing God's people before they entered the land of promise:

> But the LORD has taken you and brought you out of the iron furnace, out of Egypt, to be a people of His own inheritance [*nachălâh*], as you are this day. (Deut. 4:20)

> And I prayed to the LORD, "O Lord GOD, do not destroy your people and your heritage [*nachălâh*], whom you have redeemed through your greatness, whom you have brought out of Egypt with a mighty hand . . . For they are your people and your heritage [*nachălâh*], whom you brought out by your great power and by your outstretched arm." (Deut. 9:26-29)

The Hebrew word *nachălâh* is a feminine noun derived from the root verb *nâchal*. According to one definition, it signifies "that which is or may be passed on as an inheritance, that which is one's by virtue of ancient right, and that which is one's permanently."[4] God thus set Israel apart to be His people, His portion, and His personal possession permanently! Centuries later, when the Lord anointed Saul to be Israel's first king and "prince over His heritage [*nachălâh*]" (1 Sam. 10:1), the Prophet Samuel informed the reluctant ruler of the solemn responsibility resting upon his young shoulders:

> Has not the LORD anointed you to be prince over His people Israel? And you shall reign over the people of the LORD and you will save them from the hand of their surrounding enemies. And this shall be the sign to you that the LORD has anointed you to be prince over His heritage [*nachălâh*]. (1 Sam. 10:1)

The concept of *nachălâh* would be brought to the fore again when Solomon, the third king of Israel, dedicated the Temple in Jerusalem. On this occasion, Solomon prayed that if the people were ever banished for their sin but repented in their captivity, then God would forgive them:

> (for they are your people and your inheritance [*nachălâh*], whom you brought out of Egypt, out of the iron furnace) . . . For you separated them from among all the peoples of the earth to be your inheritance [*nachălâh*], as you spoke by your servant Moses, when you brought our fathers out of Egypt, O Lord GOD. (1 Kgs. 8:51-53, NKJV)

Tribal Inheritance

The Scriptures reveal just how important the notion of inheritance was and is to the Jewish people. We read in Genesis about Rachel and Leah lamenting their father Laban's treatment of them and their inheritance. Laban had "devoured" their money (Gen. 31:14-16). The book of Numbers tells us about the five daughters of Zelophehad who appealed to Moses so that they might inherit from the estate of their father, who had died without a son and heir. On this occasion, God instructed Moses to grant their request and issued a statute concerning *nachălâh* (Num. 27:1-11, 36:1-12; Josh. 17:3-6). During the time of the Judges, the issue of inher-

---

[4] *Theological Wordbook of the Old Testament*, ed. R. Laird Harris, Gleason L. Archer, and Bruce K. Waltke (Chicago, IL: Moody Publishers, 1980), p. 569.

itance was integral to the story of Ruth and Boaz, upon which God's redemptive plan for mankind hinged. Before Boaz was free to redeem that which belonged to Naomi's deceased husband Elimelech, he approached a closer relative to determine whether or not he was willing to fulfill the role of kinsman-redeemer. The responsibilities were made clear to him by Boaz:

> The day you buy the field from the hand of Naomi, you also acquire Ruth the Moabite, the widow of the dead, in order to perpetuate the name of the dead in his inheritance [*nachălâh*]. Then the redeemer said, "I cannot redeem it for myself, lest I impair my own inheritance [*nachălâh*]. Take my right of redemption yourself, for I cannot redeem it." (Ruth 4:5-6)

In the first book of Kings, we read about Naboth the Jezreelite, whose vineyard was coveted by Ahab, the wicked king of Israel. When Ahab asked for the vineyard to be given to him in return for full compensation, he received this response from Naboth: "The LORD forbid that I should give you the inheritance [*nachălâh*] of my fathers" (1 Kgs. 21:3). Ahab's enraged wife, Jezebel, subsequently arranged Naboth's death, and Ahab got his vineyard. However, God was so angered by this heinous crime that He sent the Prophet Elijah to the king with this message: "Thus says the LORD, 'Have you killed and also taken possession?' And you shall say to him, 'Thus says the LORD: "In the place where dogs licked up the blood of Naboth shall dogs lick your own blood"'" (1 Kgs. 21:19). In a later chapter, we will consider how God's anger was also provoked by the Edomites, who "rejoiced over the inheritance [*nachălâh*] of the house of Israel" (Ezek. 35:15) and tried to take possession of it.

While the verb *nâchal* occurs 66 times in the Old Testament, the noun *nachălâh* is used 222 times in 191 verses (according to the Hebrew concordance of the KJV). It occurs most frequently in Numbers (31x), Deuteronomy (22x), Joshua (43x), Psalms (22x), Jeremiah (12x), and Ezekiel (11x). The most common occurrence of the noun is in passages dealing with Israel's tribal inheritance in Canaan, hence the preponderance of references in Numbers, Deuteronomy, and Joshua. For example, this was the instruction that was given by God to Moses:

> Speak to the people of Israel and say to them, "When you pass over the Jordan into the land of Canaan, then you shall drive out all the inhabitants of

the land from before you ... And you shall take possession of the land and settle in it, for I have given the land to you to possess it. You shall inherit [*nâchal*] the land by lot according to your clans. To a large tribe you shall give a large inheritance [*nachălâh*], and to a small tribe you shall give a small inheritance [*nachălâh*]. Wherever the lot falls for anyone, that shall be his. According to the tribes of your fathers you shall inherit [*nâchal*]." (Num. 33:51-54)

The use of *nachălâh* in this context presupposes the Abrahamic Covenant and the everlasting nature of the promises that God made to Abraham and later confirmed to Abraham's son Isaac and grandson Jacob. It was on the basis of this everlasting covenant that God determined where the inheritors of His promises were to settle:

"And I will establish my covenant between me and you and your offspring after you throughout their generations for an everlasting covenant, to be God to you and to your offspring after you. And I will give to you and to your offspring after you the land of your sojournings, all the land of Canaan, for an everlasting possession, and I will be their God." (Gen. 17:7-8; cf. 17:13, 19; 48:4)

Each of the twelve sons of Jacob, together with the two sons of Joseph who were born in Egypt (Ephraim and Manasseh), were to be allotted their own tribal inheritance in Canaan, with one exception: Levi. This was later expounded in Numbers and Joshua, where we read about the land being apportioned by lot to each tribe. Aaron, representing the tribe of Levi and the priesthood of Israel, received the following instruction from the Lord:

"You shall have no inheritance [*nâchal*] in their land, neither shall you have any portion among them. I am your portion and your inheritance [*nachălâh*] among the people of Israel. To the Levites I have given every tithe in Israel for an inheritance [*nachălâh*] ... It shall be a perpetual statute throughout your generations, and among the people of Israel they shall have no inheritance [*nachălâh*]. For the tithe of the people of Israel ... I have given to the Levites for an inheritance [*nachălâh*]. Therefore I have said of them that they shall have no inheritance [*nachălâh*] among the people of Israel." (Num. 18:20-24)

Brought Out, Brought In

The Lord did not bring His people out of Egypt to wander and flounder in the wilderness. He brought them *out of* a land of servitude and despair in order to bring them *into* a land of peace and security, which He Himself had prepared for them. As Moses told the people,

> The LORD has taken you and *brought you out of* the iron furnace, *out of* Egypt, to be a people of His own inheritance [*nachălâh*], as you are this day ... And because He loved your fathers and chose their offspring after them and *brought you out of* Egypt with His own presence, by His great power, driving out before you nations greater and mightier than you, to *bring you in*, to give you their land for an inheritance [*nachălâh*], as it is this day, know therefore today, and lay it to your heart, that the LORD is God in heaven above and on the earth beneath; there is no other. (Deut. 4:20-39; cf. 6:10-12, 23; Josh. 24:13; Neh. 9:25)

Despite being forbidden by God from entering the verdant pastures of Canaan, Moses did not wash his hands of responsibility for "the flock of Israel," one of the metaphors that features prominently in Scripture to depict the nation's relationship with God. Moses' heart was so closely knit to God's that he earnestly entreated "the Shepherd of Israel" to appoint a man to succeed him, and Joshua was chosen:

> Let the LORD, the God of the spirits of all flesh, appoint a man over the congregation who shall *go out* before them and *come in* before them, who shall *lead them out* and *bring them in*, that the congregation of the LORD may not be as sheep that have no shepherd. (Num. 27:17)

This shepherd imagery runs like a rich vein through the Scriptures, from the Genesis accounts of the patriarchs, to the wilderness wanderings of the Israelites, to the settlement of Canaan under Joshua, to David's timeless shepherd song (Psalm 23), to the prophetic indictments of Jeremiah and Ezekiel against the worthless "shepherds" of Israel,[5] and finally to the glorious revelation and ministry of Messiah Jesus as the Good, Great, and Chief Shepherd of God's flock (Jn. 10:1-18; Heb. 13:20; 1 Pet. 5:4). Throughout His Messianic ministry, Jesus "went in and out" (Acts 1:21)

---

[5] See especially Jeremiah 23 and Ezekiel 34.

among His sheep, tending and feeding, protecting and leading, warning and restoring. The world is a dangerous place for the believer—a wilderness of temptations and snares, of pitfalls and predators—but the promise remains the same: "The LORD will keep your *going out* and your *coming in* from this time forth and forevermore" (Ps. 121:8). This promise also belongs to those who will be saved during the tribulation period after the church has been raptured. As the Apostle John was told, "the Lamb in the midst of the throne will be their shepherd, and He will guide them to springs of living water" (Rev. 7:17).

When God sent His people into Babylonian exile, He repeatedly reminded them of what He had accomplished on their behalf and how they had rebelled against Him. Yet, despite their rebellion, the Lord promised to bring them *out of* exile and back *into* the Promised Land:

> "On the day when I chose Israel . . . I swore to them that I would bring them *out of* the land of Egypt *into* a land that I had searched out for them . . . So I led them *out of* the land of Egypt and brought them *into* the wilderness . . . But the house of Israel rebelled against me in the wilderness . . . Nevertheless, my eye spared them, and I did not destroy them or make a full end of them in the wilderness . . . As I live, declares the Lord GOD . . . I will bring you *out from* the peoples and gather you *out of* the countries where you are scattered . . . And I will bring you *into* the wilderness of the peoples, and there I will enter into judgment with you face to face . . . I will purge out the rebels from among you, and those who transgress against me. I will bring them *out of* the land where they sojourn, but they shall not *enter* the land of Israel . . . As a pleasing aroma I will accept you, when I bring you *out from* the peoples and gather you *out of* the countries where you have been scattered . . . And you shall know that I am the LORD, when I bring you *into* the land of Israel, the country that I swore to give to your fathers." (Ezek. 20:6-42)

The shepherd-sheep metaphor is reflected in 2 Samuel 5 and Psalm 78, which recall the divine commissioning of David as shepherd-king of Israel:

> Then all the tribes of Israel came to David at Hebron and said, "Behold, we are your bone and flesh. In times past, when Saul was king over us, it was you who *led out* and *brought in* Israel. And the LORD said to you, 'You shall be shepherd of my people Israel, and you shall be prince over Israel.'" So all the elders of Israel came to the king at Hebron, and King David made a covenant

with them at Hebron before the LORD, and they anointed David king over Israel. (2 Sam. 5:1-3)

Then [God] *led out* His people like sheep and guided them in the wilderness like a flock ... And He *brought them to* His holy land ... He chose David His servant and took him from the sheepfolds; from following the nursing ewes He brought him to shepherd Jacob His people, Israel His inheritance [*nachălâh*]. With upright heart he shepherded them and guided them with his skillful hand. (Ps. 78:52-72)

David understood that he was merely an under-shepherd to the true Shepherd of Israel. On one occasion, he made this impassioned plea to God: "Oh, save your people and bless your heritage [*nachălâh*]! Be their shepherd and carry them forever" (Ps. 28:9). David understood that God's people, like sheep, could not make it on their own but needed to be led and fed "with knowledge and understanding" (Jer. 3:15). This is why Ezekiel was later told to "prophesy against the shepherds of Israel" who had neglected God's flock (Ezek. 34:2). The people had, by that time, become spiritually malnourished and fallen prey to their enemies. Led astray and "scattered over all the face of the earth, with none to search or seek for them" (Ezek. 34:6), they were like "lost sheep" (Jer. 50:6). In His prophetic and Messianic indictment against Israel's leaders, God emphatically declared that He was going to personally contend against them and seek after His flock:

"And I will *bring them out* from the peoples and gather them from the countries, and will *bring them into* their own land ... I will feed them with good pasture, and on the mountain heights of Israel shall be their grazing land ... I myself will be the shepherd of my sheep, and I myself will make them lie down, declares the Lord GOD ... And I will set up over them one shepherd, my servant David, and He shall feed them: He shall feed them and be their shepherd." (Ezek. 34:13-23; cf. Jn. 10:1-16)

In the wonderfully consoling prophecies of Isaiah 40 and Jeremiah 31, the prophets speak of a future time when the great Shepherd will decisively intervene on behalf of His people:

He will tend His flock like a shepherd; He will gather the lambs in His arms; He will carry them in His bosom, and gently lead those that are with young. (Isa. 40:11)

Hear the word of the LORD, O nations, and declare it in the coastlands far away; say, "He who scattered Israel will gather him, and will keep him as a shepherd keeps his flock." For the LORD has ransomed Jacob and has redeemed him from hands too strong for him. (Jer. 31:10-11)

It is clear, then, that the shepherd-sheep metaphor employed in these and many other scriptures is tied to the concept of *nachălâh*, both historically and prophetically. This is encapsulated in the petition that the Prophet Micah offered to the Lord on behalf of the nation and in the Lord's response:

> Shepherd your people with your staff, the flock of your inheritance [*nachălâh*], who dwell alone in a forest in the midst of a garden land; let them graze in Bashan and Gilead as in the days of old. "As in the days when you came out of the land of Egypt, I will show them marvelous things." (Mic. 7:14-15)

A Valuable Inheritance

God's mighty deliverance of the Hebrew slaves from Egypt happened overnight. According to one translation, that night was "a night of watching by the Lord, to bring them out of the land of Egypt" (Ex. 12:42, ESV). According to another, "the LORD kept vigil that night to bring them out of Egypt" (NIV). Miraculous plagues, destroying angels, and a dramatic dialogue between God's appointed deliverer and Egypt's obdurate king tell only half the story, for God was keeping vigil. This is why the psalmist could later exclaim, "Behold, He who keeps Israel will neither slumber nor sleep" (Ps. 121:4).

The concept of Israel as God's inheritance would have been a purely nebulous one had the Lord not displayed His mighty power on behalf of the people and made His dwelling among them. By regularly communicating to the Israelites through Moses, God made His people aware just how precious they were to Him. When the Lord gave Moses instructions about the tabernacle and tent of meeting, He revealed to him His purpose:

> "There [at the tent of meeting] I will meet with the people of Israel, and it shall be sanctified by my glory... I will dwell among the people of Israel and will be their God. And they shall know that I am the LORD their God, who brought them out of the land of Egypt that I might dwell among them. I am the LORD their God." (Ex. 29:43-46; cf. 25:8)

The Ten Commandments, along with an additional 603 that followed, were given by God to Moses at Mount Sinai. They comprised the moral, legal, and ceremonial code that underpinned God's covenant with Israel. No doubt we can all recall the first commandment: "You shall have no other gods before me" (Ex. 20:3). However, this is not how the Ten begin! The law of God did not commence with a commandment but a revelation: "I am the LORD your God, who brought you out of the land of Egypt, out of the house of slavery" (Ex. 20:2; Deut. 5:6). So crucial was this revelation that God repeated it time and again before His people crossed into Canaan.[6] Without it, Israel would have been left with a lifeless code and an unknowable God.

Many of us will, at some point in our lives, receive an earthly inheritance. It may take the form of a cash endowment, a piece of real estate, a business, a car, a watch, a piece of jewelry, a work of art, an item of clothing, an antique, or maybe some kind of military memorabilia. We may appreciate the inheritance for its financial and/or sentimental value, but more than that, we will cherish the one who bequeathed it to us and perhaps realize at a deeper level how valuable we ourselves were to our benefactor. When God was preparing His people to claim their earthly inheritance beyond the Jordan, He made it clear how special the land of Canaan was. By bequeathing it to them, His people would have a daily reminder of how precious an inheritance *they themselves* were to Him. As Moses declared,

> For the land that you are entering to take possession of it is not like the land of Egypt, from which you have come, where you sowed your seed and irrigated it, like a garden of vegetables. But the land that you are going over to possess is a land of hills and valleys, which drinks water by the rain from heaven, a land that the LORD your God cares for. The eyes of the LORD your God are always upon it, from the beginning of the year to the end of the year. (Deut. 11:10-12)

In God's estimation, Canaan was "the most glorious of lands" (Ezek. 20:6, 15) and one that He Himself had personally searched out for His people to inherit. But is the Most High, whom "the highest heaven cannot contain" (2 Chron. 6:18), really that interested in hills and valleys, in rainfall, grain,

---

[6] Ex. 6:7; 20:2; 29:46; Lev. 11:45; 19:36; 22:33; 23:43; 25:38, 42, 55; 26:13, 45; Num. 15:41; Deut. 5:6; 6:12; 8:14; 13:5, 10; 20:1; cf. Ps. 81:10; Am. 2:10.

wine, oil, and livestock? According to many in the church, the answer would be "No!" But according to the Lord, the answer is a resounding "Yes!" for these were the things that were to occupy the people on a daily basis. It was how they were to live, work, and interact as a predominantly agricultural people.

The cultivated land of Canaan, which would yield so abundantly to the Israelites as long as they loved the Lord and kept His commandments, would be a perpetual reminder of their worth as His *nachălâh*. Out of "all the families of the earth" (Am. 3:2), they alone had been chosen to be a people, distinct "from every other people on the face of the earth" (Ex. 33:16). As God declared through Moses, "You shall be holy to me, for I the Lord am holy and have separated you from the peoples, that you should be mine" (Lev. 20:26). As Moses later reminded the Israelites, "the Lord set His heart in love on your fathers and chose their offspring after them, you above all peoples, as you are this day" (Deut. 10:15). For the Israelites to function as God's people, they needed a land, and for Canaan to function as God's land, it needed a people who would dwell there in perpetual gratitude, carefully tending the soil and demonstrating complete dependence upon God.

A Treasured People

With our main Hebrew noun, *nachălâh*, we need to include another unique word, *seˈgullâh*. It is used to describe a personal possession that is of a peculiar, special, or treasured kind. Its meaning becomes evident if we compare the following translations of Malachi 3:17:

"They shall be mine," says the Lord of hosts, "On the day that I make them my jewels [*seˈgullâh*]." (NKJV)

"They shall be mine, says the Lord of hosts, my special possession [*seˈgullâh*] on the day when I act." (RSV)

"They shall be mine, says the Lord of hosts, in the day when I make up my treasured possession [*seˈgullâh*]." (ESV)

"And they shall be unto me a peculiar treasure [*seˈgullâh*], saith Jehovah of hosts, in the day that I prepare." (DBY)

According to one theological reference book, "while the word occurs only eight times, it is filled with theological and spiritual treasures."[7] Consider these additional references:

> "Now therefore, if you will indeed obey my voice and keep my covenant, you shall be my treasured possession [s^{e}gullâh] among all peoples, for all the earth is mine." (Ex. 19:5)

> For you are a people holy to the LORD your God. The LORD your God has chosen you to be a people for His treasured possession [s^{e}gullâh], out of all the peoples who are on the face of the earth. (Deut. 7:6; cf. 14:2, 26:18)

> For the LORD has chosen Jacob for Himself, Israel as His own possession [s^{e}gullâh]. (Ps. 135:4)

Thus, we have in these two Hebrew words—*nachălâh* and *s^{e}gullâh*—a beautiful portrait of Israel as God's earthly inheritance and treasured possession. One of the points I will be repeatedly making throughout this book is that if this is the way in which *God* looks at Israel, then every believer is required to show Israel the same kind of appreciation. God will yet judge, purge, and refine His chosen people before they are fully and finally reconciled to Him. However, as far as the church is concerned, Israel ought to be cherished, not chided; treasured, not trampled upon; defended, not demonized; comforted, not condemned; provoked to jealousy, not outrage; and driven to Jesus, not despair. Tragically, this is not happening in many parts of the church, and that is surely an offense to our God and Savior.

Conclusion

As we proceed, we will be looking at the way in which the concept of *nachălâh* interacts with many other features of God's covenant relationship with Israel. In the process, we will excavate from the biblical soil several other Hebrew word-gems. But let me say from the outset that the notion of "inheritance" is also central to a New Covenant understanding of the church's relationship with Jesus. As Paul wrote in his letter to the Ephesians,

---

[7] *Theological Wordbook of the Old Testament*, p. 617.

> In Him we have obtained an inheritance, having been predestined according to the purpose of Him who works all things according to the counsel of His will ... In Him you also, when you heard the word of truth, the gospel of your salvation, and believed in Him, were sealed with the promised Holy Spirit, who is the guarantee of our inheritance until we acquire possession of it, to the praise of His glory. (Eph. 1:11-14)

Paul prayed that every believer would fully comprehend "the riches of His glorious inheritance in the saints" (Eph. 1:18) and never cease to give thanks to the Father, who had qualified them "to share in the inheritance of the saints in light" (Col. 1:12; cf. 3:24). Jesus is portrayed in the letter to the Hebrews as "the mediator of a new covenant, so that those who are called may receive the promised eternal inheritance" (Heb. 9:15), while in Peter's first letter, we read this opening benediction:

> Blessed be the God and Father of our Lord Jesus the Messiah! According to His great mercy, He has caused us to be born again to a living hope through the resurrection of Jesus the Messiah from the dead, to an inheritance that is imperishable, undefiled, and unfading, kept in heaven for you, who by God's power are being guarded through faith for a salvation ready to be revealed in the last time. (1 Pet. 1:3-5)

The concept of the church as the inheritance of Jesus clearly merits a separate volume, but we close this opening chapter with David's prayer of thanksgiving after Nathan the prophet had relayed to him God's message concerning the future of his house and throne. It is my hope that this book will inspire many similar prayers of thanksgiving as we reflect upon the great goodness and faithfulness of our God:

> And who is like your people Israel, the one nation on earth whom God went to redeem to be His people, making Himself a name and doing for them great and awesome things ... ? And you established for yourself your people Israel to be your people forever. And you, O LORD, became their God. And now, O LORD God, confirm forever the word that you have spoken concerning your servant and concerning his house, and do as you have spoken. And your name will be magnified forever, saying, "The LORD of hosts is God over Israel," and the house of your servant David will be established before you. (2 Sam. 7:23-26)

Chapter 2:

The Irrevocable Blessing, Part 1

> Blessed is the nation whose God is the LORD, the people whom He has chosen for His own inheritance [*nachălâh*] ... Blessed are the people to whom such blessings fall! Blessed are the people whose God is the LORD! (Ps. 33:12; 144:15)

> Remember your congregation, which you have purchased of old, which you have redeemed to be the tribe of your inheritance [*nachălâh*] ... Remember this, O LORD, how the enemy scoffs, and a foolish people reviles your name. (Ps. 74:2, 18)

The biblical account of a talking donkey is one of the most unusual, well-known, somewhat amusing, but critically important episodes in Israel's history. The donkey's owner was a Mesopotamian seer by the name of Balaam, whose life was spared when his faithful beast took evasive action after she had seen the angel of the Lord standing before them. Balaam had been on his way to meet Balak, king of Moab, who wanted him to curse the Israelites as they encamped in the plains of Moab. Amidst these strange goings-on, a truth of God, pivotal to the canon of Scripture and the whole course of human history, was revealed.

In Numbers 22, we find the Israelites encamped east of the Jordan Valley opposite Jericho. Having just defeated the Amorites, the Moabites were now in fear of God's people. Knowing he could not defeat the Israelites militarily, Balak sent messengers to Balaam with an invitation that effectively drew the spiritual battle lines: "Come now, curse this people for me, since they are too mighty for me. Perhaps I shall be able to defeat them and drive them from the land, for I know that he whom you bless is blessed, and he whom you curse is cursed" (Num. 22:6). I believe this was a direct challenge from Satan himself to the promise that God had sovereignly made to Abraham centuries earlier:

Now the LORD said to Abram, "Go from your country and your kindred and your father's house to the land that I will show you. And I will make of you a great nation, and I will bless you and make your name great, so that you will be a blessing. I will bless those who bless you, and him who dishonors you I will curse, and in you all the families of the earth shall be blessed." (Gen. 12:1-3)

Blessed Beginnings

How crucial it was for Abraham and his descendants to know that they were living under the blessing of God! They understood that all of life was governed by the One who alone had the power to give and to withhold, to build up and to tear down, to bless and to curse. In fact, as Michael Brown notes, "All religious or superstitious peoples (in other words, virtually the entire ancient world, along with most of the world to this day) have actively sought the blessing of a specific deity or spirit . . . The more powerful the deity, the more important the blessing."[1] Through Abraham and his descendants, God would show the peoples of the world that their gods were no gods at all, just "worthless idols" (1 Chron. 16:26; Ps. 97:7).

From the opening chapters of Genesis, we discover the centrality of the divine blessing. We are told that on the fifth day of creation God blessed all marine life and the birds of the air, commanding them to be fruitful and multiply (Gen. 1:22). On the sixth day, He blessed Adam and Eve, having created them in His own image (Gen. 1:28; 5:2; 9:1). Finally, "God blessed the seventh day and made it holy" (Gen. 2:3) as He rested from His work. In other words, all of creation was blessed, for it was good in God's sight. Adam and Eve's disobedience in the Garden of Eden, however, was to have catastrophic consequences. The ground was cursed by God, making man's labor difficult, while the pain of childbearing was multiplied for future generations of women. God's blessing had been forfeited.

Disqualified from the garden but never from grace, Adam and Eve were physically *and* spiritually covered by God (Gen. 3:21; cf. Jn. 1:29-36; 1 Pet.

---

[1] Michael L. Brown, "1385 ברך," in *The New International Dictionary of Old Testament Theology and Exegesis, Volume 1*, ed. Willem A. VanGemeren (Carlisle, UK: Paternoster Press, 1997), p. 758.

1:18-20; Rev. 5:6-14). We are later told that Enoch and Noah were among those who lived under God's favor, but the corruption of mankind only increased until God intervened in a cataclysmic manner by flooding the earth. Starting again with Noah, the Lord eventually called forth from the line of Noah's son Shem a man by the name of Abram (later Abraham), through whom blessing would be restored to mankind. What happened with Abraham's grandson Jacob, however, would be a constant reminder that God's blessing would no longer be secured as readily as it was in the beginning.

A Tale of Two Brothers

Having "struggled together" in their mother Rebekah's womb, the twins Jacob and Esau were born (Gen. 25:22). In time, they would father two great peoples, and the world would never be the same again! By divine election, the older (Esau) would serve the younger (Jacob).[2] As the firstborn, Esau had been entitled to a double portion of his father's inheritance (see Deut. 21:17). However, he despised his birthright and frivolously sold it to his brother for some of his lentil stew. Jacob, not Esau, would now inherit not only his father's wealth but also the covenant promises once given to his grandfather Abraham and confirmed to his father, Isaac. Through Rebekah's deception, a frail and elderly Isaac was tricked into bestowing the blessing of the firstborn upon his youngest son. Jacob, not Esau, would be the one who would assume the role of head of the family. The promises given to Abraham were reaffirmed to Jacob through his father Isaac's pronouncements:

> Let peoples serve you, and nations bow down to you . . . Cursed be everyone who curses you, and blessed be everyone who blesses you! (Gen. 27:29)

> God Almighty bless you and make you fruitful and multiply you, that you may become a company of peoples. May he give the blessing of Abraham to you and to your offspring with you, that you may take possession of the land of your sojournings that God gave to Abraham! (Gen. 28:3-4)

---

[2] Gen. 25:23; Mal. 1:2,3; Rom. 9:10-13.

Through an extraordinary sequence of events, God's purposes for the embryonic nation of Israel were fulfilled, but not without a struggle. This was epitomized in Jacob's encounter with an angel immediately before he was reunited with his estranged brother. Having taken his family across the brook called Jabbok, Jacob crossed back and was left alone to wrestle all night with the angel, who appeared to him in human form. The account continues:

> When the man saw that he did not prevail against Jacob, he touched his hip socket, and Jacob's hip was put out of joint as he wrestled with him. Then he said, "Let me go, for the day has broken." But Jacob said, "I will not let you go unless you bless me." And he said to him, "What is your name?" And he said, "Jacob." Then he said, "Your name shall no longer be called Jacob, but Israel, for you have striven with God and with men, and have prevailed." Then Jacob asked him, "Please tell me your name?" But he said, "Why is it that you ask my name?" And there he blessed him. (Gen. 32:25-29; cf. 35:9-12; Hos. 12:3,4)

Through this extraordinary encounter, the name "Israel" was announced to the world. Its precise meaning is disputed, a common suggestion being "he struggles with God." As Jacob wrestled with the angel that night, one thing was clear: Without God's blessing, there could be no fulfillment of God's promise and no future for Israel. Weary, wounded, and battle-worn, "Jacob" lives to this day by the mercy, faithfulness, and blessing of God. In the words of the nineteenth-century bishop of Liverpool, J. C. Ryle (1816-1900),

> God has many witnesses to the truth of the Bible, if men would only examine them and listen to their evidence. But you may depend on it, there is no witness so unanswerable as one who always keeps standing up, and living, and moving before the eyes of mankind. That witness is the Jew.[3]

---

[3] J. C. Ryle, "And So All Israel Shall Be Saved," in *Are You Ready for the End of Time? Understanding Future Events from Prophetic Passages of the Bible* (Fearn, Scotland: Christian Focus Publications, 2001), p. 150.

A Divine Eulogy

When Balak appealed to Balaam to curse the Israelites, I believe Balaam heard the same sinister voice that Eve had heard in the garden, when the serpent asked her: "Did God really say. . .?" (Gen. 3:1). Through the Moabite king, a similar kind of diabolical question was posed, which might be reworded this way: "Did God really say that only those *God* blesses are blessed, and only those *God* curses are cursed? Is it really true that only those who *bless* Israel will be blessed, while those who *curse* Israel will be cursed?" Satan, through Balak, attempted to curse God's people, but God, through Balaam, issued a decisive and unambiguous riposte:

> From Aram Balak has brought me, the king of Moab from the eastern mountains: "Come, curse Jacob for me, and come, denounce Israel!" How can I curse whom God has not cursed? How can I denounce whom the LORD has not denounced? (Num. 23:7-8)

The backdrop to all this is Genesis 12:1-3, when God committed Himself to one man and through that one man a nation. But when God told Abraham that He was going to make his name "great," what did He mean? Consider what the Lord declared through the Prophet Isaiah centuries later: "For my own sake, for my own sake, I do it, for how should my name be profaned? My glory I will not give to another" (Isa. 48:11). In making Abraham's name great, then, God's intention was to magnify His own name in the sight of the nations! Thus, in Genesis 12, God laid out the ground rules for the way the nations of the world were to relate to Israel. By blessing Abraham and his descendants, they would be blessing Him and vice-versa, for the way a nation responded to them would indicate the degree of their acquiescence with God's election of Israel. It has been said that from Haman to Hitler, "history shows how dangerous it is to hate [God's] chosen people."[4]

The Hebrew word for "bless" in Genesis 12 is *barâk*. The Septuagint (LXX) uses the verb *eulogeō*, meaning "to speak a good word." It is from this verb that we derive our English words "eulogize" and "eulogy." The

---

[4] Allan A. MacRae, "Hath God Cast Away His People?" in *Prophetic Truth Unfolding Today*, ed. by Charles L. Feinberg (Westwood, NJ: Fleming H. Revell, 1968), p. 95.

LXX uses *kataraomai* to denote the opposite of *eulogeō*, namely, "to speak ill of/wish evil against/curse." Sadly, the progeny of Ishmael and Esau, from whom the Arab nations are descended, continually forfeited the blessing they would have received had they "eulogized" Israel. Instead of embracing God's chosen people and worshiping the true and living God, they despised Israel and embraced all manner of false gods and religions, most notably Islam, and they continue to reap the consequences. As for the way in which the Gentile nations as a whole have treated the Jewish people, Arnold Fruchtenbaum has made this poignant observation: "One thing history bears witness to many times over is that every nation that has ever dared to raise its hand against the Jew has fallen. The Jew 'has stood at the graveside of all his enemies.'"[5]

The divine principle of "bless and be blessed, curse and be cursed" can be traced through Old Testament history on into the New Testament and church age, through the tribulation period to come, and to the end of the millennial kingdom (Rev. 20:7-10). The supreme exposition of this principle was given, unsurprisingly, by Jesus on the Mount of Olives. On that occasion, the Lord spoke to His disciples about His second coming and announced that upon His return, He would judge the "sheep" and "goat" nations according to how they had treated His brethren. The Lord's brethren, in this particular context, are the Jewish people. Those nations that had blessed the Jewish people would be blessed by the Father and welcomed into the millennial kingdom, while those who had neglected Jesus' brethren would face a terrifying judgment:

> When the Son of Man comes in His glory, and all the angels with Him, then He will sit on His glorious throne. Before Him will be gathered all the nations, and He will separate people one from another as a shepherd separates the sheep from the goats. And He will place the sheep on His right, but the goats on the left. Then the King will say to those on His right, "Come, you who are blessed [*eulogeō*] by my Father, inherit the kingdom prepared for you from the foundation of the world. For I was hungry and you gave me food, I was thirsty and you gave me drink, I was a stranger and you welcomed me, I was naked and you clothed me, I was sick and you visited me, I was in prison and

---

[5] Arnold G. Fruchtenbaum, *Israelology: The Missing Link in Systematic Theology* (Tustin, CA: Ariel Ministries Press, 1993), p. 838.

you came to me." Then the righteous will answer Him, saying, "Lord, when did we see you hungry and feed you, or thirsty and give you drink? And when did we see you a stranger and welcome you, or naked and clothe you? And when did we see you sick or in prison and visit you?" And the King will answer them, "Truly, I say to you, as you did it to one of the least of these my brothers, you did it to me." Then He will say to those on His left, "Depart from me, you cursed [*kataraomai*], into the eternal fire prepared for the devil and his angels. For I was hungry and you gave me no food, I was thirsty and you gave me no drink, I was a stranger and you did not welcome me, naked and you did not clothe me, sick and in prison and you did not visit me." Then they also will answer, saying, "Lord, when did we see you hungry or thirsty or a stranger or naked or sick or in prison, and did not minister to you?" Then He will answer them, saying, "Truly, I say to you, as you did not do it to one of the least of these, you did not do it to me." And these will go away into eternal punishment, but the righteous into eternal life. (Mt. 25:31-46)

A State of Blessing

After he had received Balak's messengers and the promise of Moabite money for services anticipated, Balaam received a word of instruction and warning from God: "You shall not go with them. You shall not curse the people, for they are blessed" (Num. 22:12). Balaam later received permission from the Lord to go, but the warning remained in force. The way was now set for a series of oracles to be proclaimed in the presence of an enemy who was seeking to curse and ultimately destroy God's people.

The initial instruction given by God to Balaam made at least three things clear from the outset:

1. God had the power to prevent His people from being cursed.
2. What God blesses should never be cursed.
3. The people of Israel exist in *a state of blessing* before God. They are blessed *positionally* because they are chosen. This state or position of blessing was neither merited nor earned but sovereignly bestowed.

To help us understand what positional blessing entails, let us read these words that Paul wrote to the churches in Rome and Ephesus:

> For what does the Scripture say? "Abraham believed God, and it was counted to him as righteousness" . . . just as David also speaks of the blessing of the one to whom God counts righteousness apart from works: "Blessed are those whose lawless deeds are forgiven, and whose sins are covered; blessed is the man against whom the Lord will not count his sin." (Rom. 4:3-8; cf. Ps. 32:1-2)
>
> Blessed be the God and Father of our Lord Jesus the Messiah, who has blessed us in Messiah with every spiritual blessing in the heavenly places, even as He chose us in Him before the foundation of the world, that we should be holy and blameless before Him. In love He predestined us for adoption to Himself as sons through Jesus the Messiah, according to the purpose of His will, to the praise of His glorious grace, with which He has blessed us in the Beloved. (Eph. 1:3-6)

This promised state or position of blessing is for every individual—Jew or Gentile—who repents of their sin and puts their faith and trust in Jesus as Lord and Savior. That individual will be eternally blessed by God on account of His mercy and forgiveness, but that same person may, at times, incur His displeasure and discipline if they disobey Him. In this way, then, we see the difference between *positional* blessing, which is eternal and dependent entirely on God's mercy and Messiah's obedience, and *practical* blessing, which is temporal and dependent entirely on each individual's walk with the Lord.

This distinction is important when we consider God's promises to Abraham in Genesis 12. Abraham's descendants, as a nation, were to be forever blessed because they had been sovereignly set apart/sanctified/chosen/elected by God, whose covenant with them was unilateral, unconditional, and everlasting. Their disobedience, on the other hand, would incur God's discipline, even His fury and wrath, because of the privileged status they enjoyed. As we know, calamitous judgments were indeed to befall Israel. However, rather than abrogating the covenant promises—or causing them to be reinterpreted and reapplied to the church—Jesus *confirmed* them through His sinless life, sacrificial death, and glorious resurrection, thereby guaranteeing their literal fulfillment (Rom. 15:8). In the words of Paul, "all the promises of God find their Yes in Him" (2 Cor. 1:20), and they include God's promises to Israel! This fundamental truth has been sadly overlooked or shamefully rejected by those who fail to understand the difference between Israel's *positional blessing* and the blessings that are linked to the nation's obedience.

Consider the following illustration:

> It is a beautiful moonlit night. The moon is at full, and shining in more than ordinary silver brightness. A man is gazing intently down a deep, still well, where he sees the moon reflected, and thus remarks to a friendly bystander: 'How beautifully fair and round she is tonight! how quietly and majestically she rides along!' He has just finished speaking, when suddenly his friend drops a small pebble into the well, and he now exclaims, 'Why, the moon is all broken to shivers, and the fragments are shaking together in the greatest disorder!' 'What gross absurdity!' is the astonished rejoinder of his companion. '*Look up, man!* the moon hasn't changed one jot or tittle. *It is the condition of the well* that reflects her that has changed.'[6]

Too many believers are looking at Israel like the man in the story, who was left with a distorted vision of the moon when the waters of the well were suddenly disturbed. The man was all confused until his friend stepped in and directed his attention upwards. In the church today, many have looked at Israel's reflection in the "well" of God's Word. They have read the history of God's dealings with His chosen people and the abundant promises He has made about their national restoration. All appeared calm and clear for a time until a pastor, preacher, theologian, author, friend, church council, denominational assembly, or social media platform came along and dropped a "pebble" into the well. That pebble was replacement theology. These believers were now being told that the promises given to Israel, which they had once taken at face value, needed to be reinterpreted in line with the allegorism of "church fathers" like Augustine of Hippo (354-430) and the amillennialism of Protestant Reformers like John Calvin (1509-1564). The church was now said to be the new, true, or spiritual Israel, while the nation that had once given the world the patriarchs, the covenants, the law, the prophets, and supremely the Messiah was to be considered no more important than any other nation on earth. The well had been disturbed and God's promises broken into fragments.

---

[6] George Cutting, *Christian Privileges* (London: W.H. Broom and Rouse, n.d.), pp. 23-24.

To anybody reading this whose vision has been impaired by the effects of the aforementioned "pebble," may the words of the friend in the story resonate: "What gross absurdity! Look up, man!" May your gaze be lifted heavenwards to the One who gave us the well of His Word and away from the rippled confusion of man-made theology. Then, and only then, will the waters settle again to reveal Israel's true reflection against the clear night-sky of God's sovereignty, faithfulness, mercy, and love.

The Divine Right to Curse

Having highlighted the blessing of God that permanently rests upon Israel, it is important to note that God Himself promised to curse His own people if they proved unfaithful to Him. Through the Prophet Malachi, God brought a stern warning to—and through—the priests of Israel, whose responsibility it was to guard the knowledge of God:

> "If you will not listen, if you will not take it to heart to give honor to my name, says the LORD of hosts, then I will send the curse upon you and I will curse your blessings. Indeed, I have already cursed them, because you do not lay it to heart . . . You are cursed with a curse, for you are robbing me, the whole nation of you." (Mal. 2:2; 3:9)

Unlike His blessing, however, God's curse would only be temporary, for it was designed not to destroy Israel but to draw her back. As Moses declared to the people in the wilderness,

> See, I am setting before you today a blessing and a curse: the blessing, if you obey the commandments of the LORD your God, which I command you today, and the curse, if you do not obey the commandments of the LORD your God, but turn aside from the way that I am commanding you today, to go after other gods that you have not known. (Deut. 11:26-28)

The incremental curse was proclaimed from Mount Ebal after the Israelites had crossed into Canaan (Deut. 27:13-26, 28:15-68). Many years later, during the Babylonian captivity, the Prophet Daniel humbly acknowledged before God that the people had failed to heed the warning and had broken the covenant:

> All Israel has transgressed your law and turned aside, refusing to obey your voice. And the curse and oath that are written in the Law of Moses the servant

of God have been poured out upon us, because we have sinned against Him. He has confirmed His words, which He spoke against us and against our rulers who ruled us, by bringing upon us a great calamity. (Dan. 9:11-12)

As noted earlier, Balaam warned Balak from the outset that he would only speak what God gave him to speak and could not curse those whom God had not cursed. Let us not forget that the Lord had already endured much rebellion from His people in the wilderness. However, He was not going to allow any other nation to curse His own. Our English word "curse" may immediately suggest to our minds something hostile and violent or incantational and devilish. Few believers would therefore entertain the thought that they, as believers, have ever "cursed" anyone, never mind an entire nation. However, English translations in general have failed to alert us to the fact that different Hebrew words are used in the blessing/cursing formula of Genesis 12:3, upon which the Balaam-Balak account stands. Here is how it reads in the New King James Version: "I will bless those who bless you, and I will curse him who *curses you*." When we compare this with other translations, the difference is immediately apparent:

> I will bless those who bless you, and him who *dishonors you* I will curse. (ESV)
>
> I will bless those who bless you, but the one who *treats you lightly* I must curse. (NET)
>
> I will bless those who bless you and curse those who *treat you with contempt*. (NLT)
>
> And I bless those blessing thee, and him who is *disesteeming thee* I curse. (YLT)

Although the same Hebrew word *bârak* is used in the "blessing" component, two Hebrew words, *'ârar* and *qâlal*, are used in the "cursing" part. I believe this is because the Lord intended to make an important, albeit subtle, distinction. A number of different Hebrew words are used throughout the Scriptures to denote cursing, but as one theological wordbook has noted, "To group all of them together under the one general English equivalent 'to curse' is much too superficial."[7] Whether in deterrence or in judgment,[8] the word *'ârar* can mean "to ban, bind, condemn, or render powerless" and is used, for example, of the judicial cursing by God of the serpent (Gen. 3:14), the ground (Gen. 3:17), Cain (Gen. 4:11), and Noah's grandson Canaan (Gen. 9:25). This word also predominates in the Deuteronomic curses that were proclaimed from Mount Ebal (Deut. 27:15-26, 28:16-19). The word *qâlal*, on the other hand, is more nuanced. It can mean "to lightly esteem," "to treat as being of little account," or "to despise," or it can be used to describe a condition "less than that deserved by, or divinely intended for, the object."[9] It is used, for example, of Hagar's contempt toward her barren mistress Sarai after Hagar had conceived (Gen. 16:4-5). It was also used by King David when he told his wife Michal, who despised him for dancing before God as the Ark of the Covenant was being brought up to Jerusalem, that he would make himself "yet more contemptible [*qâlal*] than this" (2 Sam. 6:22).

The main reason for drawing attention to this distinction in Genesis 12:3 is because many professing Christians who typically scoff at this text, display an appalling attitude toward the modern State of Israel. Those embroiled in the Christian Palestinianist movement would never admit to *cursing* Israel, but they are biblically mistaken; the word *qâlal* fits what they are doing perfectly. Through various forms of pro-Palestinian activism and propaganda, underpinned by theologies of replacement and liberation, they are expressing unbridled contempt for the Jewish nation. Without question, they are cursing Israel!

With Balaam's first oracle in Numbers 23, the distinction is even more apparent. According to various English translations, verse 8 reads as follows:

How shall I curse, whom God hath not cursed? or how shall I *defy*, whom the LORD hath not defied? (Bishops 1568, KJV, RV, ASV)

---

[7] *Theological Wordbook of the Old Testament*, p. 75.

[8] *The New International Dictionary of Old Testament Theology and Exegesis, Volume 1*, p. 525.

[9] *Theological Wordbook of the Old Testament*, p. 800.

> How shal I curse, where God hath not cursed? or howe shall I *detest*, where the Lorde hath not detested? (Geneva 1560)
>
> How shall I curse whom God has not cursed? And how shall I *denounce* whom the LORD has not denounced? (NKJV, DBY, RSV, ESV, NASB, NIV, NET)
>
> But how can I curse those whom God has not cursed? How can I *condemn* those whom the LORD has not condemned? (NLT)
>
> What—do I pierce?—God hath not pierced! And what—am I *indignant*?— Jehovah hath not been indignant! (YLT)

The Hebrew word translated "defy," "detest," "denounce," "condemn," or "be indignant" is zâ'am. It speaks of intense anger, rage, and abhorrence. We hear this anger being expressed all around the world toward Israel and in many parts of the church, and the decibels are rising. However, according to the Prophet Isaiah, God Himself will one day "show indignation [zâ'am] against His enemies" (Isa. 66:14), against those who defied, detested, denounced, and condemned His people. We will return to this later, but for now, let us consider another cardinal truth that can be gleaned from Balaam's first oracle.

As the seer looked out from his vantage point, he referred to the Israelites as "a people dwelling alone, and not counting itself among the nations!" (Num. 23:9). The KJV is more emphatic, perhaps even prophetic: "the people *shall* dwell alone, and *shall* not be reckoned among the nations." Through Balaam, God was making it clear that *His* nation was not to be viewed or treated like any other nation on earth. We may recall that this was the basis of Moses' intercession following the golden-calf episode, when God told him that He was no longer going to accompany His people. Moses responded by pleading with the Lord:

> If your presence will not go with me, do not bring us up from here. For how shall it be known that I have found favor in your sight, I and your people? Is it not in your going with us, so that we are distinct, I and your people, from every other people on the face of the earth? (Ex. 33:15-16)

Moses was only praying back to the Lord what the Lord Himself had told him to declare to the people while they were encamped at Mount Sinai:

> Now therefore, if you will indeed obey my voice and keep my covenant, you shall be my treasured possession [*s^egullâh*] among all peoples, for all the earth

is mine; and you shall be to me a kingdom of priests and a holy nation. (Ex. 19:5-6)

Moses later repeated the call when the Israelites were about to enter the Promised Land:

> For you are a people holy to the LORD your God. The LORD your God has chosen you to be a people for His treasured possession [*s^egullâh*], out of all the peoples who are on the face of the earth. (Deut. 7:6; cf. Deut. 14:2; 26:18-19; Ps. 135:4; Am. 3:2)

From exodus to exile, God made it abundantly clear that He would never countenance behavior from His people resembling that of the nations. They were to be recognizably different:

> "When my angel goes before you and brings you to the Amorites and the Hittites and the Perizzites and the Canaanites, the Hivites and the Jebusites, and I blot them out, you shall not bow down to their gods nor serve them, nor do as they do, but you shall utterly overthrow them and break their pillars in pieces . . . You shall make no covenant with them and their gods. They shall not dwell in your land, lest they make you sin against me; for if you serve their gods, it will surely be a snare to you." (Ex. 23:23-33; cf. Deut. 12:29-30)

> "Therefore say to the house of Israel, Thus says the Lord GOD: 'Are you defiling yourselves in the manner of your fathers, and committing harlotry according to their abominations? . . . So shall I be inquired of by you, O house of Israel? As I live,' says the Lord GOD, 'I will not be inquired of by you. What you have in your mind shall never be, when you say, "We will be like the Gentiles, like the families in other countries, serving wood and stone."'" (Ezek. 20:30-32)

The warning to Israel was stark because God's honor was at stake. But what the Lord pronounced through the Prophet Ezekiel concerning Moab and Seir would be a reminder both to Israel *and* to the rest of the world that He is no respecter of persons or nations. Ultimately God's glory is what matters:

> "Thus says the Lord GOD: Because Moab and Seir said, 'Behold, the house of Judah is like all the other nations,' therefore I will lay open the flank of Moab from the cities . . . I will give it along with the Ammonites to the people of the East as a possession . . . and I will execute judgments upon Moab. Then they will know that I am the LORD." (Ezek. 25:8-11)

The attitude of Moab and Seir was an affront to God. By regarding Israel as a nation no different from their own, they had despised God's people. In this way, then, and with our Hebrew words in mind, we can say that they had despised and therefore cursed God. This is precisely what many in the church today are doing who consider Israel to be no different than any other nation on earth. They have no idea what they are doing!

Fickle Man, Faithful God

Infuriated by Balaam's first oracle, Balak took the seer to another vantage point, only to be disappointed once more by the words he proclaimed:

> God is not man, that He should lie, or a son of man, that He should change His mind. Has He said, and will He not do it? Or has He spoken, and will He not fulfill it? Behold, I received a command to bless: He has blessed, and I cannot revoke it. He has not beheld misfortune in Jacob, nor has He seen trouble in Israel. The LORD their God is with them, and the shout of a king is among them . . . For there is no enchantment against Jacob, no divination against Israel; now it shall be said of Jacob and Israel, "What has God wrought!" (Num. 23:19-23)

As a believer, I cherish the words written by Paul to the Philippians: "He who began a good work in you will bring it to completion at the day of Jesus the Messiah" (Phil. 1:6). If that promise still holds true for the church after *two* thousand years, then why, after *four* thousand years, would the One who began a good work with Israel be anything but faithful to complete it as well? I believe this is one of the lessons that God was teaching the world through Balaam's second oracle.

In his commentary, Plymouth Brethren preacher, author, and editor Charles Henry Mackintosh (1820-1896) wrote:

> This places Israel upon safe ground. God must be true to Himself. Is there any power that can possibly prevent Him from fulfilling His word and oath? Surely not. '*He hath blessed*; and I cannot reverse it.' God *will* not, and Satan *can* not reverse the blessing. Thus all is settled.[10]

---

[10] Charles Henry Mackintosh, *Notes on the Book of Numbers* (London: G. Morrish, 1869), p. 384.

To God's pronouncement through Balaam, we could add the words of Joshua: "Not one word has failed of all the good things that the LORD your God promised concerning you" (Josh. 23:14); of Jeremiah: "I am watching over my word to perform it" (Jer. 1:12); and of Jesus: "Truly, I say to you, until heaven and earth pass away, not an iota, not a dot, will pass from the Law until all is accomplished" (Mt. 5:18). Scripture is unequivocal: God finishes what He begins!

According to certain translations[11] of Balaam's second oracle, God was not going to behold "misfortune" or "trouble" in Israel (Num. 23:20). This is a difficult verse. If it is translated this way, then it seems to imply that God was not going to allow anything injurious or calamitous to happen to His people as they journeyed toward the Promised Land. Other translations favor an alternative reading: "He has not observed iniquity in Jacob, nor has He seen wickedness in Israel."[12] If we take this translation instead, then even greater care is needed. Clearly the Israelites were far from blameless, the golden-calf episode being a case in point. Whenever iniquity was found amongst His people, God addressed it and dealt with it either immediately or in time, for He can *never* turn a blind eye to sin. However, the Hebrew word *nâbaṭ* ("to behold" or "to observe") speaks of looking intently at something or scanning it with great care. This verse in Numbers, using our second translation, suggests that God did not look at the wickedness of the Israelites to such an extent that He would have had to destroy them. He loved His people, having redeemed them from slavery, and He remembered the everlasting covenant He had made with their fathers.

Whatever the true meaning of this verse may be, by taking a panoramic view of the Bible and the whole course of human history, we can conclude that God never *focuses* on the sin of His people. If He did, then Israel—and the church—would not survive! On the contrary, God looks intently at the way His name is either being honored or profaned. Above all, He looks at His Son. Even in Balaam's time, God foresaw the day of days when Jesus, the spotless Lamb of God, would bear upon Himself all of the sin, guilt, and shame of His people Israel and of the whole world (Isa. 53:5-8; Jn. 1:29;

---

[11] Including the RSV, ESV, NASB, NIV, and NLT.

[12] NKJV; see also KJV, ASV, DBY, and YLT.

3:16; 1 Jn. 2:2; 4:14). So how could Israel survive back then, how can Israel survive today, and how will Israel survive tomorrow and through the tribulation to come? The answer is gloriously simple: Jesus!

What God Has Done

Balaam's second oracle includes a remarkable statement that demands our attention: "For there is no enchantment against Jacob, no divination against Israel; now it shall be said of Jacob and Israel, 'What has God wrought!'" (Num. 23:23). Who was to make such an exclamation concerning Jacob/Israel?[13] Was it to be the Israelites themselves after they had experienced God's mighty deliverance from Egypt and from every threat made against them during their wilderness wanderings? The difficulty with this answer is that no sooner had Balaam delivered his oracles than the Israelites yoked themselves to the Baal of Peor, incurring God's immediate judgment (Num. 25). Were the words to be spoken by Israel's neighbors when they witnessed God's people possessing and prospering in the land of Canaan? We do know that Rahab and many of her people feared the Lord when they heard what He had done for Israel. As she told the two Israelite spies in Jericho, "our hearts melted, and there was no spirit left in any man because of you, for the LORD your God, He is God in the heavens above and on the earth beneath" (Josh. 2:11). The Queen of Sheba was another who extolled the Lord when she visited Jerusalem during Solomon's reign. Upon hearing the king's wisdom and beholding the people's prosperity, we are told that "there was no more spirit in her." The queen then publicly blessed the One who, as she said, "loved Israel for ever" (1 Kgs. 10:1-13). The difficulty with these answers, however, is that the Israelites turned away from God after the time of Joshua and the elders who outlived him; as for Solomon, his reign ended in disgrace, Israel was divided, and the nation was never the same again. Therefore, trying to pinpoint a time

---

[13] I recommend listening to the following extract from a sermon that was preached by the much-loved founder of the Calvary Chapel movement, Pastor Charles "Chuck" Smith (1927-2013). See Chuck Smith, "Numbers 21-28 (1979-82 Audio)," www.blueletterbible. org/audio_video (frame 50:00 – 54:40).

past that *precisely* and *fully* fits this particular part of Balaam's oracle is problematic.

Having made these caveats, I still believe the words "What has God wrought!" do apply, in the first instance, to what happened with Israel millennia ago, including the responses of Rahab and the Queen of Sheba. However, I propose that this exclamation is ultimately the custodianship of the church, especially the generation of believers that has witnessed Israel's miraculous rebirth as a nation. This is because Israel's national restoration is directly linked to the second coming of Jesus and His thousand-year reign on earth. There could be no second coming if Israel did not exist as a sovereign nation! Whenever God makes pronouncements like those He made through Balaam, there is invariably a triple aspect to them: the immediate, the ongoing, and the future. God's Word is living, active, and enduring. A prophecy may be specific to an individual, group, or nation at the time it is given, but more often than not, there are prophetic *elements* that have an ongoing application throughout the generations, with an ultimate end in view. This is clearly seen with Israel since God declared that His people would continue to exist as a nation before Him for as long as the fixed order of the earth endures (Jer. 31:35-37) and until He ushers in "new heavens and a new earth" (Isa. 66:17). In other words, some of the prophecies concerning Israel have had their fulfillment in times past, as we read in biblical history; some have only been partially fulfilled;[14] some are continuing to be fulfilled in our time;[15] and the majority will only be fulfilled once the rapture has taken place and the tribulation period has begun.[16]

I therefore maintain that every believer without exception, regardless of their ethnic, cultural, or ecclesiastical background, should be giving the

---

[14] One example is Isaiah 61, only part of which Jesus read out in the Nazareth synagogue before declaring Himself to be the fulfillment (Lk. 4:16-21). The portion of the prophecy that deals with "the day of vengeance of our God" still awaits its fulfillment.

[15] Most notably, the prophecies that speak about the return of the Jewish people to their ancient homeland.

[16] Including Daniel's prophecy of "the abomination of desolation," which Jesus spoke about to His disciples on the Mount of Olives (Mt. 24:15; Dan. 9:27; 12:11).

same wholehearted response whenever they contemplate or converse about Israel: "What has God wrought!"

Scripture is clear: A day is coming when Balaam's second oracle will have its ultimate fulfillment. On that day, God will be acknowledged by all nations for what He will have done for Israel throughout the nation's history, including the supernatural intervention of His Son at the end of the tribulation period when Israel will be on the brink of annihilation. Let us consider the words of the song of Moses and the Israelites after God had delivered them from Pharaoh's armies:

> The peoples have heard; they tremble; pangs have seized the inhabitants of Philistia. Now are the chiefs of Edom dismayed; trembling seizes the leaders of Moab; all the inhabitants of Canaan have melted away. Terror and dread fall upon them; because of the greatness of your arm, they are still as a stone, till your people, O LORD, pass by, till the people pass by whom you have purchased. (Ex. 15:14-16)

Now let us recall the words of the psalmist after God had brought a remnant of His people back from Babylonian captivity:

> When the LORD restored the fortunes of Zion, we were like those who dream. Then our mouth was filled with laughter, and our tongue with shouts of joy; then they said among the nations, "The LORD has done great things for them." (Ps. 126:1-3)

Only around fifty thousand Jewish exiles returned from Babylon following King Cyrus' decree (Ezra 2:64-65; Neh. 7:66-67), and yet the psalmist declared that it would be said *among the nations* what great things the Lord had done for His people. If we compare that event to what we see today with nearly seven million Jews living in the Land of Israel, then surely the nations have a lot more to say about what God has done for His people! This is a staggering population statistic, but it is only the fulfillment, at least in part, of what the Lord promised long ago. As we read in the book of Jeremiah, for example,

> "Therefore, behold, the days are coming, declares the LORD, when it shall no longer be said, 'As the LORD lives who brought up the people of Israel out of the land of Egypt,' but 'As the LORD lives who brought up the people of Israel out of the north country and out of all the countries where he had driven them.' For I will bring them back to their own land that I gave to their fathers." (Jer. 16:14-15)

Only when the Messiah returns to Jerusalem and the kingdom is restored to Israel (Acts 1:6-8) will *all* nations finally acknowledge *everything* that God has done for His people. C. H. Mackintosh put it well when he wrote:

> It is not 'What hath Israel wrought!' Balak and Balaam would have found plenty to do in the way of cursing, had Israel's work been in question. The Lord be praised, it is on what He hath wrought that His people stand, and their foundation is as stable as the throne of God.[17]

Irrevocable Blessing, Irreversible Decree

> What then shall we say to these things? If God is for us, who can be against us?... Who shall bring any charge against God's elect? It is God who justifies. Who is to condemn? Messiah Jesus is the one who died — more than that, who was raised — who is at the right hand of God, who indeed is interceding for us. Who shall separate us from the love of Messiah? (Rom. 8:31-35)

These words of Paul to the Romans assure believers of every generation that nothing can cause their spiritual blessings in the heavenly realms to be revoked. For all her faults and failings—and there are many—the body of Messiah, the church, cannot be cursed. However, this does not mean that individual believers, local assemblies, Christian ministries, and global denominations are immune from God's censure and discipline. So it is with Israel *as a nation*. Remember that shortly after the episode with Balak and Balaam, many individual Israelites were judged by God on account of their idolatry. Furthermore, an entire generation that came out of Egypt never entered the Promised Land.[18] But *as a nation*, Israel cannot be cursed to the point of destruction, having been forever covered by God's blessing. As we read in Jeremiah,

> Thus says the LORD, who gives the sun for light by day and the fixed order of the moon and the stars for light by night, who stirs up the sea so that its waves roar — the LORD of hosts is His name: "If this fixed order departs from before me, declares the LORD, then shall the offspring of Israel cease from being a nation before me forever." Thus says the LORD: "If the heavens above can be measured, and the foundations of the earth below can be explored, then I will

---

[17] Mackintosh, *Notes*, pp. 384-85.
[18] See 1 Cor. 10:1-10; Heb. 3:7 – 4:11.

cast off all the offspring of Israel for all that they have done, declares the LORD." (Jer. 31:35-37; cf. 33:23-26)

The psalmist was equally emphatic:

O offspring of Abraham, His servant, children of Jacob, His chosen ones! ... He remembers His covenant forever, the word that He commanded, for a thousand generations, the covenant that He made with Abraham, His sworn promise to Isaac, which He confirmed to Jacob as a statute, to Israel as an everlasting covenant, saying, "To you I will give the land of Canaan as your portion for an inheritance [*nachălâh*]." (Ps. 105:6-11)

Absolute statements like these could have and should have prevented two thousand years of theological debate in the church. Could God have made Israel's position any clearer? All that is required to understand what God has declared concerning Israel is a faith that has not been clogged, cluttered, or corrupted by the theological novelties of men who have mishandled God's Word or by the demonically inspired media. Our faith as believers must be grounded in a sound, consistent, and predominantly literal interpretation of Scripture. This is the only hermeneutic that is reasonable, sensible, logical, and dependable. All other systems of interpretation generate error, create division, and damage our witness. Without the progressive revelation of God's Word *and* of God's character, and without distinguishing between Israel and the church whenever we read the Bible, everything is muddle and confusion.

Conclusion

The final book of the Old Testament (according to the order of books in our English Bibles) expresses God's indignation toward His people who were robbing Him of what was rightfully His. Yet, for all their spiritual profanity and pollution, the Lord still desired to pour out His blessings upon them. He promised to do just that if His people heeded the warning:

"Bring the full tithe into the storehouse, that there may be food in my house. And thereby put me to the test, says the LORD of hosts, if I will not open the windows of heaven for you and pour down for you a blessing until there is no more need. I will rebuke the devourer for you, so that it will not destroy the fruits of your soil, and your vine in the field shall not fail to bear, says the

LORD of hosts. Then all nations will call you blessed, for you will be a land of delight, says the LORD of hosts." (Mal. 3:10-12)

We will pick up this thread in a later chapter, but for now let us read the solemn promise that God gave through the Prophet Zechariah. Its fulfillment may seem impossible to imagine, but the Lord never asks His people to imagine anything, only to believe what He has spoken:

> "And as you have been a byword of cursing among the nations, O house of Judah and house of Israel, so will I save you, and you shall be a blessing" ... For thus says the LORD of hosts: "As I purposed to bring disaster to you when your fathers provoked me to wrath, and I did not relent, says the LORD of hosts, so again have I purposed in these days to bring good to Jerusalem and to the house of Judah; fear not." (Zech. 8:13-15)

On March 17, 2019, with his country's economy severely ailing, Islamist Iranian President Hassan Rouhani urged his people to "put all your curses on those who created the current situation," blaming the United States, "the Zionists," and Saudi Arabia.[19] Two days later, torrential rains hit Iran and continued to fall, breaking all meteorological records. The result was unprecedented flash flooding in twenty-six of the country's thirty-one provinces, with 1,900 cities and villages damaged and over seventy civilians killed. As we read in the book of Isaiah, there will come a day when every attempt to curse Israel will cease, and Israel will finally be acknowledged as the nation uniquely and irrevocably blessed by God:

> Their offspring shall be known among the nations, and their descendants in the midst of the peoples; all who see them shall acknowledge them, that they are an offspring the LORD has blessed ... For as the earth brings forth its sprouts, and as a garden causes what is sown in it to sprout up, so the Lord GOD will cause righteousness and praise to sprout up before all the nations. (Isa. 61:9-11)

---

[19] "Rouhani urges Iranians to 'put all your curses on Zionists, US,'" *The Times of Israel*, March 18, 2019, www.timesofisrael.com/rouhani-urges-iranians-to-put-all-your-curses-on-zionists-us/.

Chapter 3:

The Irrevocable Blessing, Part 2

Before we return to the scene of the attempted crime above the plains of Moab, I would like to spotlight three of the momentous words that the Messiah spoke on the cross. In John's account of the crucifixion, we read the following: "After this, Jesus, knowing that all was now finished, said (to fulfill the Scripture), 'I thirst' . . . When Jesus had received the sour wine, He said, 'It is finished,' and He bowed His head and gave up His spirit" (Jn. 19:28-30).

Before any consideration is given to what it was that was finished on the cross, we can say unequivocally that it was not finished by command of Caiaphas, the high priest of Israel, or Pontius Pilate, the Roman governor of Judea. Caiaphas had torn his robes and charged Jesus with blasphemy before handing Him over to Pilate. Pilate in turn had washed his hands and pronounced himself innocent before delivering Jesus over to be crucified. But that which was finished on the cross was only finished when the Messiah uttered those anguished words and yielded His spirit to the Father.

According to the New Testament, we are told that the Son of God came to this earth to:

- ✡ Seek and save the lost (Lk. 19:10)
- ✡ Call sinners to repentance (Lk. 5:32)
- ✡ Baptize with the Holy Spirit and fire (Mt. 3:11)
- ✡ Fulfill the Law and the Prophets (Mt. 5:17)
- ✡ Do the will of the One who sent Him (Jn. 6:38)
- ✡ Lay down His life for the sheep (Jn. 10:15-17)
- ✡ Give them eternal life (Jn. 10:28)
- ✡ Bear witness to the truth (Jn. 18:37)

- ✧ Destroy the works of the devil (1 Jn. 3:8)

This list is by no means exhaustive, but can it be said that any of the above was "finished" in the way we typically understand our English word? Is the Lord not continuing to do all of the above? Many in the church would have us believe that God's work with Israel, for example, terminated when Jesus died and rose again. I may be unable to fully comprehend and articulate all that the Savior accomplished, but the Bible tells me this:

- ✧ Through the sinless life of the most righteous Jew who ever walked the earth;
- ✧ through the miracles, signs, and wonders of Israel's long-awaited Messiah;
- ✧ through the compassionate ministry of the Good Shepherd of God's sheep;
- ✧ through the substitutionary, atoning sacrifice of the spotless Lamb of God;
- ✧ and through the glorious resurrection of the Great High Priest

... all that was necessary for every human being to be saved from their sin and reconciled to God was completed on the cross. As the Apostle John wrote, "Now Jesus did many other signs in the presence of the disciples, which are not written in this book; these are written so that you may believe that Jesus is the Messiah, the Son of God, and that by believing you may have life in His name" (Jn. 20:30-31).

The point I wish to make here is simply this: No believer, theologian, author, campaigner, church leader, NGO, or denominational assembly/council/synod has *any* right or authority to declare God's work finished until God Himself has explicitly said so! This applies to the church on an individual and corporate basis, and to Israel and the peoples of the world on a national basis. If God is seen to be working or has promised to work in a particular way in the future, then it is in our best interest not to interrupt Him, contradict Him, or tell Him that His work is already done.[1]

---

[1] I pray that this may encourage any brother or sister in the Lord whom God has called to a particular work but who may be feeling discouraged, demoralized, or in despair right now. God has not finished the work He began in and through you, no matter what the enemy may have you believe.

The work that God began with Israel when He set Abraham and his descendants apart to be His earthly inheritance did not end at Calvary, as so many in the church have mistakenly believed. That unique sovereign work of God was *completed* by Jesus on the cross in the sense that He *finished* everything that was required for the nation of Israel to fulfill its calling. Since that national calling extends to the end of time according to God's prophetic Word, then we can say for certain that God's work with Israel is far from done. As Paul wrote in his letter to the Romans, "For I tell you that Messiah became a servant to the circumcised [the people of Israel] to show God's truthfulness, in order *to confirm the promises* given to the patriarchs, and in order that the Gentiles might glorify God for His mercy" (Rom. 15:8-9).

In Satan's Service

Two of the Gospels record an astonishing episode when one of the twelve disciples, Simon Peter, took Jesus aside and rebuked Him. The Lord had just informed them all that He was going to Jerusalem to suffer and be killed but on the third day be raised from the dead. Matthew 16:22 contains Simon's reaction: "Far be it from you, Lord! This shall never happen to you." These may have been Simon's words, but they originated from another source, which is why Jesus' response was immediate, firm, and quite shocking: "Get behind me, Satan! You are a hindrance to me. For you are not setting your mind on the things of God, but on the things of man" (Mt. 16:23; Mk. 8:33). To Simon's unredeemed mind and the minds of his fellow disciples whom he represented, the path that Jesus was proposing and pursuing was incomprehensible—as indeed it would have been to anyone of us had we been standing in their sandals. But what makes this episode even more compelling is that Simon Peter had earlier confessed Jesus to be the Messiah and Son of God (Mt. 16:16), a confession that the Lord Himself had attributed to the revelation of His Father. Now, at Caesarea Philippi, Jesus was publicly reprimanding Simon, who had unwittingly allowed Satan to manipulate his emotions in an attempt to keep the Messiah from fulfilling His mission.

For nearly two thousand years, many who have professed Jesus as Lord and Savior have been unwittingly used by Satan to make the church a stumbling block to the Jewish people, perhaps no more so than in our own time. By reinterpreting, spiritualizing, or allegorizing the very name "Israel," they have erroneously claimed that Jesus theologically and prophetically replaced, redefined, fulfilled, or enlarged Israel when He established the church. In recent years, this doctrine of demons[2] has been manifesting itself in all kinds of nefarious campaigns and crusades against the modern State of Israel. The Jewish people are now struggling to differentiate between the enduring and escalating anti-Semitism of the nations and the anti-Zionism that has become increasingly prevalent within the church. The reason for their difficulty is simple: Anti-Zionism *is* a form of anti-Semitism, a manifestation of the spirit of Antichrist and not the Holy Spirit. All who claim to follow Jesus but treat Israel in such an appalling manner are clearly being used by Satan to try to obstruct God's purposes for His chosen people.

What a Question!

At the beginning of Romans 11, Paul rhetorically asked the church a question that is still relevant and of critical importance. This is how it reads in our English Bibles:

> I say then, Hath God cast away his people? God forbid! (KJV)
>
> I say then, has God cast away His people? Certainly not! (NKJV)
>
> I say then, Did God cast off his people? God forbid! (ASV)
>
> I say then, God has not rejected His people, has He? May it never be! (NASB)
>
> I ask, then, has God rejected his people? By no means! (RSV, ESV)
>
> I say then, Has God cast away his people? Far be the thought! (DBY)

---

[2] "Now the Spirit expressly says that in later times some will depart from the faith by devoting themselves to deceitful spirits and teachings of demons" (1 Tim. 4:1). "For the time is coming when people will not endure sound teaching, but having itching ears they will accumulate for themselves teachers to suit their own passions, and will turn away from listening to the truth and wander off into myths" (2 Tim. 4:3-4).

I ask then: Did God reject his people? By no means! (NIV)

So I ask, God has not rejected his people, has he? Absolutely not! (NET)

I ask, then, has God rejected his own people, the nation of Israel? Of course not! (NLT)

On ten occasions in his letter to the Romans, Paul used the subjunctive "God forbid!" He did so in order to expound the truth concerning the righteousness of God. This series of subjunctives closes with three statements he made in chapters 9-11, the final two of which related specifically to Israel. In other words, what we read about Israel in these three chapters is both the continuation *and* conclusion to Paul's whole argument; it is *not* a parenthesis, as many scholars have mistakenly argued. Here is that series of ten, as found in the King James Version:

1. For what if some [Jews] did not believe? Shall their unbelief make the faith of God without effect? God forbid! (Rom. 3:3-4)

2. Is God unrighteous who taketh vengeance? (I speak as a man) God forbid! (Rom. 3:5-6)

3. Do we then make void the law through faith? God forbid! (Rom. 3:31)

4. Shall we continue in sin, that grace may abound? God forbid! (Rom. 6:1-2)

5. Shall we sin, because we are not under the law, but under grace? God forbid! (Rom. 6:15)

6. Is the law sin? God forbid! (Rom. 7:7)

7. Was then that which is good made death unto me? God forbid. (Rom. 7:13)

8. What shall we say then? Is there unrighteousness with God? God forbid! (Rom. 9:14)

9. I say then, Hath God cast away His people? God forbid! (Rom. 11:1)

10. I say then, Have they stumbled that they should fall? God forbid! (Rom. 11:11)

Although Paul had not finished dictating his letter to Tertius (his amanuensis)—and despite bearing "great sorrow and unceasing anguish" in his heart for his fellow Jews (Rom. 9:2)—he was suddenly enraptured with the glory of God's dealings with Israel when he said in Romans 11:33-36, "Oh, the depth of the riches and wisdom and knowledge of God! How unsearchable are His judgments and how inscrutable His ways! . . . To Him be glory forever. Amen."

Satan's primary and perennial objective is to rob God of His glory, and the annihilation of Israel is integral to his achieving that goal. If the physical destruction of the Jewish people is on his agenda for the nations, then the theological destruction of "Israel" is part of his agenda for the church. The two go hand in hand. This is because what happens in the spiritual or heavenly realm invariably has its counterpart in the physical or earthly realm. Israel's miraculous reestablishment as a state in 1948 did not come about without the earnest prayers and faithful preaching and teaching of many believers. The political movement among the nations to secure a homeland for the Jewish people ran parallel with a move of God's Spirit within the church. But the reverse has also been true. Satan's nefarious attempt to physically destroy the Jewish State has been working in tandem with his malevolent campaign to deceive men, ministries, and movements within the church into jumping on the pro-Palestinian bandwagon.

God's Word tells us plainly that Satan is "the god of this world," who has "blinded the minds of the unbelievers, to keep them from seeing the light of the gospel of the glory of Messiah, who is the image of God" (2 Cor. 4:4). This means that if man is left to himself, without the gracious intervention of God's Spirit, then he will inevitably set his mind on things that run counter to God's will. As Paul wrote, "The natural person does not accept the things of the Spirit of God, for they are folly to him, and he is not able to understand them because they are spiritually discerned" (1 Cor. 2:14). This is evident all around us in society today. It is also evident in relation to God's chosen nation, for unless a person is truly born again, he or she will never be able to understand Israel—past, present, or future. Having said that, even those who *are* born again will fall short if they are not constantly submitting to the authority of God's Word and allowing God's Spirit to shape their thinking. They may even find themselves unwittingly serving Satan's agenda, not God's.

Back to Balak

We closed the previous chapter by looking at Balaam's second oracle (Num. 23:13-24) and the persistent attempt by the king of Moab to make him curse Israel. By the time Balaam gave his third pronouncement, something significant had changed.

Up until then, Balaam had been using divination to seek the word of God, and on each occasion, "the LORD put a word in Balaam's mouth" (Num. 23:5, 12, 16). This was clearly not God's *modus operandi* or prescribed way of communicating, but Balaam was not one of His holy prophets. However, as soon as "Balaam saw that it pleased the LORD to bless Israel" (Num. 24:1), he stopped searching for omens. We are then told that he set his face toward the wilderness and for the first time saw the whole nation of Israel encamped according to its tribal divisions. Previously, Balak had restricted Balaam's view to the outskirts of the encampment (Num. 22:41; 23:13). This was in keeping with Moabite belief that only part of the nation needed to be seen when pronouncing a curse. Balaam, of course, would have happily obliged Balak and reaped the financial rewards had God not restrained him, for he "loved the wages of wickedness" (2 Pet. 2:15, NIV). However, once it became clear that God's blessing was never going to be revoked, Balaam's approach (if not his heart) changed.

I believe God wanted Balaam to witness the full extent of His people, including the awesome sight of the Tabernacle in their midst, the great symbol of God's abiding presence with Israel. There was to be no more dabbling with divination, at least for the time being. We are not told what Balaam thought as he lifted up his eyes and beheld the Israelites at that moment. Perhaps he reflected for the first time on the scale of what God had already revealed to him. He was no longer distracted by enchantments but enchanted by the distraction of a nation set apart, dwelling alone, and enjoying the protective blessing of God. Now for the first time, "the Spirit of God came upon him" (Num. 24:2-3) to reveal the glorious zenith of Israel's history. There was more of a poetic flourish with the third oracle, for Balaam was shown what he could not perceive with his natural eye—namely, the way God Himself sees His people. As we read the following extract, let us keep in mind that the tents of Israel were not encamped in the land of milk and honey at this stage but in the desert wasteland of Moab:

> How lovely are your tents, O Jacob, your encampments, O Israel! Like palm groves [or valleys] that stretch afar, like gardens beside a river, like aloes that the LORD has planted, like cedar trees beside the waters. Water shall flow from his buckets, and his seed shall be in many waters. (Num. 24:5-7)

At the close of his oracle, Balaam addressed Israel with the words: "Blessed are those who bless you, and cursed are those who curse you" (Num. 24:9). This was now the third time that Balak had instructed Balaam to curse and the third time God had constrained him to bless. The king was furious and sought to dispense with Balaam's services, but God had not finished speaking! Another oracle was imminent that would spell the end for Balak and the Moabites at the hand of One who would arise from the very nation he was trying to curse. But before we consider this fourth and final oracle, I believe an application can be made here. The church must never interrupt God when He speaks in His Word about *judging* Israel because promises of national *restoration* and future *blessing* invariably follow! A case in point is Jeremiah 32:

> "Therefore, thus says the LORD: Behold, I am giving this city [Jerusalem] into the hands of the Chaldeans and into the hand of Nebuchadnezzar king of Babylon, and he shall capture it . . . For the children of Israel and the children of Judah have done nothing but evil in my sight from their youth . . . This city has aroused my anger and wrath, from the day it was built to this day, so that I will remove it from my sight . . . **[Church, keep reading!]** Now therefore thus says the LORD, the God of Israel . . . Behold, I will gather them from all the countries to which I drove them in my anger and my wrath and in great indignation. I will bring them back to this place, and I will make them dwell in safety. And they shall be my people, and I will be their God. I will give them one heart and one way, that they may fear me forever . . . I will make with them an everlasting covenant, that I will not turn away from doing good to them . . . I will rejoice in doing them good, and I will plant them in this land in faithfulness, with all my heart and all my soul. For thus says the LORD: Just as I have brought all this great disaster upon this people, so I will bring upon them all the good that I promise them . . . for I will restore their fortunes, declares the LORD." (Jer. 32:28-44)

Let us combine this remarkable prophecy with what we read in the book of Ezekiel, where we find prophecies addressed not only to *the people* of Israel but also to *the mountains* of Israel. This becomes even more compelling when we realize that so many in the church today are claiming that the Land of Israel has been made theologically and prophetically redundant.[3] The following prophecy from Ezekiel 6, if read in isolation, would certainly appear to corroborate such a claim:

> The word of the LORD came to me: "Son of man, set your face toward the mountains of Israel, and prophesy against them, and say, You mountains of Israel, hear the word of the Lord GOD! Thus says the Lord GOD to the mountains and the hills, to the ravines and the valleys: Behold, I, even I, will bring a sword upon you, and I will destroy your high places ... And you shall know that I am the LORD, when their slain lie among their idols around their altars, on every high hill, on all the mountaintops." (Ezek. 6:1-13)

But chapter 6 does not conclude the prophecies of Ezekiel. God had not finished speaking! Here is an extract from chapter 36:

> "And you, son of man, prophesy to the mountains of Israel, and say, 'O mountains of Israel, hear the word of the LORD' ... 'Thus says the Lord GOD to the mountains and the hills, the ravines and the valleys, the desolate wastes and the deserted cities, which have become a prey and derision to the rest of the nations all around ... I swear that the nations that are all around you shall themselves suffer reproach. But you, O mountains of Israel, shall shoot forth your branches and yield your fruit to my people Israel, for they will soon come home. For behold, I am for you, and I will turn to you, and you shall be tilled and sown. And I will multiply people on you, the whole house of Israel, all of it.'" (Ezek. 36:1-10)

In the light of these prophecies, why would anyone take chapter 6 literally but then spiritualize chapter 36 and apply it to the church? Moreover, why would anyone believe that "the whole house of Israel" returned to the mountains of Israel when approximately fifty thousand Jews returned from Babylonian exile in the sixth century B.C.? To spiritualize this prophecy defies both reason and grammatical convention. More importantly, it

---

[3] I have addressed these claims in my previous book, *Israel Betrayed, Volume 2: The Rise of Christian Palestinianism.*

robs the nation of Israel of its future blessing and the God of Israel of His future glory.

A Star out of Jacob, a Scepter out of Israel

Before delivering his final oracle, Balaam ominously announced to an angry Balak, "Come, I will let you know what this people will do to your people in the latter days" (Num. 24:14). A sentence was to be pronounced not only upon the Moabites but also upon all of Israel's hostile neighbors:

> I see Him, but not now; I behold Him, but not near: a star shall come out of Jacob, and a scepter shall rise out of Israel; it shall crush the forehead of Moab and break down all the sons of Sheth. Edom shall be dispossessed; Seir also, his enemies, shall be dispossessed. Israel is doing valiantly. And One from Jacob shall exercise dominion and destroy the survivors of cities! (Num. 24:17-19)

We know today what Balak did not know then, that the One whom Balaam beheld from afar was Israel's Messiah, Jesus. God sees what we do not see—namely, the end from the beginning. There is no past, present, or future with the One who dwells outside of time. As Moses declared, "a thousand years in your sight are but as yesterday when it is past, or as a watch in the night" (Ps. 90:4), and as Peter wrote, "with the Lord one day is as a thousand years, and a thousand years as one day" (2 Pet. 3:8).

The fact that the Balaam-Balak episode is referred to in four other books of the Bible not only illustrates how important it *was* in Israel's past but also how important it *is* in Israel's present and how important it *will be* in Israel's future. Here are those additional references:

When Moses laid out certain exclusion laws to prepare for the Israelites' crossing into Canaan, he made the following stipulation:

> No Ammonite or Moabite may enter the assembly of the LORD . . . because they did not meet you with bread and with water on the way, when you came out of Egypt, and because they hired against you Balaam the son of Beor from Pethor of Mesopotamia, to curse you. But the LORD your God would not listen to Balaam; instead the LORD your God turned the curse into a blessing for you, because the LORD your God loved you. (Deut. 23:3-5)

When Joshua assembled the tribes of Israel at Shechem to renew the covenant, he brought the word of the Lord to them. In that word, the Lord reminded His people of some critical moments in their history:

> Then Balak the son of Zippor, king of Moab, arose and fought against Israel. And he sent and invited Balaam the son of Beor to curse you, but I would not listen to Balaam. Indeed, he blessed you. So I delivered you out of his hand. (Josh. 24:9-10)

When God indicted His people through the Prophet Micah, He brought to their remembrance how He had once intervened to prevent them from being cursed:

> "O my people, remember what Balak king of Moab devised, and what Balaam the son of Beor answered him, and what happened from Shittim to Gilgal, that you may know the saving acts of the LORD" (Mic. 6:5).

When Nehemiah made his final reforms in Jerusalem, he reminded the people of what had taken place above the plains of Moab:

> On that day they read from the Book of Moses in the hearing of the people. And in it was found written that no Ammonite or Moabite should ever enter the assembly of God, for they did not meet the people of Israel with bread and water, but hired Balaam against them to curse them — yet our God turned the curse into a blessing. (Neh. 13:1-2)

God will never listen to any man or malevolent spirit that seeks to curse and destroy His people. In Psalms 2 and 83, we read about the perennial conspiracy of the nations against the Lord and His Messiah and their futile attempts to defy God, thwart His purposes, and destroy Israel:

> Why do the nations rage and the peoples plot in vain? The kings of the earth set themselves, and the rulers take counsel together, against the LORD and against His anointed, saying, "Let us burst their bonds apart and cast away their cords from us." (Ps. 2:1-3)

> They lay crafty plans against your people; they consult together against your treasured ones. They say, "Come, let us wipe them out as a nation; let the name of Israel be remembered no more!" (Ps. 83:3-4)

David's response in Psalm 2 was to "tell of the decree" (Ps. 2:7) and stand resolutely on what God had already spoken. Asaph's response in Psalm 83 was to recall what God had done in times past and to pray that the enemies of both Israel and of God would know that He alone is "the Most High over all the earth" (Ps. 83:18). As we read in the book of Isaiah, "The grass withers, the flower fades, but the word of our God will stand forever" (Isa. 40:8).

The *Aaronic* Blessing?

In many local churches, the benediction recorded at the end of Numbers 6 is often recited by pastors over their congregations or sung by the people to one another at the close of a service. This benediction is generally referred to as "the Aaronic blessing" and reads as follows:

> The LORD spoke to Moses, saying, "Speak to Aaron and his sons, saying, Thus you shall bless the people of Israel: you shall say to them, The LORD bless you and keep you; the LORD make His face to shine upon you and be gracious to you; the LORD lift up His countenance upon you and give you peace. So shall they put my name upon the people of Israel, and I will bless them." (Num. 6:22-27)

Since the benediction pronounced upon Israel was the blessing of God, then perhaps a more appropriate designation would be "God's blessing," "Yahweh's blessing," or "the divine blessing." This would certainly help keep the focus on the One who initiated the benediction and who guarantees its ongoing efficacy. Although Aaron and his sons were the anointed mediators, their priesthood was only temporary, anticipating the more excellent and permanent priesthood of the Messiah. If the blessing had originated with Aaron, then it would certainly have expired when Messiah Jesus, "a priest forever, after the order of Melchizedek" (Heb. 7:17), cut the New Covenant on the cross—or perhaps much earlier when God judged Aaron for his unfaithfulness at the waters of Meribah (Num. 20:10-13, 23-29). The blessing remains in effect to this day because it was initiated by and is dependent upon God, and its mediation continues through the heavenly intercession of the Jewish Messiah, Jesus.

God's blessing in this particular context is tied to Israel's *position* as a nation chosen, sanctified, and precious to Him and not to the obedience of the people themselves. This important distinction was made in the previous chapter. However, the blessing of God upon Israel cannot be understood solely by reading the words of the benediction itself. Through the pronouncements of the prophets in particular, God has communicated to us what that blessing looks like from His perspective. Using the most evocative language, the Lord refers to Israel as His "chosen people,"[4] His "chosen ones,"[5] and His "treasured possession."[6] Metaphorically, God speaks of Israel as being His "darling child,"[7] His "children,"[8] His "dear son,"[9] His "firstborn son,"[10] His "sons and daughters,"[11] His "wife,"[12] His "flock,"[13] and "the apple of His eye."[14] This kind of tender language speaks so powerfully of the way in which God sees Israel and therefore of the way in which He wants the church to see Israel too. This brings us to the crux of the divine blessing.

God told Moses what would happen the moment Aaron and his sons proclaimed the benediction: "So shall they put my name upon the people of Israel, and I will bless them" (Num. 6:27). For the eternal, omnipotent, and transcendent God of all creation to stoop in this way and set His hallowed name upon a sinful nation is beyond extraordinary. We will be considering the name of God in more detail in a later chapter. Within the context of the divine blessing, we simply need to observe at this point that in putting His name upon His people, God was emphasizing at least three things:

1. Divine ownership and obligation
2. Divine possession and privilege
3. Divine permanency and continuity

---

[4] Isa. 43:20; cf. Dt. 7:6, 14:2; 1 Kgs. 3:8; Ps. 33:12.

[5] 1 Chron. 16:13; Ps. 105:6, 43; 106:5.

[6] Ex. 19:5; Deut. 7:6; 14:2; 26:18.

[7] Jer. 31:20; cf. Hos. 11:1.

[8] Deut. 32:20; Isa. 1:2-4; 30:1; 45:11.

[9] Jer. 31:20.

[10] Ex. 4:22; Jer. 31:9.

[11] Deut. 32:19; Isa. 43:6; cf. 2 Cor. 6:18.

[12] Isa. 54:6; cf. Hos. 2:2, 16.

[13] Isa. 40:11; 63:11; Jer. 23:2-3; 31:10; Ezek. 34:12-22; 36:37; Mic. 2:12; 5:4; 7:14; Zech. 9:16; 10:3; cf. Ps. 68:10; 77:20; 78:52; 80:1.

[14] Deut. 32:10; Zech. 2:8.

No other nation on earth has ever stood in such intimate relationship with God the way Israel has. No other nation on earth has ever been so blessed and privileged by God the way Israel has. No other nation on earth has ever incurred so much divine discipline and judgment for its sin as Israel has, and no other nation on earth has ever been subjected to as much hostility and hatred from the rest of the nations as Israel has. Despite being cut off and separated from God for a season, Paul used the present tense—not past tense—when explaining to the church the privileged position his people *still held* as a nation before God:

> They *are* Israelites, and to them *belong* the adoption, the glory, the covenants, the giving of the law, the worship, and the promises. To them *belong* the patriarchs, and from their race, according to the flesh, *is* the Messiah, who is God over all, blessed forever. Amen . . . As regards the gospel, they are enemies for your sake. But as regards election, they *are* beloved for the sake of their forefathers. For the gifts and the calling of God *are irrevocable*. (Rom. 9:4; 11:28-29)

From these words alone, the church is without excuse in terms of her understanding of Israel's present status before God. The Lord has *never* revoked His calling and election of Israel (impossible), and He has *never* withdrawn His name from Israel (unthinkable), and He has *never* reinterpreted the meaning of "Israel" and reapplied the nation's promises to the church (inconceivable). The fervent supplication of the psalmist springs to mind:

> Rise up, O judge of the earth; repay to the proud what they deserve! . . . They crush your people, O LORD, and afflict your heritage [*nachălâh*] . . . Understand, O dullest of the people! Fools, when will you be wise? . . . For the LORD will not forsake His people; He will not abandon His heritage [*nachălâh*]; for justice will return to the righteous, and all the upright in heart will follow it. (Ps. 94:2-14)

The Blessed One

Scripture clearly identifies the source of all true blessing. As we read in the Psalms, "Blessed be the LORD, the God of Israel, who alone does wondrous things. Blessed be His glorious name forever" (Ps. 72:18-19; cf. 89:52). The

Prophet Daniel, upon receiving from God the revelation and interpretation of Nebuchadnezzar's dream, prayed, "Blessed be the name of God forever and ever, to whom belong wisdom and might" (Dan. 2:19-20). In his letters to the churches in Rome and Corinth, Paul exalted "the Creator, who is blessed forever!" (Rom. 1:25), and "the God and Father of the Lord Jesus, He who is blessed forever" (2 Cor. 11:31), and "the Messiah, who is God over all, blessed forever" (Rom. 9:5). He also began his letter to the Ephesians with the following benediction:

> Blessed be the God and Father of our Lord Jesus the Messiah, who has blessed us in Messiah with every spiritual blessing in the heavenly places, even as He chose us in Him before the foundation of the world, that we should be holy and blameless before Him. (Eph. 1:3)

The triune God—Father, Son, and Holy Spirit—is *the Blessed One* because of who He is. Everything good, pure, holy, honorable, lovely, righteous, just, and true comes from Him because He is, *in Himself*, all these things. The innumerable host of angels in heaven never ceases to worship God, while the vast assembly of saints on earth daily offers up its praise and thanksgiving to Him. Without fault, blemish, or weakness, His excellence is unmatched, His perfection limitless, His power undiminished, His light inextinguishable, His lovingkindness everlasting, and His grace boundless. He is forever blessed and forever worthy of all praise!

Toward the end of David's reign, after abundant provision had been made by the Israelites for the building of the Temple in Jerusalem, the king acknowledged that everything had come from God. The king then blessed the Lord in the presence of the people:

> Blessed are you, O LORD, the God of Israel our father, forever and ever. Yours, O LORD, is the greatness and the power and the glory and the victory and the majesty, for all that is in the heavens and in the earth is yours. Yours is the kingdom, O LORD, and you are exalted as head above all. Both riches and honor come from you, and you rule over all ... And now we thank you, our God, and praise your glorious name. But who am I, and what is my people, that we should be able thus to offer willingly? For all things come from you, and of your own have we given you ... O LORD our God, all this abundance that we have provided for building you a house for your holy name comes from your hand and is all your own ... O LORD, the God of Abraham, Isaac, and Israel, our fathers, keep forever such purposes and thoughts in the

hearts of your people, and direct their hearts toward you. (1 Chron. 29:10-18)

David then called upon the assembly to bless the Lord, and the people bowed their heads and paid homage to Him (1 Chron. 29:20). Few moments in Israel's tempestuous history have ever eclipsed what happened that day in Jerusalem as the people, with one accord, blessed the God of Abraham, Isaac, and Jacob. But that day will forever be eclipsed when they finally bless the holy name of their Messiah Jesus and hail Him, as doubting Thomas once did, with these words: "My Lord and my God!" (Jn. 20:28).

Over the years, I have had the privilege of speaking at a number of conferences around the world and have often closed my presentations by playing a recording of one of the songs written by my late pastor, Andrew Robinson (1951-2016). Andrew's first song was inspired by David's benedictory prayer. As a true pastor, he never stopped exhorting his flock to bless the Lord at all times. Time and again in the book of Psalms, we hear the psalmist telling his own soul, his own people, and even the angels in heaven to "bless the Lord." As we read in Psalms 103 and 135:

> Bless the LORD, O my soul, and all that is within me, bless His holy name! Bless the LORD, O my soul, and forget not all His benefits . . . Bless the LORD, O you His angels, you mighty ones who do His word, obeying the voice of His word! Bless the LORD, all His hosts, His ministers, who do His will! Bless the LORD, all His works, in all places of His dominion. Bless the LORD, O my soul! (Ps. 103:1-2, 20-22)

> O house of Israel, bless the LORD! O house of Aaron, bless the LORD! O house of Levi, bless the LORD! You who fear the LORD, bless the LORD! Blessed be the LORD from Zion, He who dwells in Jerusalem! Praise the LORD! (Ps. 135:19-21)

Thus, whenever we think of Israel as being a blessed nation, our focus should not be on Israel herself but on the One who has bestowed an irrevocable blessing upon His people, the One who is blessed forever.

Conclusion

Israel's blessing is irrevocable because God is unchangeable. Israel is blessed as a nation, even when under judgment, because of the inherent goodness and faithfulness of God and not Israel. In His infinite wisdom, the Lord set apart for Himself a nation of slaves through whom He intended to proclaim liberty to the world. With David, we can therefore proclaim:

> May His name endure forever, His fame continue as long as the sun! May people be blessed in Him, [may] all nations call Him blessed! Blessed be the LORD, the God of Israel, who alone does wondrous things. Blessed be His glorious name forever; may the whole earth be filled with His glory! Amen and Amen! (Ps. 72:17-19)

On that momentous Palm Sunday two thousand years ago, as Jesus rode into Jerusalem with deep anguish in His heart, the crowds triumphantly exclaimed: "Hosanna to the Son of David! Blessed is He who comes in the name of the Lord! Hosanna in the highest!" (Mt. 21:9). But these words were to herald Messiah's crucifixion, not His coronation. As the Lord lamented over Jerusalem, "See, your house is left to you desolate. For I tell you, you will not see me again, until you say, 'Blessed is He who comes in the name of the Lord'" (Mt. 23:38-39).

In the spirit of Balak and supremely of the Antichrist, the world will never stop condemning and cursing Israel until Israel blesses the name of Jesus. Then, and only then, will He return to deliver His people and silence the nations. How scandalous it is that this same spirit has been allowed to quietly drift in through the doors of "Christian" hearts, homes, and halls of worship. It is critically important, especially at this late hour, that as many believers as possible are taken to the vantage point of God's Word to see spiritually what Balaam saw physically: Israel through God's eyes. Every believer needs to understand where the Jewish people have come from, how they got to where they are today, where they are going according to God's prophetic roadmap, and most important of all, who it is that has blessed them and why. As believers in the Jewish Messiah, we cannot, must not, and dare not denounce those whom God has not denounced and think there will be no repercussions. Let the world condemn and curse, but let the church comfort and bless. I close this chapter with the words of the Prophet Samuel:

> For the LORD will not forsake His people, for His great name's sake, because it has pleased the LORD to make you a people for Himself. Moreover, as for

me, far be it from me that I should sin against the LORD by ceasing to pray for you, and I will instruct you in the good and the right way. (1 Sam. 12:22-23)

Chapter 4:

For His Name's Sake

So I lay prostrate before the LORD for these forty days and forty nights, because the LORD had said He would destroy you. And I prayed to the LORD, "O Lord GOD, do not destroy your people and your heritage [*nachălâh*], whom you have redeemed through your greatness, whom you have brought out of Egypt with a mighty hand. Remember your servants, Abraham, Isaac, and Jacob. Do not regard the stubbornness of this people, or their wickedness or their sin, lest the land from which you brought us say, 'Because the LORD was not able to bring them into the land that He promised them, and because He hated them, He has brought them out to put them to death in the wilderness.' For they are your people and your heritage [*nachălâh*], whom you brought out by your great power and by your outstretched arm." (Deut. 9:25-29)

If ever there were a man—apart from Jesus the Messiah!—who wrestled in prayer before God on behalf of His people, then it was Moses. He did so at great personal cost to himself, but the Israelites had reached a perilous moment in their forty-year wilderness wanderings. The very survival of the nation was at stake, but not because of any external threat. God Himself was threatening to "destroy them and blot out their name from under heaven" (Deut. 9:14). While Moses had been receiving the stone tablets from God on Mount Sinai, the Israelites had been corrupting themselves before a golden calf. For forty days and nights, Moses fasted and implored the Lord on behalf of those who had "sinned a great sin" (Ex. 32:30). As the psalmist records, God would have destroyed His people "had not Moses, His chosen one, stood in the breach before Him, to turn away His wrath from destroying them" (Ps. 106:23). What was the basis of Moses' intercession? God's honor was at stake!

I believe this is of paramount importance today in understanding how and why Christians should pray for Israel. It is all too easy for believers to be swept along by emotion and sentiment or even by a misguided sense of collective guilt for all that the Jewish people have suffered at the hands of "the Church," but we need to ensure that we are being informed by God's Word and inspired by the Holy Spirit. If the nation of Israel becomes the focus instead of the God of Israel, then we can all too quickly lose sight of God's glory.

In the Sight of the Nations

As the prophetic books of the Bible make clear, God never promised Israel restoration *for Israel's sake*. Looking back to the nation's redemption from Egypt, the psalmist wrote:

> Our fathers, when they were in Egypt, did not consider your wondrous works; they did not remember the abundance of your steadfast love, but rebelled by the sea, at the Red Sea. Yet He saved them for His name's sake, that He might make known His mighty power. (Ps. 106:7-8)

There are many wonderful prophecies yet to be fulfilled for the nation of Israel, which are laid out so beautifully and powerfully in God's Word. In Isaiah 60, for example, we read about the day when God's glory will rise upon the nation (Isa. 60:1-2), when nations and kings will come to Israel's light (Isa. 60:3), when the wealth of the nations will be brought to Israel (Isa. 60:5), when the nations and kingdoms that refuse to serve Israel will be "utterly laid waste" (Isa. 60:12), and when all who have despised and afflicted God's people "will bow down" before them (Isa. 60:14). These prophecies are all the more remarkable when we consider what Israel has suffered *and* perpetrated. However, the Lord made it clear *why* His people will be restored: "that I might be glorified" (Isa. 60:21). Restoration will come, but at great cost:

> "For my name's sake I defer my anger, for the sake of my praise I restrain it for you, that I may not cut you off. Behold, I have refined you, but not as silver; I have tried you in the furnace of affliction. For my own sake, for my own sake, I do it, for how should my name be profaned? My glory I will not give to another." (Isa. 48:9-11; cf. 42:8; 43:25; Ps. 115:1)

> "In the whole land," declares the LORD, "two thirds shall be cut off and perish, and one third shall be left alive. And I will put this third into the fire, and

refine them as one refines silver, and test them as gold is tested. They will call upon my name, and I will answer them. I will say, 'They are my people'; and they will say, 'The LORD is my God.'" (Zech. 13:8-9)

The double repetition "For my own sake, for my own sake" in Isaiah 48:11 highlights the cardinal truth that will be the focus of this chapter. There are thirty-three references in the Old Testament to God doing, or not doing, something *for His own sake*, such as forgiving, atoning, delivering, saving, defending, hearing, remembering, leading, not forsaking, and not destroying His people. This truth is made even more emphatic in the book of Ezekiel.

During the Babylonian exile, God commanded Ezekiel to teach the Jewish elders a history lesson they would never forget. On that occasion, they were told three times why God's mercy had prevailed over His wrath.

First, while dwelling in Egypt, the Israelites had been warned by God to forsake the idols that were all around them, but they refused to listen:

"Then I said I would pour out my wrath upon them and spend my anger against them in the midst of the land of Egypt. But I acted for the sake of my name, that it should not be profaned in the sight of the nations among whom they lived, in whose sight I made myself known to them in bringing them out of the land of Egypt." (Ezek. 20:8-9)

Second, when the Israelites were in the wilderness, they rejected the statutes and commandments that God had given them, even profaning His Sabbaths:

"Then I said I would pour out my wrath upon them in the wilderness, to make a full end of them. But I acted for the sake of my name, that it should not be profaned in the sight of the nations, in whose sight I had brought them out." (Ezek. 20:13-14)

Third, the children of those who perished in the wilderness were admonished by the Lord not to follow in their fathers' footsteps, but they refused to listen:

"Then I said I would pour out my wrath upon them and spend my anger against them in the wilderness. But I withheld my hand and acted for the sake of my name, that it should not be profaned in the sight of the nations, in whose sight I had brought them out." (Ezek. 20:21-22)

One thing is clear from this threefold repetition: Although God will never turn a blind eye or a deaf ear when His people profane His "great and awesome name" (Ps. 99:3), His ultimate concern is that all nations should glorify Him. The earth trembled when God delivered His people from Egypt. So great was His deliverance that not only the Egyptians but also the surrounding peoples feared the Lord. As Rahab testified to the two Israelite spies in Jericho,

> I know that the LORD has given you the land, and that the fear of you has fallen upon us, and that all the inhabitants of the land melt away before you. For we have heard how the LORD dried up the water of the Red Sea before you when you came out of Egypt, and what you did to the two kings of the Amorites who were beyond the Jordan, to Sihon and Og, whom you devoted to destruction. And as soon as we heard it, our hearts melted, and there was no spirit left in any man because of you, for the LORD your God, He is God in the heavens above and on the earth beneath. (Josh. 2:9-11)

Rahab's incorporation into the Messianic line shows how much the Lord delighted in her humble and reverent testimony.[1]

The Prophetic Panorama

In chapter 36 of Ezekiel, we reach one of the great mountain peaks of Bible prophecy. From the summit, we can see the landscape as it will appear one day, after Israel has passed through the tribulation judgments and been renewed by the Holy Spirit (Ezek. 36:25-27; cf. 37:14). In this astonishing chapter, God made thirty-one unconditional "I will" promises to His people, which are sometimes coupled together. Here is a sample:

> "I will . . . vindicate the holiness of my great name . . . take you from the nations and gather you from all the countries [not just Babylon!] and bring you into your own land . . . sprinkle clean water on you . . . give you a new heart . . . remove the heart of stone from your flesh and give you a heart of flesh . . . put my Spirit within you, and cause you to walk in my statutes and be careful to obey my rules." (Ezek. 36:23-27; cf. 11:19)

---

[1] See Josh. 6:25; Mt. 1:5; Heb. 11:31; James 2:25.

Strikingly, the Lord also made eighteen "you shall" promises to the mountains/Land of Israel, including "you shall be their inheritance [*nachălâh*], and you shall no longer bereave them of children" (Ezek. 36:12). Over this prophetic landscape hangs a resplendent banner that God has unfurled. It serves as an everlasting reminder that Israel's national restoration, including the land's regeneration, will be for His glory alone:

> "But I had concern for my holy name, which the house of Israel had profaned among the nations to which they came. Therefore say to the house of Israel, 'Thus says the Lord GOD: It is not for your sake, O house of Israel, that I am about to act, but for the sake of my holy name, which you have profaned among the nations to which you came. And I will vindicate the holiness of my great name, which has been profaned among the nations, and which you have profaned among them. And the nations will know that I am the LORD, declares the Lord GOD, when through you I vindicate my holiness before their eyes' . . . It is not for your sake that I will act, declares the Lord GOD; let that be known to you. Be ashamed and confounded for your ways, O house of Israel." (Ezek. 36:21-32)

In fifty-seven of the psalms, we find ninety-seven direct references to God's name. This tells us how precious and central the name of the Lord was to Israel's worship. These songs speak of knowing, loving, praising, fearing, seeking, glorifying, worshiping, rejoicing in, exalting, thanking, trusting in, declaring, calling upon, singing to, blessing, taking refuge in, petitioning, testifying to, waiting for, remembering, exulting in, being saved by, conquering in, and declaring the majesty of God's name. Psalm 113 begins with an exhortation:

> Praise the LORD! Praise, O servants of the LORD, praise the name of the LORD! Blessed be the name of the LORD from this time forth and forevermore! From the rising of the sun to its setting, the name of the LORD is to be praised! (Ps. 113:1-3)

I wonder if a lot of prayer for Israel today is actually drawing more attention to the names of particular individuals, ministries, organizations, and churches than to the name of God. May we truly be able to say with the psalmist, "Not to us, O LORD, not to us, but to your name give glory, for the sake of your steadfast love and your faithfulness!" (Ps. 115:1).

Introducing God

We cannot read the Bible without encountering, time and again, "the God of Abraham, Isaac, and Jacob" or "the God of Israel" or "the Holy One of Israel." But how often do we pause and consider names and titles like these? Let us consider the frequency with which these particular names and others occur in Scripture, specifically as they relate to Israel. According to the King James Version, this is what we find:

- Lord God of Israel (108)
- God of Israel (95)
- Holy One of Israel (31)
- God of Jacob (18)
- King of the Jews (18)
- God of Abraham (10)
- God of Abraham, Isaac, and Jacob (9)
- God of the Hebrews (6)
- King of Israel (6)
- God of Abraham, Isaac, and Israel (3)
- God of Isaac (3)
- Fear of Isaac (2)
- Mighty One of Jacob (2)
- Hope of Israel (2)
- Mighty One of Israel (2)
- Holy One of Jacob (1)
- God of Jeshurun (1)
- Shepherd of Israel (1)
- Creator of Israel (1)
- Redeemer of Israel (1)
- Stone of Israel (1)
- Rock of Israel (1)

The list only includes exact matches and therefore could be much longer. For example, God is never directly named as "Father of Israel," but as He declared through the Prophet Jeremiah, "I am a father to Israel" (Jer. 31:9). There is also only one depiction of God as "Shepherd of Israel," but there are numerous references in the Old Testament to God being Israel's Shepherd, a title that was magnified in the ministry of "the Good Shepherd" Himself (Jn. 10:11, 14). I share this simply to highlight the ways in which God has uniquely identified Himself with the nation of Israel. If we now consider some of the Lord's high and exalted names, this identification becomes even more apparent.

The lofty names of God include "LORD of hosts," "God of hosts," and "LORD God of hosts." In Hebrew, we have *Yahweh* (LORD), *Elohim* (God), and *tsebā'ôt* (of hosts). Together, they occur 285 times in the Old Testament. In at least fifty verses, we find one of these three names being coupled with "God of Israel" or "God of Jacob." The book of Jeremiah, more than any other, makes this connection. In thirty-one instances, the prophecies of Jeremiah begin this way: "Thus says the LORD of hosts, the God of Israel." To these prophecies we may add the following:

The LORD of hosts is with us; the *God of Jacob* is our fortress. (Ps. 46:7, 11)

Thou, LORD God of hosts, art *God of Israel.* (Ps. 59:5, RSV)

O LORD of hosts, *God of Israel*, enthroned above the cherubim, you are the God, you alone, of all the kingdoms of the earth; you have made heaven and earth. (Isa. 37:16)

For your Maker is your husband, the LORD of hosts is His name; and the *Holy One of Israel* is your Redeemer, the God of the whole earth He is called. (Isa. 54:5)

"Therefore, as I live," declares the LORD of hosts, the *God of Israel*, "Moab shall become like Sodom, and the Ammonites like Gomorrah . . . The remnant of my people shall plunder them, and the survivors of my nation shall possess them." (Zeph. 2:9)

How easy it is when reading through Bible prophecies to skim through the introduction and head straight for what we may instinctively feel is the heart of a particular prophecy: the who, what, when, why, and how. I wonder if we are not missing the most important part when we do so—namely, the identity of the Author. It is not enough to know that God is speaking, for the simple reason that He uses different titles at different times to address different people. Why does He do this? I believe it is because the names and titles God uses are intended to bear witness to His attributes and have a direct bearing on the content of the prophetic word itself. I believe this is the key to unlocking Bible prophecy as a whole.

Whenever I receive a personal letter through the mail, the first thing I do is go straight to the end to see *who* has written it. The author's name will immediately affect the way I read *what* has been written. All that I know about the author will then be in my mind, either consciously or subconsciously, as I read through the letter. In Bible prophecy, the recipients of God's messages knew straightaway who they were from. In 416 verses of the Old Testament, the words "Thus says the Lord" are used either alone or with other names and titles appended. The majority of these are found in Jeremiah (150) and Ezekiel (126). We can see this pattern of introduction first emerging in many of the formative texts in Genesis and Exodus as the following examples illustrate:

> When Abram was ninety-nine years old the LORD appeared to Abram and said to him, "I am God Almighty; walk before me, and be blameless, that I may make my covenant between me and you, and may multiply you greatly." Then Abram fell on his face. (Gen. 17:1-3)
>
> And behold, the LORD stood above it [the ladder] and said, "I am the LORD, the God of Abraham your father and the God of Isaac. The land on which you [Jacob] lie I will give to you and to your offspring" . . . And he [Jacob] was afraid and said, "How awesome is this place!" (Gen. 28:13-17)
>
> And He said, "I am the God of your father, the God of Abraham, the God of Isaac, and the God of Jacob." And Moses hid his face, for he was afraid to look at God. (Ex. 3:6)
>
> God spoke to Moses and said to him, "I am the LORD. I appeared to Abraham, to Isaac, and to Jacob, as God Almighty, but by my name the LORD I did not make myself known to them." (Ex. 6:2-3)
>
> Then the LORD said to Moses, "Rise up early in the morning and present yourself before Pharaoh and say to him, 'Thus says the LORD, the God of the Hebrews, "Let my people go, that they may serve me."'" (Ex. 9:13)
>
> And God spoke all these words, saying, "I am the LORD your God, who brought you out of the land of Egypt, out of the house of slavery. You shall have no other gods before me." (Ex. 20:1-3)

This pattern is most apparent at the end of the Bible in the letters to the seven churches. The way in which the Lord Jesus introduced Himself in each letter was pivotal and not incidental to the matters He was about to address:

> "To the angel of the church in Ephesus write: 'The words of Him who holds the seven stars in His right hand, who walks among the seven golden lampstands.'" (Rev. 2:1)
>
> "And to the angel of the church in Smyrna write: 'The words of the first and the last, who died and came to life.'" (Rev. 2:8)
>
> "And to the angel of the church in Pergamum write: 'The words of Him who has the sharp two-edged sword.'" (Rev. 2:12)
>
> "And to the angel of the church in Thyatira write: 'The words of the Son of God, who has eyes like a flame of fire, and whose feet are like burnished bronze.'" (Rev. 2:18)
>
> "And to the angel of the church in Sardis write: 'The words of Him who has the seven spirits of God and the seven stars.'" (Rev. 3:1)
>
> "And to the angel of the church in Philadelphia write: 'The words of the holy one, the true one, who has the key of David, who opens and no one will shut, who shuts and no one opens.'" (Rev. 3:7)
>
> "And to the angel of the church in Laodicea write: 'The words of the Amen, the faithful and true witness, the beginning of God's creation.'" (Rev. 3:14)

Once we have given thought to *how* God introduces Himself, we can begin to understand *what* He was trying to communicate. Therefore, in the thirty-one references in Jeremiah alluded to above, the coupling of titles like "Lord God of hosts" and "God of Israel" tells us, at the very least, that the One who is transcendent over His creation is also immanent in His relationship with Israel; that the One who holds all power and authority as Sovereign is also the One who holds the paternal and inheritance rights to His chosen people; and that the One to whom the nations "are like a drop from a bucket" (Isa. 40:15) is ever watching, protecting, and preserving the one nation He set apart for Himself as His *nachălâh*. Pry apart any of these couplets, which is what replacement theologians in the church have been doing for nearly two thousand years, and God's self-revelation is obscured and His true identity eclipsed.

Consider the time when God called Moses and a select group of Israelites to approach Mount Sinai to worship Him. As we read in the book of Exodus,

> Then Moses and Aaron, Nadab, and Abihu, and seventy of the elders of Israel went up, and they saw *the God of Israel*. There was under His feet as it were a pavement of sapphire stone, like the very heaven for clearness. And He did not lay His hand on the chief men of the people of Israel; they beheld God, and ate and drank. (Ex. 24:9-11)

We are not told that these men saw "I AM" or "the Most High" or "the Lord of hosts." Of course, that *was* who they saw because God bears all His names and titles concurrently. However, on this occasion, the name Moses used in his account was "the God of Israel."

In his farewell address and solemn admonition to the people of Israel, the Prophet Samuel made a statement that has stood the test of time: "For the LORD will not forsake His people, for His great name's sake, because it has pleased the LORD to make you a people for Himself" (1 Sam. 12:22). The man whom Samuel anointed king famously celebrated God's identification with Israel after he had been told by Nathan the prophet that the Lord was going to establish his name, his dynasty, and his throne forever. As David humbly prayed,

> There is none like you, O LORD, and there is no God besides you, according to all that we have heard with our ears. And who is like your people Israel, the one nation on earth whom God went to redeem to be His people, making for yourself a name for great and awesome things, in driving out nations before your people whom you redeemed from Egypt? And you made your people Israel to be your people forever, and you, O LORD, became their God. And now, O LORD, let the word that you have spoken concerning your servant and concerning his house be established forever, and do as you have spoken, and your name will be established and magnified forever, saying, "The LORD of hosts, the God of Israel, is Israel's God," and the house of your servant David will be established before you. (1 Chron. 17:20-24)

When we come to the New Testament, we find that not one of the names and titles of God is ever revoked, redefined, or reinterpreted! Matthew, for example, tells us that when great crowds brought the lame, blind, mute, crippled, and diseased to Jesus, He healed them all, and "they glorified the God of Israel" (Mt. 15:31). Luke begins his Gospel with a record of events surrounding the birth of John the Baptist. Following John's birth, we are told that his father Zechariah "was filled with the Holy Spirit and prophesied, saying, 'Blessed be the Lord God of Israel, for He has visited and redeemed His people and has raised up a horn of salvation for us in the house of His servant David.'" (Lk. 1:67-68). To put it bluntly, I believe it is impossible to truly know God as "the Lord of hosts" without knowing Him as "the God of Israel," for the two go hand in hand—past, present, and future!

Resurrection

In his first letter to the Corinthians, Paul did not hold back: "If Messiah has not been raised, then our preaching is in vain and your faith is in vain . . . and you are still in your sins. Then those also who have fallen asleep in Messiah have perished" (1 Cor. 15:14-18). It surely follows, then, that if Jesus the Messiah did not rise from the dead, then the nation of Israel is also without hope and destined to perish. However, as Paul went on to triumphantly exclaim, "But in fact Messiah has been raised from the dead, the firstfruits of those who have fallen asleep . . . Thanks be to God, who gives us the victory through our Lord Jesus the Messiah" (1 Cor. 15:20, 57). The Prophet Jeremiah declared God to be "the hope of Israel" (Jer. 17:13; 14:8). Paul was imprisoned in Rome because of this hope (Acts 28:20). Through the life, death, and resurrection of Messiah, God has ensured that Israel's hope will never be extinguished, because Yeshua/Jesus *is* the Hope of Israel!

Matthew's Gospel informs us that earthquakes attended both the crucifixion and resurrection of Jesus (Mt. 27:51-28:2). While the Son of God hung between heaven and earth, creation went into mourning. The sun's light failed at midday, and the earth trembled at the sound of His death cry. Immediately following His resurrection, the earth was shaken again as two angels rolled back the stone that had sealed the tomb where His body lay, not to let the risen Lord out but to let His grieving followers in. The resurrection validates and vindicates Jesus' every word, deed, claim, and promise. It conclusively demonstrates that His death was far more than an appalling miscarriage of justice. First and foremost, it was a pure, unblemished, atoning sacrifice for the sin of the world. It forcefully declares to the nations that all their gods, religions, philosophies, and theories are false, foolish, and futile. Furthermore, it seals and certifies everything that was spoken by the prophets concerning Israel's restoration and Messiah's return.

Through the messages He proclaimed and the miracles He performed, Jesus revealed the truth about life and death. As He declared to Martha, who was grieving the death of her brother Lazarus, "I am the resurrection and the life" (Jn. 11:25). When the Sadducees confronted the Messiah over the question of resurrection, the response they received was one of the most breathtaking statements I believe Jesus ever made about Israel:

> "You are wrong, because you know neither the Scriptures nor the power of God... And as for the resurrection of the dead, have you not read what was said to you by God: 'I am the God of Abraham, and the God of Isaac, and the God of Jacob?' He is not God of the dead, but of the living." (Mt. 22:29-32)

What a supreme demonstration of divine wisdom and authority! Jesus rebuked the Sadducees for not only failing to understand the Scriptures and God's power to resurrect but also for not recognizing how integral resurrection is to the very name of God. The bodies of Abraham, Isaac, and Jacob had long since returned to the earth, but as Jesus made clear, they themselves were very much alive in God's presence; and if the patriarchs were alive, then all the promises that God had made to them were still in play. The Author of life does not lend His name to death.

It was at the burning bush that God first revealed the name that Jesus brought to the Sadducees' attention. As we read in the book of Exodus,

> Then Moses said to God, "If I come to the people of Israel and say to them, 'The God of your fathers has sent me to you,' and they ask me, 'What is His name?' what shall I say to them?" God said to Moses, "I AM WHO I AM." And He said, "Say this to the people of Israel: 'I AM has sent me to you.'" God also said to Moses, "Say this to the people of Israel: 'The LORD, the God of your fathers, the God of Abraham, the God of Isaac, and the God of Jacob, has sent me to you.' *This is my name forever*, and thus I am to be remembered throughout all generations. Go and gather the elders of Israel together and say to them, 'The LORD, the God of your fathers, the God of Abraham, of Isaac, and of Jacob, has appeared to me.'" (Ex. 3:13-16)

There on Mount Sinai, the transcendent "I AM" declared Himself to be the immanent God of Abraham, Isaac, and Jacob. Not only did the Lord declare His transcendent name to be eternal, but He also announced that His immanent name was everlasting, too, and was to be remembered forever. Tragically, the Sadducean spirit is flourishing in the church today where Israel is concerned, for this revelation is being obscured from many believers. But let us remain with Moses and spotlight yet another glorious revelation that was given to him, this time when God told him what to say to Pharaoh:

> And the LORD said to Moses, "When you go back to Egypt, see that you do before Pharaoh all the miracles that I have put in your power. But I will harden his heart, so that he will not let the people go. Then you shall say to Pharaoh, 'Thus says the LORD, *Israel is my firstborn son*, and I say to you, "Let my son go that he may serve me." If you refuse to let him go, behold, I will kill your firstborn son.'" (Ex. 4:21-23)

I suspect the words "Let my people go!" will be more familiar to us than "Let my son go!" especially if we have ever watched Charlton Heston (Moses) addressing Yul Brynner (Pharaoh) in Cecil B. DeMille's biblical epic, *The Ten Commandments* (1956). Moses and Aaron were certainly not acting when they proclaimed these words to Egypt's tyrannical king. Out of all the families of the earth, Israel alone had been chosen by God to be His treasured possession, even His "firstborn," who would inherit from Him and partake of His blessing. This privileged status was never rescinded, even when Israel was under God's judgment. As the Lord declared through the Prophet Jeremiah, "With weeping they shall come, and with pleas for mercy I will lead them back, I will make them walk by brooks of water, in a straight path in which they shall not stumble, for I am a father to Israel, and Ephraim is my firstborn" (Jer. 31:9).

To the One who is eternal and dwells outside time, the promises made to the patriarchs, the commissioning of Moses on Mount Sinai, and the warning given to Pharaoh must be as if they had just happened. The passage of time may have dulled the memory of nations and allowed amillennial amnesia to affect a significant part of the church, but as Moses expressed to God in his psalm, "a thousand years in your sight are but as yesterday when it is past, or as a watch in the night" (Ps. 90:4). The church of replacement theology, which has held Israel in theological chains for nearly two millennia, needs to hear God's warning to Pharaoh as if it had been given to her: "Israel is my firstborn son, and I say to you, 'Let my son go that he may serve me' . . . You are still exalting yourself against my people and will not let them go" (Ex. 4:22-23, 9:17; cf. Rom. 11:17-25).

God's ZIP Code

Not only did God allot Himself a piece of land and set apart for Himself a people to inherit that land, but He also singled out a city in which to make His dwelling among them. Before crossing the Jordan, the Israelites received the following instruction through Moses: "But you shall seek the place that the Lord your God will choose out of all your tribes to put His name and make His habitation there. There you shall go, and there you shall bring your burnt offerings and your sacrifices" (Deut. 12:5; cf. Dan. 12:11; 14:23; 16:6, 11; 26:2; Ex. 20:24; 1 Kgs. 8:29; 2 Chron. 12:13; Neh. 1:9). That place, of course, was Jerusalem. God's choice of the city was to become a prominent theme of the Psalms:

> On the holy mount stands the city He founded; the LORD loves the gates of Zion more than all the dwelling places of Jacob. Glorious things of you are spoken, O city of God. (Ps. 87:1-3; cf. Ps. 78:67-68)

> For the LORD has chosen Zion; He has desired it for His dwelling place: "This is my resting place forever; here I will dwell, for I have desired it." (Ps. 132:13-14)

> O mountain of God, mountain of Bashan; O many-peaked mountain, mountain of Bashan! Why do you look with hatred, O many-peaked mountain, at the mount that God desired for His abode, yes, where the LORD will dwell forever? (Ps. 68:15-16)

Following the dedication of the Temple in Jerusalem, God appeared to Solomon in a dream and made this astonishing declaration: "I have consecrated this house that you have built, by putting my name there forever. My eyes and my heart will be there for all time" (1 Kgs. 9:3; 2 Chron. 7:16). As we know, the Temple was later destroyed by the Babylonians in 586 B.C. as an outworking of God's judgment. Centuries later in A.D. 70, the

Second Temple was similarly destroyed, this time by the Romans. On numerous occasions in its history, Jerusalem itself was razed to the ground, either in part or completely, but on no occasion did God ever withdraw His name or seek out another city for His dwelling. Even the Persian king Darius understood the connection between Jerusalem and "the God of heaven" (Ezra 6:9) when he decreed that the Jews could continue to rebuild the Temple: "May the God who has caused His name to dwell there overthrow any king or people who shall put out a hand to alter this, or to destroy this house of God that is in Jerusalem. I Darius make a decree; let it be done with all diligence" (Ezra 6:12).

In the words of my late pastor, Andrew Robinson, if God has an earthly address, then it is Temple Mount, Jerusalem, Israel.

Conclusion

We can but marvel at what God has done with His chosen people, especially in the wake of the Holocaust. The Lord God of Israel has returned millions of His exiles to the land of their forefathers. He has revived the land itself through their phenomenal exploits. He has restored the Hebrew language as their spoken tongue. He has miraculously defeated or repelled Israel's enemies in successive wars, and He has prospered the nation economically to the point where Israel is now recognized as one of the most powerful nations on earth. Yet for all this "blessing," the nation has still not returned to God or turned to the Messiah. Jesus declared on one occasion, "The Father judges no one, but has given all judgment to the Son, that all may honor the Son, just as they honor the Father. Whoever does not honor the Son does not honor the Father who sent Him" (Jn. 5:22-23). The Apostle John wrote in his first letter, "No one who denies the Son has the Father. Whoever confesses the Son has the Father also . . . Whoever has the Son has life; whoever does not have the Son of God does not have life" (1 Jn. 2:23; 5:12). Notwithstanding the burgeoning Messianic community in the land today, Israel as a nation presently denies the Son and is therefore bereft of the Father's presence and the life that can only come through Jesus. The Jewish people remain God's chosen people *positionally*, as we have already considered, but they are forfeiting daily communion with God and the New Covenant blessings that He longs to bestow upon them. This means that for all the benefits that have undoubtedly accrued to Israel since its miraculous rebirth in 1948, the nation remains under judgment and is set to endure the tribulation period. As Jesus said, "Whoever does not obey the Son shall not see life, but the wrath of God remains on him" (Jn. 3:36). According to the words spoken by the Lord to His disciples on the Mount of Olives, the nation has *yet* to endure its darkest hour, a truth that does not sit well with many believers who stand with Israel. However, God's Word and not our emotions or sensibilities must be our final authority.

Having drawn His disciples' attention to Daniel's prophecy of the seventy "weeks" of years (Dan. 9:24-27) and having specifically pinpointed the middle of the *seventieth* "week," or final seven years, of that prophecy, Jesus made a startling declaration: "For then there will be great tribulation, such as has not been from the beginning of the world until now, no, and never will be. And if those days had not been cut short, no human being would be saved" (Mt. 24:21-22; cf. Dan. 12:1). We must never forget that a lost eternity—the greatest tribulation of all—is what awaits everyone who spurns "the free gift of God," which is "eternal life in Messiah Jesus our Lord" (Rom. 6:23).[2] But let us remember where we have been in this chapter. We have considered what it means to honor or disgrace the "holy and awesome" name of the Lord (Ps. 111:9). From Genesis to Revelation, from the dawn of creation six thousand years ago to the eternal state yet to be, it is God's glory that is ultimately at stake—not man's, not Israel's, not the church's, but God's!

Let us also remember that the suffering that awaits Israel will *not* result in the nation's destruction, though many of the people will perish during that dreadful time. According to God's own promise, "that day is great, so that none is like it; and it is the time of Jacob's trouble, but he shall be saved out of it" (Jer. 30:7, NKJV). A remnant of Israel will be saved, and their estrangement from God will finally be ended when they "look on me, on Him whom they have pierced" and "mourn for Him, as one mourns for an only child, and weep bitterly over Him, as one weeps over a firstborn" (Zech. 12:10). Israel will at last acknowledge and bless the holy name of

---

[2] See also: Jn. 3:15-18; 5:24; 6:40-68; 10:28; 17:3; 1 Jn. 5:11-13.

Jesus (Mt. 23:29), and He, in turn, will cleanse them from all their sin and idolatry (Zech. 13:1-2). He will fight for them against the nations that will have gathered against Jerusalem at that time (Zech. 14:2-3), and His feet will stand once again on the Mount of Olives (Zech. 14:4). Only then will He make a truly triumphal entry into Jerusalem, from where He will reign as King over all the earth (Zech. 14:9; cf. Isa. 33:17).

In closing, the answer to the question "Why Israel?" is very simple: God's glory! As the Lord made clear through the Prophet Isaiah,

> "Your people shall all be righteous; they shall possess the land forever, the branch of my planting, the work of my hands, that I might be glorified." (Isa. 60:21)

> "The Spirit of the Lord GOD is upon me, because the Lord has anointed me ... to comfort all who mourn; to grant to those who mourn in Zion — to give them a beautiful headdress instead of ashes ... that they may be called oaks of righteousness, the planting of the LORD, that He may be glorified." (Isa. 61:1-3)

The Hebrew word translated "glorified" in these scriptures is *pâ'ar*, meaning "to adorn" or "to display the beauty of something." Israel's restoration is therefore tied to God's glory. Who God is must be seen and acknowledged by all. One day Israel, as a remnant nation, will hallow the name of the Lord, as we read again in Isaiah:

> Therefore thus says the LORD, who redeemed Abraham, concerning the house of Jacob: "Jacob shall no more be ashamed, no more shall his face grow pale. For when he sees his children, the work of my hands, in his midst, they will sanctify my name; they will sanctify the Holy One of Jacob and will stand in awe of the God of Israel." (Isa. 29:22-23)

As for the nations, the Lord had this to say through the Prophet Malachi, and with these words we close this chapter:

> "For from the rising of the sun to its setting my name will be great among the nations, and in every place incense will be offered to my name, and a pure offering. For my name will be great among the nations, says the LORD of hosts ... For I am a great King, says the LORD of hosts, and my name will be feared among the nations." (Mal. 1:11-14)

Chapter 5:

The Loyal Love of the Lord

> Give thanks to the LORD, for He is good, for His steadfast love endures forever; . . . to Him who struck down great kings, for His steadfast love endures forever; . . . and gave their land as a heritage [*nachălâh*], for His steadfast love endures forever; a heritage [*nachălâh*] to Israel His servant, for His steadfast love endures forever; . . . Give thanks to the God of heaven, for His steadfast love endures forever. (Ps. 136:1, 17-22, 26)

Psalm 136 is a timeless, inspirational summons to thank God for His steadfast love, which never ceases. In his commentary on the psalm, Charles Spurgeon wrote:

> Most hymns with a solid, simple chorus become favourites with congregations, and this is sure to have been one of the best beloved. It contains nothing but praise. It is tuned to rapture, and can only be fully enjoyed by a devoutly grateful heart.[1]

This psalm appears to have been sung, at least in part, by the people and priests of Israel after Solomon had dedicated the Temple in Jerusalem. On that momentous occasion, fire from heaven came down and consumed the burnt offering and sacrifices. As we read in the Chronicles account,

> When all the people of Israel saw the fire come down and the glory of the LORD on the temple, they bowed down with their faces to the ground on the pavement and worshipped and gave thanks to the LORD, saying, "For He is good, for His steadfast love endures forever" . . . The priests stood at their posts; the Levites also, with the instruments for music to the LORD that King David had made for giving thanks to the LORD — for His steadfast love endures forever. (2 Chron. 7:3-6)

---

[1] Spurgeon, *The Treasury of David, Vol. III*, p. 204.

God's love for His people is faithful, unconditional, enduring, trustworthy, and completely undeserved. His love is dependent entirely upon His character, and without it, neither Israel nor the church nor the world could survive. There is no sentimentality attached to God's love, for He is holy and just, requiring a sacrifice for sin and repentance from all who would fellowship with Him! Two thousand years ago, a sacrifice was made once and for all that fulfilled and superseded all previous sacrifices. As we read in the book of Hebrews:

> He has appeared once for all at the end of the ages to put away sin by the sacrifice of Himself. And just as it is appointed for man to die once, and after that comes judgment, so Messiah, having been offered once to bear the sins of many, will appear a second time, not to deal with sin but to save those who are eagerly waiting for Him . . . For by a single offering He has perfected for all time those who are being sanctified. (Heb. 9:26-28; 10:14)

A nineteenth-century writer put it this way: "Wondrous altar! wondrous offering! A richer sacrifice it infinitely was, than an eternity of Adam's innocency would have been."[2] If *Christos* is the Greek New Testament word that is used to designate the One through whom God's love was supremely manifested, then *chesed* is the Hebrew word through which that same love was prophetically anticipated and so beautifully expressed in the Old Testament.[3]

The Loyalty of God

In the first book of Samuel, we read the account of King Saul's relentless pursuit of David. Before parting from each other, Saul's son Jonathan made the following impassioned plea to David, who was not only the king-in-waiting but also his covenanted friend:

> If I am still alive, show me the loyal love [*chesed*] of the LORD, that I may not die; and do not cut off your loyalty [*chesed*] from my house for ever. When the LORD cuts off every one of the enemies of David from the face of the

---

[2] John Gifford Bellett, *A Short Meditation on the Moral Glory of the Lord Jesus Christ*, 17*th* ed. (Kingston-on-Thames, England: Stow Hill Bible and Tract Depot, 1963), pp. 65-66.

[3] Another way of transliterating this Hebrew word is *cheçed*.

earth, let not the name of Jonathan be cut off from the house of David. (1 Sam. 20:14-16, RSV)

I have specifically cited the Revised Standard Version (RSV) because of its unique translation. The words "loyal love" and "loyalty" were finally decided upon by the RSV translation committee after they had labored to render into English the beautifully rich, deeply absorbing, and almost-impossible-to-translate Hebrew word *chesed*. Such was the degree of difficulty they encountered, that after several months' work, the committee finally agreed on one thing: No single English noun could do it justice. *Chesed* proved to be the final word they voted on before completing their translation of the Old Testament.

A comparison of other English translations, from the earliest to the more modern, reveals how multilayered this Hebrew word is. In our selected text, *chesed* is variously translated "mercy" (Coverdale, Geneva, Bishops), "kindness" (KJV, NKJV, DBY, YLT, NIV), "lovingkindness" (ASV, NASB), "steadfast love" (ESV), "faithful love" (NLT), and "loyalty" (NET). The RSV committee generally favored "steadfast love" when translating *chesed* elsewhere in Scripture, but in this particular case, I believe they made an insightful choice.

Wherever Bible students excavate in the Old Testament, sooner or later their exegetical trowel will strike *chesed*, which appears 248 times. Half of these occurrences are in the book of Psalms alone. This theological gem sparkles to the glory of God, for its true meaning can only be found by digging deep into the rich seam of God's covenant relationship with Israel. In the text above, it is important to note that Jonathan did not ask David for *his* loyalty but for the loyalty *of the* LORD (1 Sam. 20:14), and David did not disappoint. Following the death of Jonathan and Saul on the mountains of Gilboa, David acceded to the throne. The man after God's own heart asked Saul's servant Ziba a question: "Is there not still someone of the house of Saul, that I may show the kindness [*chesed*] of God to him?" (2 Sam. 9:3). Mephibosheth, the crippled son of Jonathan, was to be the recipient of God's kindness through David. The king restored Saul's land to Mephibosheth and gave him a permanent place at his table.

Before we proceed, it is important to highlight another significant aspect of Jonathan's appeal to David: his use of the tetragrammaton YHWH. Often pronounced "Yahweh" but usually translated "Lord" in our English Bibles, it is the name by which God reveals Himself to those with whom He is in covenant relationship. With this in mind, let us consider the following definition of *chesed* by William O. E. Oesterley (1866-1950), a Church of England vicar, theologian, and professor of Hebrew and Old Testament at King's College, London:

> [*Chesed* is] an essential quality of soul, a spiritual endowment which goes deep down into the very nature of him who has it . . . No other word means so much to the Hebrew ear, and its cultivation in the human heart is the highest demand of the prophetic morality. In all its completeness it can be seen only in Yahweh.[4]

The Superabundance of God's Mercy

A study of the Scriptures reveals just how consistently the loyal love of God was shown to His covenanted people *and* to those outside Israel who were being drawn into relationship with Him. Genesis 24, for example, tells the beautiful story of the search for a wife for Abraham's son Isaac. Upon meeting Rebekah and her family in the Mesopotamian city of Nahor, Abraham's servant thanked God for showing *chesed* to his master: "Blessed be the Lord, the God of my master Abraham, who has not forsaken His lovingkindness [*chesed*] and His truth toward my master" (Gen. 24:27, NASB).

Later in Genesis, we read how this same love sustained Joseph during his imprisonment in Pharaoh's dungeons: "But the Lord was with Joseph and showed him steadfast love [*chesed*], and gave him favor in the sight of the keeper of the prison" (Gen. 39:21, RSV).

The book of Joshua records what happened to the two Israelite spies when they arrived in Jericho. Finding themselves in a dangerous situation, they promised the prostitute Rahab that if she hid them from her king, they would remember her when Jericho was taken: "Our life for yours even to

---

[4] W. O. E. Oesterley, *The Psalms* (London: SPCK, 1953), p. 80.

death! If you do not tell this business of ours, then when the LORD gives us the land, we will deal kindly [*chesed*] and faithfully with you" (Josh. 2:14).

It was the same merciful kindness of God that was shown to Naomi and her deceased husband Elimelech through Boaz, their kinsman-redeemer in Bethlehem. As Naomi joyfully declared to her Moabite daughter-in-law Ruth, "May he be blessed by the LORD, whose kindness [*chesed*] has not forsaken the living or the dead!" (Ruth 2:20). Many years later, Ruth's great-grandson David gratefully acknowledged God's loyal love after being delivered from the hand of all his enemies: "Great salvation He brings to His king, and shows steadfast love [*chesed*] to His anointed, to David and his offspring forever" (2 Sam. 22:51).

It was the *chesed* of God that the psalmists repeatedly acknowledged when recounting God's saving acts on behalf of His people:

> Many times He delivered them, but they were rebellious in their purposes and were brought low through their iniquity. Nevertheless, He looked upon their distress, when He heard their cry. For their sake He remembered His covenant, and relented according to the abundance of His steadfast love [*chesed*]. (Ps. 106:43-45)

> The LORD is merciful and gracious, slow to anger and abounding in steadfast love [*chesed*]. He will not always chide, nor will He keep His anger forever. He does not deal with us according to our sins, nor repay us according to our iniquities. For as high as the heavens are above the earth, so great is His steadfast love [*chesed*] toward those who fear Him; as far as the east is from the west, so far does He remove our transgressions from us. (Ps. 103:8-11)

Wherever we turn in Scripture, God's *chesed* glistens. It is integral both to the law of God and to His very name and nature. From Mount Sinai, the Lord declared that He would visit the iniquity of the fathers on the children and on the third and the fourth generations of those who hate Him, but that He would show "lovingkindness [*chesed*] to thousands"—to those who love Him and keep His commandments (Ex. 20:5-6, NASB). When Moses ascended the mountain a second time, the Lord passed by and proclaimed His name:

> "The LORD, the LORD, a God merciful and gracious, slow to anger, and abounding in steadfast love [*chesed*] and faithfulness, keeping steadfast love

[*chesed*] for thousands, forgiving iniquity and transgression and sin, but who will by no means clear the guilty." (Ex. 34:6, RSV)

Forty years later, Moses gave the Israelites a solemn reminder before they crossed the Jordan River into Canaan:

> Know therefore that the LORD your God is God, the faithful God who keeps covenant and steadfast love [*chesed*] with those who love Him and keep His commandments, to a thousand generations, and repays to their face those who hate Him, by destroying them. (Deut. 7:7-9)

This self-revelation of God is integral to our understanding of Israel's chosenness. It is also the key to the nation's survival. If it were not for God's *chesed*, then Israel would not exist today as a sovereign state in the Middle East because of the nation's lamentable history of covenant-breaking infidelity. No matter where we turn in the prophetic scriptures, *chesed* takes center stage. Consider the following examples, which serve to illustrate both the richness of this word and the greatness of our God:

> "In an outburst of anger I hid my face from you for a moment, but with everlasting lovingkindness [*chesed*] I will have compassion on you," says the LORD, your Redeemer. (Isa. 54:8, NASB)

> Long ago the LORD said to Israel: "I have loved you, my people, with an everlasting love. With unfailing love [*chesed*] I have drawn you to myself. I will rebuild you, my virgin Israel." (Jer. 31:3-4, NLT)

> For the LORD will not cast off for ever, but, though He cause grief, He will have compassion according to the abundance of His steadfast love [*chesed*]. (Lam. 3:31-32, RSV)

> "I will betroth you to me forever; yes, I will betroth you to me in righteousness and justice, in lovingkindness [*chesed*] and mercy." (Hos. 2:19-20, NKJV)

> You will be loyal to Jacob and extend your loyal love [*chesed*] to Abraham, which you promised on oath to our ancestors in ancient times. (Mic. 7:20, NET)

Whenever prayer for Israel was urgently needed, God's *chesed* was at the heart of every supplication. Whether we read Solomon's prayer of dedication after the Temple was completed (1 Kgs. 8:23) or Daniel's prayer for the restoration of the Babylonian exiles (Dan. 9:4) or Nehemiah's prayer for the favor of King Artaxerxes (Neh. 1:5) or Ezra's prayer on behalf of the returning exiles who had intermarried (Ezra 9:9), we learn that the common denominator was neither Israel's merit nor Israel's plight, but God's loyal love.

I invite the reader to pause at this point and read these accounts carefully to see how each intercessor appealed to God on the basis of the revelation He had given to Moses at Sinai.

A Bridge into the New Covenant

Although the New Testament was written in Greek, I believe the Hebrew word *chesed* serves as a bridge between the Old and the New in understanding God's dealings with His people. The New Testament counterpart is *éleos*, which was also the word generally favored by the compilers of the Septuagint (LXX) when they translated *chesed*. This Greek word is found in the opening chapter of Luke's Gospel when Mary magnified the Lord for having "helped His servant Israel, in remembrance of His mercy [*éleos*]" (Lk. 1:54). It is also found in the account of Zechariah who blessed the Lord for having shown "the mercy [*éleos*] promised to our fathers" (Lk. 1:72). In this way, then, we can say that the good news of the Jewish Messiah is inextricably bound to the loyal love of God. In His virgin birth, sinless life, atoning death, glorious resurrection, and heavenly ascension, Jesus personified *chesed*. When He returns, He will fill this word up with meaning, for as Paul wrote in his letter to the Romans, "Messiah became a servant to the circumcised to show God's truthfulness, in order to confirm the promises given to the patriarchs, and in order that the Gentiles might glorify God for His mercy [*éleos*]" (Rom. 15:8-9). In making such a statement, I believe Paul was also pulling the theological rug out from under those in the church who have refused to glorify God for His mercy toward Israel.

The Loyal Love of the Church?

In recent times, an alarming number of professing Christians have been quick to point an accusing finger at Israel. Acting as judge and jury, they have held the Jewish nation to account for not upholding the biblical commandments of God. At the same time, they have turned a blind eye to the atrocities committed against the Jewish people and a deaf ear to the endless cycle of annihilationist threats, fallacious accusations, and mindless resolutions made against Israel. It should be noted that many of these self-appointed prosecutors in the church do not believe that the modern State of Israel is even related to the Israel of the Bible or that the Jews in the land today are really Jews!

Israel as a nation is currently hardened in unbelief, blind to the light of the gospel, and deaf to the life-transforming message of Jesus (Rom. 9:30-33; 10:1-4, 18-21; 11:7-10, 25-31). Why, then, do these belligerent "Christians" expect Israel to behave like the nation it will be only after the tribulation judgments have run their course and the Messiah has returned? Is there not a deeply Pharisaical "plank-in-the-eye"[5] attitude among those who are trying to hold Israel to account in this way?

Let us consider the following statements that Jesus made to the early church, either directly or through His apostles. We can then ask whether or not the same kinds of indictments could be laid at the door of many believers, churches, denominations, and Christian NGOs today:

> Do not be arrogant toward the branches ... For if God did not spare the natural branches, neither will He spare you. (Rom. 11:18-21)

> O foolish Galatians! Who has bewitched you? ... Having begun by the Spirit, are you now being perfected by the flesh? (Gal. 3:1-3)

> For many ... walk as enemies of the cross of Messiah ... with minds set on earthly things. (Phil. 3:18-19)

> Now the Spirit expressly says that in later times some will depart from the faith by giving heed to deceitful spirits and doctrines of demons. (1 Tim. 4:1)

---

[5] Jesus said, "Judge not, that you be not judged. For with what judgment you judge, you will be judged; and with the measure you use, it will be measured back to you. And why do you look at the speck in your brother's eye, but do not consider the plank in your own eye? Or how can you say to your brother, 'Let me remove the speck from your eye'; and look, a plank is in your own eye? Hypocrite! First remove the plank from your own eye, and then you will see clearly to remove the speck from your brother's eye." (Mt. 7:1-5, NKJV)

For the time is coming when people will not endure sound teaching, but having itching ears they will accumulate for themselves teachers to suit their own passions, and will turn away from listening to the truth and wander off into myths. (2 Tim. 4:3-4)

But false prophets also arose among the people, just as there will be false teachers among you, who will secretly bring in destructive heresies, even denying the Master who bought them, bringing upon themselves swift destruction. And many will follow their sensuality, and because of them the way of truth will be blasphemed. (2 Pet. 2:1-2)

"But I have this against you, that you have abandoned the love you had at first." (Rev. 2:4)

"But I have a few things against you: you have some there who hold the teaching of Balaam . . . So also you have some who hold the teaching of the Nicolaitans. Therefore repent." (Rev. 2:14-16)

"But I have this against you, that you tolerate that woman Jezebel, who calls herself a prophetess and is teaching and seducing my servants to practice sexual immorality and to eat food sacrificed to idols." (Rev. 2:20)

"I know your works. You have the reputation of being alive, but you are dead." (Rev. 3:1)

"So, because you are lukewarm, and neither hot nor cold, I will spew you out of my mouth. For you say, I am rich, I have prospered, and I need nothing; not knowing that you are wretched, pitiable, poor, blind, and naked." (Rev. 3:16-17, RSV)

These scriptures make for uncomfortable reading, but the church needs to urgently wake from its slumber and put its own house in order before it casts a disapproving eye on Israel. In his first epistle, the Apostle Peter declared: "It is time for judgment to begin at the household of God; and if it begins with us, what will be the outcome for those who do not obey the gospel of God?" (1 Pet. 4:17). One of the crucial lessons to be learned from our study of *chesed/éleos* is that believers dare not take God's loyal love for granted or hold others to a standard they are not keeping themselves.

God is our *Chesed*

At the heart of Israel's worship was the call to reflect upon the loyal, steadfast love of the Lord. We know from Psalm 106 that it grieved the faithful among God's people to see how poorly the nation had responded to God's loyalty:

> Both we and our fathers have sinned . . . Our fathers, when they were in Egypt, did not consider your wondrous works; they did not remember the abundance of your steadfast love [*chesed*], but rebelled by the sea, at the Red Sea. Yet He saved them for His name's sake . . . For their sake He remembered His covenant, and relented according to the abundance of His steadfast love [*chesed*]. (Ps. 106:6, 45)

It was noted earlier that over half of the references to *chesed* in the Old Testament are in the book of Psalms. According to the psalmists, the loyal love of the Lord is good, abundant, and great above the heavens. It is trustworthy, precious, and wondrously shown. It fills the earth, extends to the heavens, and endures forever. It surrounds, crowns, satisfies, preserves, and comforts the saints. It is to be declared, hoped in, and sung about, and it is "better than life" itself (Ps. 63:3). The enduring nature of God's *chesed* is emphasized more than any of its other attributes.

In Psalm 136, the loyal love of the Lord is the constant refrain throughout. A connection is also made in this psalm between *chesed* and *nachălâh*:

> Give thanks to the LORD, for He is good, for His steadfast love [*chesed*] endures forever . . . to Him who led His people through the wilderness, for His steadfast love [*chesed*] endures forever; to Him who struck down great kings, for His steadfast love [*chesed*] endures forever; . . . and gave their land as a heritage [*nachălâh*], for His steadfast love [*chesed*] endures forever; a heritage [*nachălâh*] to Israel His servant, for His steadfast love [*chesed*] endures forever; . . . Give thanks to the God of heaven, for His steadfast love [*chesed*] endures forever. (Ps. 136:1-3, 16-17, 22, 26)

But there is another crucial aspect to God's *chesed* that we need to consider, and it is one that applies to many of God's other attributes. Here is David's benediction in Psalm 144:

> Blessed be the LORD, my rock, who trains my hands for war, and my fingers for battle; He is my steadfast love [*chesed*] and my fortress, my stronghold

and my deliverer, my shield and He in whom I take refuge, who subdues peoples under me. (Ps. 144:1-2)

This is very similar to the way in which Psalm 18 begins, but here in Psalm 144 David makes an interesting and illuminating addition. He personalizes *chesed* by declaring God to be "my steadfast love," or as other translations have it, "my lovingkindness" / "my mercy." If we were seated listening to David singing this psalm, we would hear him praising God for being his *chesed*. Was he being overly poetic or sentimental at this point? Hardly—just read the rest of the psalm!

The same kind of emphasis is made in Psalm 71, where the anonymous author expresses his need for God's deliverance:

Rescue me, O my God, from the hand of the wicked, from the grasp of the unjust and cruel man. For you, O Lord, are my hope, my trust, O LORD, from my youth. Upon you I have leaned from before my birth; you are He who took me from my mother's womb. My praise is continually of you. (Ps. 71:4-5)

It is one thing to think about the Lord *showing* loyal love to His people or *giving* them hope but quite another to think of the Lord *being* loyal love to Israel, of Him *being* their hope and their trust. God did not simply *give* David strength; He *was* his strength. He did not simply *provide* a refuge for David; He *was* his refuge. This is what covenant relationship is all about: knowing God close at hand and not at a distance, but in a way that does not diminish the need for reverence. Moses, David, and Isaiah all blessed God in praise and prophecy for *being* their salvation. He not only saved them; He *was* their salvation (Ex. 15:2; Ps. 62:2; Isa. 12:2). The same distinction is made in the book of Jeremiah, where the contrast is made between those who trust in man and those who trust in God:

Blessed is the man who trusts in the LORD, *whose trust is the LORD*. He is like a tree planted by water, that sends out its roots by the stream, and does not fear when heat comes, for its leaves remain green, and is not anxious in the year of drought, for it does not cease to bear fruit. (Jer. 17:7-8)

Israel's Future Secured

In Psalm 89, Ethan the Ezrahite extolled the faithfulness and the *chesed* of God. We know that Ethan was among the wisest men of Israel because King Solomon is said to have been "wiser than Ethan the Ezrahite" (1 Kgs. 4:31). Ethan certainly fits the profile of Psalm 107, where the anonymous psalmist writes: "Whoever is wise, let him attend to these things; let them consider the steadfast love [*chesed*] of the LORD" (Ps. 107:43). Ethan's own psalm is pertinent to our discussion of Israel's place in the ongoing purposes of God, for it begins:

> I will sing of the steadfast love [*chesed*] of the LORD, forever; with my mouth I will make known your faithfulness to all generations. For I said, "Steadfast love [*chesed*] will be built up forever; in the heavens you will establish your faithfulness." (Ps. 89:1-2)

The main focus of the psalm is God's faithfulness to His covenant with David. It is clear that Israel was in a bad way at the time the psalm was written, which is why Ethan reminded himself and his people of God's promises. More importantly, he reminded God of His steadfast love for David and what He had once spoken in relation to Israel's king:

> "I have found David, my servant; with my holy oil I have anointed him, so that my hand shall be established with him ... My faithfulness and my steadfast love [*chesed*] shall be with him ... My steadfast love [*chesed*] I will keep for him forever, and my covenant will stand firm for him. I will establish his offspring forever and his throne as the days of the heavens. If his children forsake my law ... then I will punish their transgression with the rod and their iniquity with stripes, but I will not remove from him my steadfast love [*chesed*] or be false to my faithfulness. I will not violate my covenant or alter the word that went forth from my lips. Once for all I have sworn by my holiness; I will not lie to David. His offspring shall endure forever, his throne as long as the sun before me. Like the moon it shall be established forever, a faithful witness in the skies." Selah. (Ps. 89:20-37)

This psalm is a real body blow to replacement theologians in their endeavor to eliminate Israel, which is why they spiritualize it away and render it meaningless. God declared long ago that David's throne, which was inextricably tied to the city of Jerusalem and the Land of Israel, would endure *forever*. He further stated that He would never violate His covenant or alter

His word to David because He had sworn by His holiness once and for all. Although David's descendants would not be allowed to reign with impunity, even the political demise and military overthrow of the nation would not overturn the authority and privilege that God had invested in His servant. It would be possible for the physical throne itself, with a physical presence on that throne, to be removed as an act of God's judgment, but only for a season. The Lord appealed to the fixed order of creation to underline the enduring nature of His promises to David, something He later reaffirmed through the Prophet Jeremiah when all seemed lost for the southern kingdom of Judah:

> For thus says the LORD: "David shall never lack a man to sit on the throne of the house of Israel . . ." Thus says the LORD: "If you can break my covenant with the day and my covenant with the night, so that day and night will not come at their appointed time, then also my covenant with David my servant may be broken, so that he shall not have a son to reign on his throne." (Jer. 33:17-21)

This divine declaration sits between two other critically important announcements God made concerning His promise of "a new covenant with the house of Israel and the house of Judah" (Jer. 31:31):

> Thus says the LORD, who gives the sun for light by day and the fixed order of the moon and the stars for light by night, who stirs up the sea so that its waves roar — the LORD of hosts is His name: "If this fixed order departs from before me, declares the LORD, then shall the offspring of Israel cease from being a nation before me forever." Thus says the LORD: "If the heavens above can be measured, and the foundations of the earth below can be explored, then I will cast off all the offspring of Israel for all that they have done, declares the LORD." (Jer. 31:35-37)

> The word of the LORD came to Jeremiah: "Have you not observed that these people are saying, 'The LORD has rejected the two clans that He chose'? Thus they have despised my people so that they are no longer a nation in their sight. Thus says the LORD: If I have not established my covenant with day and night and the fixed order of heaven and earth, then I will reject the offspring of Jacob and David my servant and will not choose one of his offspring to rule over the offspring of Abraham, Isaac, and Jacob. For I will restore their fortunes and will have mercy on them." (Jer. 33:23-26)

Emphatic! Unambiguous! Unanswerable! Everlasting! Could God have made His point any clearer?

Conclusion

> O Israel, hope in the LORD! For with the LORD there is steadfast love [*chesed*], and with Him is plentiful redemption. And He will redeem Israel from all his iniquities. (Ps. 130:7-8)

This chapter does not do justice to God's *chesed*. Wherever we turn in Scripture, the loyal, steadfast love of the Lord confronts, challenges, comforts, and compels us to carefully consider His greatness and our own response. No wonder David was forever singing the praises of the One who was forever loyal to him, especially during the darkest times in his life. Consider Psalm 86:

> For you, O Lord, are good and forgiving, abounding in steadfast love [*chesed*] to all who call upon you . . . For great is your steadfast love [*chesed*] toward me; you have delivered my soul from the depths of Sheol. O God, insolent men have risen up against me; a band of ruthless men seeks my life . . . But you, O Lord, are a God merciful and gracious, slow to anger and abounding in steadfast love [*chesed*] and faithfulness. (Ps. 86:5, 13-15)

Therefore, when David passed through the valley of the shadow of death, which he did on many occasions, he could confidently proclaim: "Surely goodness and mercy [*chesed*] shall follow me all the days of my life: and I will dwell in the house of the LORD for ever" (Ps. 23:6, KJV). Spurgeon wrote in his devotional commentary:

> These twin guardian angels [goodness and mercy] will always be with me at my back and my beck. Just as when great princes go abroad they must not go unattended, so it is with the believer. Goodness and mercy follow him always . . . the black days as well as the bright days, the days of fasting as well as the days of feasting, the dreary days of winter as well as the bright days of summer . . . May God grant us grace to dwell in the serene atmosphere of this most blessed Psalm![6]

---

[6] Spurgeon, *The Treasury of David, Vol. I*, pp. 356-57.

The atmosphere for Israel right now is anything but serene, but it will be one day. We have that on God's oath! Goodness and mercy once followed close on the heels of the children of Israel. These "twin guardian angels," as Spurgeon called them, may have taken their leave for a season, but they were never retired by the Lord. They are ready to resume their pursuit of Israel once the people realize that they have wandered far from the ancient paths (Jer. 6:16), forsaken "the Ancient of days" (Dan. 7:9), and rejected Him "whose origin is from of old, from ancient days" (Mic. 5:2). Scripture tells us that a glorious revelation will soon break upon the hearts of God's people. In that day, the following words, spoken by psalmist and by prophet, will be filled up with meaning when Israel finally reflects upon the enduring loyalty of God's love:

> The LORD has made known His salvation; He has revealed His righteousness in the sight of the nations. He has remembered His steadfast love [*chesed*] and faithfulness to the house of Israel. All the ends of the earth have seen the salvation of our God. (Ps. 98:2-3)

> I will recount the steadfast love [*chesed*] of the LORD, the praises of the LORD, according to all that the LORD has granted us, and the great goodness to the house of Israel that He has granted them according to His compassion, according to the abundance of His steadfast love [*chesed*]. (Isa. 63:7)

We close with a hymn written in 1782 by the English Baptist pastor Samuel Medley (1738-1799). Entitled "Awake, My Soul, to Joyful Lays," the hymn found popularity in camp meetings across the United States during the nineteenth century. I believe it captures the essence of what we have been discussing in this chapter. May it be a blessing to those who have experienced for themselves the loyal, steadfast love of the Lord:

Awake, My Soul, To Joyful Lays

> And sing thy great Redeemer's praise;
> He justly claims a song from me –
> His lovingkindness [*chesed*], O how free!
> Lovingkindness, lovingkindness,
> His lovingkindness, O how free!
>
> He saw me ruined in the fall,
> Yet loved me notwithstanding all;
> He saved me from my lost estate –

His lovingkindness, O how great!
Lovingkindness, lovingkindness,
His lovingkindness, O how great!

Though numerous hosts of mighty foes,
Though earth and hell my way oppose,
He safely leads my soul along –
His lovingkindness, O how strong!
Lovingkindness, lovingkindness,
His lovingkindness, O how strong!

When trouble, like a gloomy cloud,
Has gathered thick and thundered loud,
He near my soul has always stood –
His lovingkindness, O how good!
Lovingkindness, lovingkindness,
His lovingkindness, O how good!

Often I feel my sinful heart
Prone from my Jesus to depart;
But though I have him oft forgot,
His lovingkindness changes not.
Lovingkindness, lovingkindness,
His lovingkindness changes not.

Soon I shall pass the gloomy vale,
Soon all my mortal powers must fail;
O! may my last expiring breath
His lovingkindness sing in death.
Lovingkindness, lovingkindness,
His lovingkindness sing in death.

Then let me mount and soar away
To the bright world of endless day;
And sing with raptures and surprise,
His lovingkindness in the skies.
Lovingkindness, lovingkindness,
His lovingkindness in the skies.[7]

---

[7] Samuel Medley, "Awake, My Soul, To Joyful Lays," retrieved from www.blueletter-bible.org/hymns.

Chapter 6:

"How long, O Lord?"

> O God, the nations have come into your inheritance [*nachălâh*]; they have defiled your holy temple; they have laid Jerusalem in ruins . . . How long, O LORD? Will you be angry forever? Will your jealousy burn like fire? . . . Help us, O God of our salvation, for the glory of your name; deliver us, and atone for our sins, for your name's sake! (Ps. 79:1-9)

One can only imagine the psalmist's grief as he lamented over the defilement and ruin of Jerusalem, the city of the great King. His main focus, however, was not the city itself but what the city represented. It was part of God's inheritance. But there was hope, and that hope was rooted, as always, in the covenant faithfulness of God:

> He remembers His covenant forever, the word that He commanded, for a thousand generations, the covenant that He made with Abraham, His sworn promise to Isaac, which He confirmed to Jacob as a statute, to Israel as an everlasting covenant, saying, "To you I will give the land of Canaan as your portion for an inheritance [*nachălâh*]." (Ps. 105:8-11)

> He remembers His covenant forever. He has shown His people the power of His works, in giving them the inheritance [*nachălâh*] of the nations . . . He sent redemption to His people; He has commanded His covenant forever. Holy and awesome is His name! (Ps. 111:5-9)

God never forgets that He gave Canaan to the Israelites by means of an *everlasting* covenant. This is crucial to our understanding of events like the sacking of Jerusalem, the destruction of the Temple, the exile of the Jewish people, and everything that has transpired since, up to the present day. These seismic events did not, do not, and cannot ever nullify or redefine the terms of God's covenant with Israel. In Psalm 79 above, Asaph did not downplay the gravity of what had happened to Jerusalem, but he lifted his eyes heavenwards and pleaded with God for mercy, confident that his cry would be heard and answered. What he was less sure about was the duration of God's judgment, which is why he asked the question: "How long, O Lord?"

Commissioning the Prophet

> And I heard the voice of the Lord saying, "Whom shall I send, and who will go for us?" Then I said, "Here I am! Send me." And He said, "Go, and say to this people: 'Keep on hearing, but do not understand; keep on seeing, but do not perceive.' Make the heart of this people dull, and their ears heavy, and blind their eyes; lest they see with their eyes, and hear with their ears, and understand with their hearts, and turn and be healed." Then I said, "How long, O Lord?" (Isa. 6:8-11)

At the heart of Isaiah's call and consecration to the office of prophet was an overwhelmingly fearful yet mercifully non-consuming encounter with the Holy One of Israel. The lips and heart of the man who was to be entrusted with such a momentous ministry at a critical juncture in the nation's history had to be purged of all uncleanness. The southern kingdom of Judah was in a precarious position. King Uzziah's fifty-two-year reign in Jerusalem, which had brought honor to the Lord for the most part, would end in disgrace. As a young man, Uzziah (also known as Azariah) had "set himself to seek God in the days of Zechariah, who instructed him in the fear of God, and as long as he sought the LORD, God made him prosper" (2 Chron. 26:5). The king and his people prospered greatly, and Uzziah's fame spread far and wide. However, there was a problem: "When he became strong, his heart was so proud that he acted corruptly, and he was unfaithful to the LORD his God" (2 Chron. 26:16, NASB).

In his pride, Uzziah blatantly defied God by defiling the Temple. At the height of his power and prestige, the king entered the holy sanctuary to burn incense, a duty restricted to the priesthood. While holding a censer in his hand, Uzziah vented his anger toward the eighty-one priests who valiantly withstood him. God immediately struck the king with leprosy in his forehead, and Uzziah remained a leper to the day of his death. His godly son Jotham reigned and prospered in his stead, but the people "still followed corrupt practices" (2 Chron. 27:2). Jotham's wicked son Ahaz, who as king would sacrifice his sons in the fire, was waiting in the wings. It was in the year that Uzziah died that Isaiah saw the Lord. The sudden exposure to the scrutinizing holiness of the Almighty convinced the prophet that he himself was "undone" ("lost," "ruined," or "unclean") and that his own people were in a wretched spiritual state.

We may be able to recall times in our own lives when we came under the conviction of the Holy Spirit as we quietly read God's Word. Maybe some of us can remember the inner discomfort we felt as we listened in church to a sermon and it seemed as though our lives were being exposed by the preacher. But can any of us honestly say that we have seen the Lord and experienced His presence the way Isaiah did? How could a mere mortal encounter the eternal One in this way and live? By God's grace, Isaiah did survive, just as Moses had survived centuries earlier when he stood on holy ground before the burning bush. An extraordinary calling was about to be revealed to Isaiah, one that he could never have fulfilled had his lips not been cleansed, his guilt taken away, his sin atoned for, and his mind indelibly marked by the overwhelming vision of the Holy One of Israel.

The Pastoral Prophet

I wonder what springs to mind when we think of Old Testament prophets like Isaiah? How would we characterize them? Do we think of them as austere, bronze-headed messengers of doom who had nothing very positive or encouraging to say? Do we see them as men of a bygone era who brought an early revelation of God that was eventually superseded by Jesus and the apostles? Would they be welcome in our church services and invited to speak in our pulpits? Would we have them in our own homes for fellowship and refreshment afterwards? Whatever mental portraits we may have drawn of them, the prophets were ordinary men set apart by an extraordinary God. Yes, they were clearly devout and faithful servants of the Most High who were greatly blessed by Him (James 5:10-11), but listen to the Prophet Amos as he responded to the accusations laid against him by Amaziah, the apostate priest of Bethel:

> I was no prophet, nor a prophet's son, but I was a herdsman and a dresser of sycamore figs. But the LORD took me from following the flock, and the LORD

said to me, "Go, prophesy to my people Israel." Now therefore hear the word of the LORD. (Am. 7:14-16)

Amos was not looking for a cause or a name, and he never put himself forward as a candidate for the prophetic ministry. He was a hard-working herdsman of Tekoa and a dresser of sycamore figs until God set him apart. Amos was given some very strong words to say to his people, but listen to his heart after he received visions from God of how the Lord was intending to punish Israel:

> O Lord GOD, please forgive! How can Jacob stand? He is so small! The Lord relented concerning this; "It shall not be," said the LORD . . . O Lord GOD, please cease! How can Jacob stand? He is so small! The LORD relented concerning this; "This also shall not be," said the Lord GOD. (Am. 7:2-6)

The Prophet Ezekiel was no different. In visions, he saw the wrath of God being poured out upon Jerusalem and responded the only way he knew how:

> I fell upon my face, and cried, "Ah, Lord GOD! Will you destroy all the remnant of Israel in the outpouring of your wrath on Jerusalem?" . . . Then I fell down on my face and cried out with a loud voice and said, "Ah, Lord GOD! Will you make a full end of the remnant of Israel?" (Ezek. 9:8; 11:13)

The true prophet of God needed to be touched by the pastoral heart of God before he could proclaim the prophetic word of God. Just as banknotes and coins in circulation today must have two distinct sides to be classed as legal tender, so God's messengers were required to be double-sided in their ministry, bearing both the prophetic word and the pastoral heart.

The Prophet Jonah is conspicuous as one who was rebuked by God for his unmerciful attitude toward the Ninevites. Jonah (eventually) delivered God's warning to them, the people repented, God relented, and Jonah vented his anger, much to the Lord's displeasure. God then proceeded to question his smoldering prophet:

> "Do you do well to be angry? . . . Should not I pity Nineveh, that great city, in which there are more than 120,000 persons who do not know their right hand from their left, and also much cattle?" (Jonah 4:4, 11)

With that rhetorical question the book of Jonah closes, and we hear no more about the prophet's life and ministry. Now contrast Jonah with Jesus, the supreme Prophet of God. As the Messiah beheld Jerusalem, He prophesied with words that were full of divine anguish:

> "O Jerusalem, Jerusalem, the city that kills the prophets and stones those who are sent to it! How often would I have gathered your children together as a hen gathers her brood under her wings, and you were not willing! See, your house is left to you desolate. For I tell you, you will not see me again, until you say, 'Blessed is He who comes in the name of the Lord.'" (Mt. 23:37-39)

In stark contrast to Jonah, Jesus had every right to be angry, but it was not anger that poured forth from His heart that day. The Lord foresaw that Jerusalem was going to be destroyed by the Romans forty years later as an outworking of God's judgment. However, just when all seemed desolate and hopeless, the promise of restoration sounded forth from the Savior's lips. Embedded in Jesus' prophetic pronouncement was the divine "until"—an underwhelming English word that conveys an overwhelming Hebrew promise. God had not finished with Jerusalem, for in His judgment He would remember His mercy (Hab. 3:2).

In the book of Acts and in Paul's letter to the Romans, we find two more remarkable and uplifting "untils" that relate directly to Israel's promised restoration:

> Repent therefore, and turn back, that your sins may be blotted out, that times of refreshing may come from the presence of the Lord, and that He may send the Messiah appointed for you, Jesus, whom heaven must receive *until* the time for restoring all the things about which God spoke by the mouth of His holy prophets long ago. (Acts 3:19-21)

> Lest you be wise in your own sight, I do not want you to be unaware of this mystery, brothers: a partial hardening has come upon Israel, *until* the fullness of the Gentiles has come in. (Rom. 11:25)

What, then, should have been the enduring response of believers to these divine "untils"? I believe Paul gave the church the definitive answer when he wrote:

> For I tell you that Messiah became a servant to the circumcised to show God's truthfulness, in order to confirm the promises given to the patriarchs, and in order that the Gentiles might glorify God for His mercy [*éleos*]. As it is written, "Therefore I will praise you among the Gentiles, and sing to your name." And again it is said, "Rejoice, O Gentiles, with His people." And again,

"Praise the Lord, all you Gentiles, and let all the peoples extol Him." (Rom. 15:8-11)

A Good and Godly Question

No sooner had Isaiah been commissioned by God than he asked what may appear, on the surface, to have been a rather innocuous question: "How long, O Lord?" Was Isaiah simply curious as to the timeframe of the prophecy? Was he keen to draw a line on his prophetic wall chart? I believe his question had little to do with curiosity and everything to do with the measure of grief within his own heart as he contemplated his people's predicament and the mission to which He had been appointed. Isaiah knew full well that his people were guilty and the divine sentence just, but he longed for the time when God would withdraw His hand of chastisement and spare His people.

Time and again from the lips of the psalmists and from David in particular, we hear the same kind of anguished concern being expressed in prayer to God:

> My soul also is greatly troubled. But you, O LORD — how long? (Ps. 6:3)

> How long, O LORD? Will you forget me forever? How long will you hide your face from me? How long must I take counsel in my soul and have sorrow in my heart all the day? How long shall my enemy be exalted over me? (Ps. 13:1-2)

> How long, O God, is the foe to scoff? Is the enemy to revile your name forever? (Ps. 74:10)

> How long, O LORD? Will you be angry forever? Will your jealousy burn like fire? (Ps. 79:5)

> How long, O LORD? Will you hide yourself forever? How long will your wrath burn like fire? (Ps. 89:46)

> Return, O LORD! How long? Have pity on your servants! (Ps. 90:13)

We hear the same supplicatory cry from the Prophet Habakkuk as he struggled to understand why God appeared to be unmoved by the wickedness of His people:

"O LORD, how long shall I cry for help, and you will not hear? Or cry to you 'Violence!' and you will not save?" (Hab. 1:2).

One man closer to our own time who experienced both physical and spiritual anguish throughout his life and ministry was Charles Spurgeon. In his commentary on Psalm 13, Spurgeon reflected on David's question before writing these typically insightful words:

> Time flies with full-fledged wing in our summer days, but in our winters he flutters painfully. A week within prison-walls is longer than a month at liberty. Long sorrow seems to argue abounding corruption; for the gold which is long in the fire must have had much dross to be consumed, hence the question 'how long?' may suggest deep searching of heart . . . Can God forget? Can Omniscience fail in memory? Above all, can Jehovah's heart forget his own beloved child? . . . Oh, dark thought! . . . No, his anger may endure for a night, but his love shall abide eternally . . . God may hide his face, and yet he may remember still. A hidden face is no sign of a forgetful heart. It is in love that his face is turned away; yet to a real child of God, this hiding of his Father's face is terrible, and he will never be at ease until once more he hath his Father's smile.[1]

I am sure those of us who have experienced God's discipline in our own lives will be able to identify to some degree with Spurgeon's reflections. Bodily affliction, separation from fellowship, withdrawal from public ministry, or the merciless taunt of the enemy do not compare with the abiding sense of God's distance. The thought that God's face no longer shines upon us can mercilessly torment the mind during these dark times and seasons in our lives. Nevertheless, we can take solace in the knowledge that these afflictions are only for a season and always with a view to restoration and greater fruitfulness (Heb. 12:7-11).

Where Israel is concerned, common sense and rational thought—the twin foes of sound, biblical theology—would only lead us to despair over the nation's future. If believers allow such foes to enter the courtroom of their minds, then the verdict is likely to be this: guilty as charged, deserving of judgment, and disinherited from grace. Sadly, many in the church have already reached such a verdict, and they are in "good" company. This was the sentence that was pronounced by most of the so-called early church

---

[1] Spurgeon, *The Treasury of David, Vol. I*, p. 151.

fathers, including Irenaeus (ca. A.D. 130-200), the hugely influential bishop of Lyon and leading Christian apologist. Irenaeus referred to Israel's disinheritance from grace in his celebrated work *Against Heresies*.[2] Thankfully God does not deal in common sense or with man's rational thinking, especially when they are covered with the veneer of theological respectability. The Lord only ever works in compliance with His own character. *Who* He is determines *what* He does. For that reason, we can declare confidently (whenever we preach or pray) and defiantly (whenever Israel's prosecuting attorneys in the church rise to their feet) that all God's promises will be fulfilled to the letter. When the tribes of Israel were allotted their inheritance in Canaan, Scripture states that "not one word of all the good promises that the LORD had made to the house of Israel had failed; all came to pass" (Josh. 21:45). As it was then, so it is now, and so it will be tomorrow. The court of heaven reached its verdict long ago. Israel has a future, and the end will be glorious!

The Prophetic Eye

When Isaiah asked, "How long, O Lord?" he was not kept waiting. This was God's reply:

> "Until cities lie waste without inhabitant, and houses without people, and the land is a desolate waste, and the LORD removes people far away, and the forsaken places are many in the midst of the land. And though a tenth remain in it, it will be burned again, like a terebinth or an oak, whose stump remains when it is felled." (Isa. 6:11-13)

As the prophecies of Isaiah proceed, the initial sounds of desolation and despair eventually give way to the voice of divine consolation, which grows louder and stronger until it reaches a glorious crescendo. Isaiah was later told that "the LORD's hand is not shortened, that it cannot save, or His ear dull, that it cannot hear," and that "a Redeemer will come to Zion, to those

---

[2] Irenaeus declared that "the house of Jacob and the people of Israel are disinherited from the grace of God." "Irenaeus: Against Heresies," in *Ante-Nicene Fathers*, ed. Alexander Roberts and James Donaldson, Vol. 1 (Peabody, MA: Hendrickson, 2012), Book III, Chapter XXI, p. 451.

in Jacob who turn from transgression," a prophecy that would later be imprinted on the heart and mind of Paul (Isa. 59:1, 20; cf. Rom. 11:26-27). It was further revealed to Isaiah that a remnant of Israel would remain in the land, a remnant God likened to a tree that is cut down leaving only the stump. The tree might appear dead to the onlooker, but having been carefully planted by God Himself and rooted deep in the fertile soil of His covenant promises, it would grow again.[3] In his devotional commentary, Robert Jamieson (1802-1880) wrote:

> [Isaiah's] prophetic eye was enabled to penetrate beyond that disastrous state of things, and to descry the dawn of returning prosperity and glory for Judah, so that his faith did not falter; he filled up the bright as well as the dark side of the picture, and at the moment of predicting the righteous judgments of heaven on a wicked and impenitent age, he comforted the faithful few in their affliction, as well as put it on record for the instruction of all future ages, that the desolations of Judah would be repaired.[4]

Jamieson's perceptive comments are entirely in keeping with the testimony of Scripture, for with the Lord there is always the hope of a new dawn, a new beginning, a new season of growth and fruitfulness. Consider the following:

> For there is hope for a tree, if it be cut down, that it will sprout again, and that its shoots will not cease. Though its root grow old in the earth, and its stump die in the soil, yet at the scent of water it will bud and put out branches like a young plant. (Job 14:7-9)

> I ask, then, has God rejected His people? By no means! . . . God has not rejected His people whom He foreknew . . . [A]t the present time there is a remnant, chosen by grace . . . If the dough offered as firstfruits is holy, so is the whole lump, and if the root is holy, so are the branches . . . For if you were cut from what is by nature a wild olive tree, and grafted, contrary to nature, into a cultivated olive tree, how much more will these, the natural branches, be grafted back into their own olive tree. (Rom. 11:1-24)

---

[3] See, for example: Ps. 44:2; 80:8-15; Isa. 5:1-7; 60:21; 61:3; Jer. 2:21; 11:17; Ezek. 19:10; Hos. 9:13; Mt. 21:33-46.

[4] Robert Jamieson and Edward H. Bickersteth, *The Holy Bible: With a Devotional and Practical Commentary – Isaiah to Revelation* (London & New York: Virtue & Co., n.d.), p. 180.

The biblical imagery of the tree with its roots, stump, and branches is tied to the revelation of Israel's Messiah, who is portrayed by the prophets as the righteous Branch. In the prophecies of Isaiah, Jeremiah, and Zechariah, we read how Israel's hope was rooted by God in the Messiah, who would come forth as a tender shoot from the seemingly dead stump of David's royal line:

> For He grew up before Him like a young plant, and like a root out of dry ground; He had no form or majesty that we should look at Him, and no beauty that we should desire Him. (Isa. 53:2)

> There shall come forth a shoot from the stump of Jesse, and a Branch from his roots shall bear fruit . . . In that day the root of Jesse, who shall stand as a signal for the peoples — of Him shall the nations inquire, and His resting place shall be glorious. In that day the Lord will extend His hand yet a second time to recover the remnant that remains of His people. (Isa. 11:1-11)

> Behold, the days are coming, declares the LORD, when I will raise up for David a righteous Branch, and He shall reign as king and deal wisely, and shall execute justice and righteousness in the land. In his days Judah will be saved, and Israel will dwell securely. And this is the name by which He will be called: "The LORD is our righteousness." (Jer. 23:5-6; cf. 33:15; Zech. 3:8; 6:12)

He Was Pierced!

God foreknew that Israel would break the covenant. He also foresaw the time when His own personal intervention would be necessary if His people were to survive. On account of His boundless grace, mercy, and loyal love, God's intervention would not be limited to destruction, desolation, and dispersion. It would, however, require a death—not of God's chosen nation but of God's beloved Son. We are not told, nor can we begin to imagine, what passed through Isaiah's heart and mind when the prophetic word was transfigured before him as he beheld in a vision the Word of God made flesh. Here is an excerpt from that momentous and most glorious of prophecies:

> He was despised and rejected by men; a man of sorrows, and acquainted with grief; and as one from whom men hide their faces He was despised, and we esteemed Him not. Surely He has borne our griefs and carried our sorrows;

yet we esteemed Him stricken, smitten by God, and afflicted. But He was wounded for our transgressions, He was bruised for our iniquities; upon Him was the chastisement that made us whole, and with His stripes we are healed. All we like sheep have gone astray; we have turned every one to His own way; and the LORD has laid on Him the iniquity of us all.

He was oppressed, and He was afflicted, yet He opened not His mouth; like a lamb that is led to the slaughter, and like a sheep that before its shearers is dumb, so He opened not His mouth. By oppression and judgment He was taken away; and as for His generation, who considered that He was cut off out of the land of the living, stricken for the transgression of my people? And they made His grave with the wicked and with a rich man in His death, although He had done no violence, and there was no deceit in His mouth.

Yet it was the will of the LORD to bruise Him; He has put Him to grief; when He makes Himself an offering for sin, He shall see His offspring, He shall prolong His days; the will of the LORD shall prosper in His hand; He shall see the fruit of the travail of His soul and be satisfied; by His knowledge shall the righteous one, my servant, make many to be accounted righteous; and He shall bear their iniquities.

Therefore I will divide Him a portion with the great, and He shall divide the spoil with the strong; because He poured out His soul to death, and was numbered with the transgressors; yet He bore the sin of many, and made intercession for the transgressors. (Isa. 53:3-12, RSV)

As noted previously, there came a point in Israel's wilderness wanderings when the nation's existence was under threat—from God Himself. But did Moses truly believe in the wake of the golden calf episode that the Lord was about to "destroy" the Israelites and "blot out their name from under heaven" (Deut. 9:13-14; cf. Ex. 32:9-10)? Moses was fully aware of God's promise to Abraham that his descendants would return to Canaan "in the fourth generation" (Gen. 15:13-16; Ex. 12:40-41). Knowing that promise, however, did not diminish in his mind the gravity of the situation. There was no blasé attitude in the heart of the man with whom God spoke "mouth to mouth" (Num. 12:8). The nation's rebellion was real, the threat of judgment was real, and therefore Moses' prayer on behalf of the people had to be real if there were to be any hope. For forty days and nights, Moses fasted and prostrated himself before God as Israel's future hung in the balance (Deut. 9:18, 25). As Moses later explained to his people,

> I was afraid of the anger and hot displeasure that the LORD bore against you, so that He was ready to destroy you. But the LORD listened to me that time also. And the LORD was so angry with Aaron that He was ready to destroy him. And I prayed for Aaron also at the same time ... And the LORD relented from the disaster that He had spoken of bringing on His people. (Deut. 9:19-20; Ex. 32:14)

Knowledge of God's promises did not induce apathy or indifference in the heart of God's servant—quite the opposite, in fact. This was no divinely conceived roleplay to test Moses, for the threat was genuine. If we apply this to the church's responsibility toward Israel, then we might say that knowledge of Paul's announcement that "all Israel will be saved" (Rom. 11:26) does not excuse believers from praying for Israel's salvation. The Bible leaves no room for Calvinistic complacency. Although God has declared in His Word what will come to pass in the last days, there is no such thing as a foregone conclusion with the Lord. He wants His people to fully engage with Him, with His Word, and with His people.

Conclusion

When the heat of divine displeasure is felt by the disobedient or when the faithful are enduring a fiery trial that is intended to refine, it is understandable and inevitable that the afflicted soul will yearn for an answer to the question, "How long, O Lord?" In the book of Revelation, we are told that John distinctly heard this same question being asked in heaven itself, after he was caught up in the Spirit on the island of Patmos. He wrote:

> When He [the Lamb/Messiah Jesus] opened the fifth seal, I saw under the altar the souls of those who had been slain for the word of God and for the witness they had borne. They cried out with a loud voice, "O Sovereign Lord, holy and true, how long before you will judge and avenge our blood on those who dwell on the earth?" Then they were each given a white robe and told to rest a little longer, until the number of their fellow servants and their brothers should be complete, who were to be killed as they themselves had been. (Rev. 6:9-11)

In Isaiah's day, that which was prescribed by God for the nation of Israel was so dreadful to contemplate that the prophet longed for confirmation that there would be an end. He knew that his prophetic mission was going to cost him personally, as it would all the true prophets of God. His lips may have been touched by a burning coal from the altar, but his heart was to be forever scorched by the burning jealousy of Israel's forsaken King. As we shall consider in a later chapter, the jealousy of God—for His people, His land, and His city—is key to understanding how there could ever be an end to Israel's judgment.

In the book of Zechariah, we hear the same question being asked of God, not by the prophet on this occasion but by the angel of the Lord who said, "O LORD of hosts, how long will you have no mercy on Jerusalem and the cities of Judah, against which you have been angry these seventy years?" (Zech. 1:12). The Lord's answer was remarkable. Where we might have expected only desolation, we encounter grace, mercy, and comfort—three heaven-sent "pilgrims" who have guaranteed Israel's future security and prosperity:

> And the LORD answered gracious and comforting words to the angel who talked with me. So the angel who talked with me said to me, "Cry out, Thus says the LORD of hosts: I am exceedingly jealous for Jerusalem and for Zion. And I am exceedingly angry with the nations that are at ease; for while I was angry but a little, they furthered the disaster. Therefore, thus says the LORD, I have returned to Jerusalem with mercy; my house shall be built in it, declares the LORD of hosts, and the measuring line shall be stretched out over Jerusalem. Cry out again, Thus says the LORD of hosts: My cities shall again overflow with prosperity, and the LORD will again comfort Zion and again choose Jerusalem." (Zech. 1:13-17)

We close with a poem written by the British-born Brethren evangelist James George Deck (1807-1884). Entitled "How Long, O Lord?", it is based on Jesus' parable of the ten virgins (Mt. 25:1-13). The poem expresses the personal longing of the author to see the Heavenly Bridegroom descend and his lament over the general state of indifference and unbelief within the church toward this great day. It is one thing for believers to be occupied with the "how long?" until Israel's restoration but quite another to be caught up daily with the "how long?" until the church's rapture. May our *primary* focus as believers not be on the day of Israel's salvation but on the day when the bride is caught up to meet her Heavenly Bridegroom, when she shall see Him in all His heavenly glory:

How Long, O Lord?

How long, O Lord, our Savior,
Wilt Thou remain away?
The careless world is mocking
At Thy so long delay.
Oh, when shall come the moment,
When, brighter far than morn,
The sunshine of Thy glory
Shall on Thy people dawn?

How long, O gracious Master,
Wilt Thou Thy household leave?
So long Thou now hast tarried,
Few Thy return believe:
Immersed in sloth and folly,
Thy servants, Lord, we see;
And few of us stand ready
With joy to welcome Thee.

How long, O Heav'nly Bridegroom!
How long wilt Thou delay?
And yet how few are grieving
That Thou dost absent stay:
Thy very Bride her portion
And calling hath forgot,
And seeks for ease and glory
Where Thou, her Lord, art not.

Oh, wake the slumb'ring virgins,
To heed the solemn cry;
Let all Thy saints repeat it –
"The Bridegroom draweth nigh!"
May all our lamps be burning,
Our loins well girded be;
Each longing heart preparing
With joy Thy face to see.[5]

---

[5] James G. Deck, *Hymns and Sacred Poems, 5th Ed.* (Winschoten, Netherlands: H.L. Heijkoop, n.d.), pp. 5-6.

Chapter 7:

When No One Else Cares

> "For thus says the LORD: Your hurt is incurable, and your wound is grievous. There is none to uphold your cause . . . All your lovers have forgotten you; they care nothing for you; for I have dealt you the blow of an enemy, the punishment of a merciless foe, because your guilt is great, because your sins are flagrant." (Jer. 30:12-14)

> Then He led out His people like sheep and guided them in the wilderness like a flock . . . He chose David His servant and took him from the sheepfolds; from following the nursing ewes He brought him to shepherd Jacob His people, Israel His inheritance [*nachălâh*]. (Ps. 78:52, 70-71)

In the above psalm, the *nachălâh* of God is couched in shepherding imagery. This helps us understand in a very vivid and pastoral way the level of care with which God tended the "flock of Israel." This metaphor was cherished by God's people whenever they walked in faithful obedience to Him, for they were "His people, and the sheep of His pasture" (Ps. 100:3). They understood their weakness and vulnerability and how utterly dependent they were upon their heavenly Shepherd to faithfully lead, feed, heal, defend, and deliver them. This is summed up in Psalm 100:

> Know that the LORD, He is God! It is He who made us, and we are His; we are His people, and the sheep of His pasture . . . For the LORD is good; His steadfast love [*chesed*] endures forever, and His faithfulness to all generations. (Ps. 100:3-5)

The Lord Is Israel's Shepherd

Israel's understanding of her Shepherd-sheep relationship with God was beautifully expressed in Psalm 23, which is cherished by Christians (and many non-Christians) the world over. To this day, David's shepherd psalm is read aloud, listened to, and sung at countless funerals even though this psalm is about life, not death!

> The LORD is my shepherd; I shall not want. He makes me lie down in green pastures. He leads me beside still waters. He restores my soul. He leads me in paths of righteousness for His name's sake. Even though I walk through the valley of the shadow of death, I will fear no evil, for you are with me; your rod and your staff, they comfort me. (Ps. 23:1-4)

On many occasions, the people of Israel were deprived of the level of care they should have received from their leaders, who failed to fulfill their responsibility as God's under-shepherds. In the book of Zechariah, for example, we are told that the people were "afflicted for lack of a shepherd" (Zech. 10:2) and that the Lord's anger grew "hot against the shepherds" (Zech. 10:3). God was also indignant toward nations that reproached and ill-treated His people, especially after He had exiled them from the land. In response to all of this, the Lord promised that *He Himself* would seek out, save, and shepherd His flock:

> Behold, the Lord GOD comes with might, and His arm rules for Him ... He will tend His flock like a shepherd; He will gather the lambs in His arms; He will carry them in His bosom, and gently lead those that are with young. (Isa. 40:10-11)

> Hear the word of the LORD, O nations, and declare it in the coastlands far away; say, "He who scattered Israel will gather him, and will keep him as a shepherd keeps his flock. For the LORD has ransomed Jacob and has redeemed him from hands too strong for him." (Jer. 31:10-11)

> On that day the LORD their God will save them, as the flock of His people; for like the jewels of a crown they shall shine on His land. For how great is His goodness, and how great His beauty! (Zech. 9:16-17)

At key times in Israel's history, both psalmist and prophet alike appealed to God to take up His shepherd's staff and rescue His beleaguered flock, just as He had done when leading the Israelites out of Egypt. We read in two of Asaph's psalms and in the prophecies of Micah:

> Your way was through the sea, your path through the great waters; yet your footprints were unseen. You led your people like a flock by the hand of Moses and Aaron. (Ps. 77:19-20; cf. Ex. 15:13)

> Give ear, O Shepherd of Israel, you who lead Joseph like a flock . . . Before Ephraim and Benjamin and Manasseh, stir up your might and come to save us! (Ps. 80:1-2)
>
> Shepherd your people with your staff, the flock of your inheritance [*nachălâh*], who dwell alone in a forest in the midst of a garden land. (Mic. 7:14)

Many times, the Lord wrought deliverance for Israel by raising up righteous men and women who courageously put their lives on the line. They did so in humble, loving obedience to the Lord and because they cared more about the welfare of the people than they did their own. The superintending presence and power of Israel's faithful Shepherd is unmistakable in the biblical accounts of Esther, Mordecai, and Nehemiah:

> Then Esther told them to reply to Mordecai, "Go, gather all the Jews to be found in Susa, and hold a fast on my behalf, and do not eat or drink for three days, night or day. I and my young women will also fast as you do. Then I will go to the king, though it is against the law, and if I perish, I perish." (Est. 4:15-16)
>
> For Mordecai the Jew was second in rank to King Ahasuerus, and he was great among the Jews and popular with the multitude of his brothers, for he sought the welfare of his people and spoke peace to all his people. (Est. 10:3)
>
> Then I came to the governors of the province Beyond the River and gave them the king's letters . . . But when Sanballat the Horonite and Tobiah the Ammonite servant heard this, it displeased them greatly that someone had come to seek the welfare of the people of Israel. (Neh. 2:9-10)

Seeking the welfare of the Jewish people ought to have been the practice of the church from its foundation. Sadly, those who have exhibited genuine love and concern for the flock of Israel have been the exception rather than the rule. One of the most remarkable though little-known exceptions was William Henry Hechler (1845-1931), a man recognized by the Jewish community as having been a true friend of Israel.

A Peculiar "Prophet"

On January 31, 2011, I had the privilege of attending a ceremony at New Southgate Cemetery in London, where a memorial stone was laid at the unmarked grave of William Hechler. Within the purposes of God, Hechler had been a significant human link in a sovereign chain of events that led to the establishment of the modern State of Israel in 1948, and yet so few believers have heard about him. The ceremony in London, which coincided with the eightieth anniversary of his death, was attended by Israeli officials, Jewish community leaders, and representatives from several Christian organizations in the UK. The event itself was organized by Jerry Klinger, the son of survivors of Buchenwald and Bergen Belsen concentration camps and president of the Jewish American Society for Historic Preservation. During the course of his own research into Jewish-Christian relations prior to 1948, Klinger discovered that Hechler, who had once served as chaplain to the British Embassy in Vienna, had died impoverished and without a headstone to mark his London grave. Little recognition had been given to a man who had done so much for the Jewish people, a situation that Klinger felt compelled to rectify.

William Hechler's concern for the Jewish people owed much to his father, Dietrich, who was a member of the London Society for Promoting Christianity amongst the Jews (known today as The Church's Ministry among Jewish People, or CMJ for short). When the horrific pogroms against the Jews broke out in Russia in 1881, Hechler helped establish a committee to raise funds for their resettlement. He also traveled to Russia to personally plead with the Jewish people to flee to their ancient homeland. Later that year, he published a broadsheet titled "The Restoration of the Jews to Palestine," in which he outlined his belief that the return of the Jews to their promised land was a central theme in Scripture and one that was intertwined with the second coming of Jesus. Hechler expressed his personal conviction that it was the duty of every believer "to pray earnestly and to long for the restoration of God's chosen race, and to love the Jews." He also issued this stark warning to the nations of the world: "Blessed shall that nation be, which loves the Jews . . . And let us not forget the terrible punishments which await those who 'hate' and 'persecute' the Jews."[1]

Hechler was a close friend and confidant of Theodor Herzl (1860-1904), the non-religious Austro-Hungarian journalist who founded modern political Zionism. The two men first met in 1896 following the publication of

---

[1] William Henry Hechler, *The Restoration of the Jews to Palestine* (London: 1884).

Der Judenstaat ("The Jewish State"), which was Herzl's manifesto for ending centuries of anti-Semitic persecution by establishing a homeland for his people. Hechler read *Der Judenstaat* and as an avid student of Bible prophecy was convinced that a critical juncture had been reached in Israel's turbulent history. However, by the time Hechler came knocking at his door, Herzl had grown despondent, having failed to secure the necessary financial backing for his ambitious plan. An audience with Europe's political elite had eluded him. In a letter addressed to the German Jewish banker Baron Maurice de Hirsch, dated June 18, 1895, Herzl wrote of his despair:

> For the present there is no helping the Jews. If someone were to show them the promised land, they would mock him. For they are demoralized . . . I cannot break that wall. Not with my head alone. Therefore I am giving it up. As a practical proposition I am done with the matter.[2]

Quite unexpectedly but in God's impeccable timing, William Hechler walked into Herzl's life and made an immediate and lasting impression. In his diaries, Herzl described the somewhat eccentric chaplain as a "likeable, sensitive man with the long grey beard of a prophet," who, though "peculiar and complex,"[3] was "thoroughly honest."[4] Hechler, in turn, insisted in the words of the Prophet Amos that he was "not a prophet, nor the son of a prophet, but only a humble student of prophecy, watching the signs of the times."[5] It was Hechler's acquaintance with Grand Duke Frederick Wilhelm I of Baden, Germany, that gave Herzl his first diplomatic breakthrough—an audience with the Grand Duke's nephew, Kaiser Wilhelm II. Hechler had previously tutored Frederick's son and on many occasions had discussed Bible prophecy with the Grand Duke, who was sympathetic to the plight of the Jewish people.

---

[2] Amos Elon, *Herzl* (New York: Holt, Rinehart and Winston, 1975), pp. 151-52.

[3] Raphael Patai, ed., *The Complete Diaries of Theodor Herzl: Vol. I* (London: Herzl Press & Thomas Yoseloff, 1960), pp. 310-12, 342.

[4] *The Complete Diaries of Theodor Herzl: Vol. III*, p. 1020.

[5] "Rev. W.H. Hechler to the Grand Duke Frederick of Baden. March 26, 1896," in Hermann and Bessi Ellern, *Herzl, Hechler, the Grand Duke of Baden and the German Emperor 1896-1904 / documents found by Hermann and Bessi Ellern, reproduced in facsimile* (Tel Aviv: Ellern's Bank Ltd., 1961), pp. 4-5.

Herzl held Hechler in such high esteem that the Zionist leader invited his Christian friend to write an article for the first edition of his new journal *Die Welt* ("The World"). Launched in Vienna in May 1897, the goal of Herzl's Zionist weekly was to promote his political solution to the Jewish question. Hechler obliged and in his article made an impassioned appeal:

> Children of Abraham, awake! . . . As a Christian, I believe as well as you in what is called the Zionist Movement, for according to the Bible and its ancient prophets a Jewish state must be raised in Palestine. I am convinced by the signs of our own time that the Jews will soon recover their beloved homeland . . . I am certain that the establishment of a Jewish state, with the support of the Princes of Europe, will inaugurate the salvation forecast by Isaiah, Micah, and Zechariah.[6]

Hechler was with Herzl the day before he died. One of Herzl's dying wishes was for the Jewish community to express their full gratitude to a man who had done so much to help them. Following the dedication of Hechler's memorial stone in London in 2011, David Breakstone, vice chairman of the World Zionist Organization, said in an interview:

> Rev. Hechler played a vital role in advancing the Zionist cause at the crucial, early stage of the movement's emergence. In honoring him as we did this week, we not only paid him the respect that was long overdue, making good on an historical debt of gratitude, but also publicly recognized the vital role that so many Christians have played — first in the establishment of the Jewish state, and since then, in support of it.[7]

A People Sought Out

One of the most striking themes running through Scripture is the deep concern that God has for the forsaken, mistreated, and deprived. As the psalmist confidently asserted, "He will regard the prayer of the destitute,

---

[6] Quoted in Paul C. Merkley, *The Politics of Christian Zionism 1891-1948* (London: Frank Cass, 1998), p. 31.

[7] Jonny Paul, "Christian leader pivotal to Herzl's work recognized," *Jerusalem Post*, February 2, 2011, www.jpost.com/international.

and will not despise their supplication" (Ps. 102:17). This concern was enshrined in the laws of justice and restitution that were given by God at Mount Sinai and summed up in the following commandment:

> "If ever you take your neighbor's cloak in pledge, you shall return it to him before the sun goes down, for that is his only covering, and it is his cloak for his body; in what else shall he sleep? And if he cries to me, I will hear, for I am compassionate." (Ex. 22:26-27)

We have an early and very vivid illustration of God's compassion in the book of Genesis when Hagar and her son Ishmael were banished by Abraham's wife Sarah and left to wander in the wilderness of Beersheba. With supplies exhausted and her son's death anticipated, Hagar lifted up her voice and wept. As the account continues,

> God heard the voice of the boy, and the angel of God called to Hagar from heaven and said to her, "What troubles you, Hagar? Fear not, for God has heard the voice of the boy where he is. Up! Lift up the boy, and hold him fast with your hand, for I will make him into a great nation." Then God opened her eyes, and she saw a well of water. And she went and filled the skin with water and gave the boy a drink. And God was with the boy, and he grew up. (Gen. 21:17-20)

Another illustration can be found in the compelling account of David's wilderness trial when he was fleeing for his life from Saul. We read how God's compassion was shown on one occasion through David to a beleaguered company of men who were like sheep without a shepherd. They found solace and safety with David, whose sufferings brought him ever closer to God's heart:

> David departed from there and escaped to the cave of Adullam ... And everyone who was in distress, and everyone who was in debt, and everyone who was bitter in soul, gathered to him. And he became commander over them. And there were with him about four hundred men. (1 Sam. 22:1-2)

God hears the cry of *every* man, woman, and child and makes no distinction according to ethnicity or gender when that cry is raised heavenwards. It was, after all, His love for *the whole world* that moved Him to give His only begotten Son, "that *whoever* believes in Him should not perish but have eternal life" (Jn. 3:16). God desires that no man or woman should perish but that all should come to Him in repentance and be saved—even though many will, in the end, reject the free gift of God and choose death rather than life.[8]

The unfathomable depth of divine compassion was magnified whenever God's people found themselves in dire straits. When Israel's sin had reached its full measure, God told the Prophet Jeremiah that even if Moses and Samuel were interceding on behalf of the nation, He would not relent from bringing disaster on Jerusalem. As the Lord rhetorically asked,

> "Who will have pity on you, O Jerusalem, or who will grieve for you? Who will turn aside to ask about your welfare? You have rejected me, declares the LORD; you keep going backward, so I have stretched out my hand against you and destroyed you — I am weary of relenting." (Jer. 15:5-6)

But the prophecies of Jeremiah did not end in chapter 15. There were another 37 chapters to go! Remarkably, after pronouncing judgment upon the southern kingdom of Judah, whose "wound" of sin had become "incurable" (Jer. 30:12; cf. Isa. 1:6; Jer. 14:19; Hos. 5:13), God promised that *He Himself* would heal His people and restore them. The reason He gave was striking: It was because the surrounding nations cared little for His people. More than that, these nations had celebrated Israel's demise, even taking God out of the equation by claiming that *no one* was interested in the nation's plight. How wrong they were! As the Lord declared to His people,

> "There is none to uphold your cause, no medicine for your wound, no healing for you. All your lovers have forgotten you; they care nothing for you . . . [T]hose who plunder you shall be plundered, and all who prey on you I will make a prey. For I will restore health to you, and your wounds I will heal, declares the LORD, because they have called you an outcast: 'It is Zion, for whom no one cares!'" (Jer. 30:13-17)

I personally prefer the KJV rendering of verse 17 because it reveals more clearly the essence of what God was saying: "For I will restore health unto thee, and I will heal thee of thy wounds, saith the LORD; because they called thee an Outcast, saying, This is Zion, whom no man seeketh after." The Hebrew word in view here is *dârash*, which occurs 164 times in the Old Testament. It can mean "to seek after diligently," "to enquire about," or "to

---

[8] See, for example, Ezek. 18:23; 33:11; Jn. 1:12-13; 1 Tim. 2:3-4; 2 Pet. 3:9; 1 Jn. 2:2.

care for." It is used, for example, by David when he lamented in the cave that there was "none who takes notice of me; no refuge remains to me; no one cares [*dârash*] for my soul" (Ps. 142:4) and again when he admonished his son and successor, Solomon, with these words: "If you seek [*dârash*] Him, He will be found by you, but if you forsake Him, He will cast you off forever" (1 Chron. 28:9).

Some of the most significant occurrences of this word are to be found in the book of Deuteronomy. There *dârash* is used, for example, in a prophetic context when Moses spoke about the Israelites seeking the Lord in the latter days:

> And the LORD will scatter you among the peoples, and you will be left few in number among the nations where the LORD will drive you ... But from there you will seek the LORD your God and you will find Him, if you search [*dârash*] after Him with all your heart and with all your soul. (Deut. 4:27-29)

Moses also used the word in connection with the land of Canaan and the city of Jerusalem. The following examples illustrate the double-sided aspect to *dârash*—namely, of caring for and seeking out, both from a divine and human perspective:

> But the land that you are going over to possess is a land of hills and valleys, which drinks water by the rain from heaven, a land that the LORD your God cares for [*dârash*]. The eyes of the LORD your God are always upon it, from the beginning of the year to the end of the year. (Deut. 11:11-12)

> But you shall seek [*dârash*] the place that the LORD your God will choose out of all your tribes to put His name and make His habitation there. (Deut. 12:5)

The word is later used in Kings and Chronicles in relation to certain rulers of the southern kingdom of Judah (Asa, Jehoshaphat, Uzziah, Hezekiah, and Josiah), all of whom prospered greatly when they were wholeheartedly *seeking* the Lord. In the days of King Asa, for example, we read that the nation "entered into a covenant to seek [*dârash*] the LORD, the God of their fathers, with all their heart and with all their soul" (2 Chron. 15:12). They even made a solemn vow that "whoever would not seek [*dârash*] the LORD, the God of Israel, should be put to death, whether young or old, man or woman" (2 Chron. 15:13).

The word is used twenty-four times in the book of Psalms alone. In Psalm 105, for example, the people of Israel were exhorted to remember and make known all of God's wondrous works, including the everlasting covenant He had made with Abraham:

> Glory in His holy name; let the hearts of those who seek the LORD rejoice! Seek [*dârash*] the LORD and His strength; seek His presence continually! (Ps. 105:4)

Dârash is also integral to Psalm 24, in which David announced the prerequisites for ascending the hill of the Lord and the reward for those with clean hands and a pure heart:

> He will receive blessing from the LORD and righteousness from the God of his salvation. Such is the generation of those who seek [*dârash*] Him, who seek the face of the God of Jacob. (Ps. 24:5-6)

Among believers, arguably the most popular and cherished occurrence of *dârash* is to be found in the book of Jeremiah:

> "For I know the plans I have for you," declares the LORD, "plans to prosper you and not to harm you, plans to give you hope and a future. Then you will call on me and come and pray to me, and I will listen to you. You will seek me and find me when you seek [*dârash*] me with all your heart." (Jer. 29:11-13, NIV)

These verses have been imprinted on cards, bookmarks, keyrings, diaries, mugs, Bible covers, jewelry, clocks, paintings, and probably a host of other items, such is the comfort and strength that millions of believers have derived from them—even though God gave the promise specifically to the Jewish exiles in Babylon! I certainly believe that we are at liberty to make an *application* for our own encouragement, provided we do not forget that the primary meaning depends on the original context.

In the Jeremiah 30 prophecy alluded to above, God told His people in no uncertain terms that the surrounding nations to which Judah had turned for help in times of crisis would be conspicuously absent when the armies of Babylon invaded. The impotent gods and idols of these nations would not be there to help God's people. Yet, for all their infidelity, the Lord still cared, even yearned, for His chosen ones. The book of Obadiah, the shortest in the Old Testament, along with other prophecies like Ezekiel 25-26 and 35-36, express God's indignation toward Israel's proud neighbors: the Ammonites, the Moabites, the Edomites, the Philistines, the Cherethites, and the people of Tyre. These nations gloated when calamity, ruin, and desolation befell God's people. Conspiring against them "with wholehearted joy and spiteful minds" (Ezek. 36:5, NKJV), they even sought to devour "the inheritance [*nachălâh*] of the house of Israel" (Ezek. 35:15). But as God declared in His righteous anger,

> "Because you [Ammonites] have clapped your hands and stamped your feet and rejoiced with all the malice in your soul against the land of Israel, therefore, behold, I have stretched out my hand against you . . . And I will cut you off from the peoples and will make you perish out of the countries; I will destroy you . . . I will execute judgments upon Moab . . . I will lay my vengeance upon Edom by the hand of my people Israel . . . I will stretch out my hand against the Philistines, and I will cut off the Cherethites and destroy the rest of the seacoast . . . Then they will know that I am the LORD, when I lay my vengeance upon them." (Ezek. 25:6-17)

Does any of this sound familiar? Is there not a very sober warning here to Israel's present-day foes? In Ezekiel's time, the Lord had a word of consolation for Israel in the face of such overwhelming hatred:

> "And for the house of Israel there shall be no more a brier to prick or a thorn to hurt them among all their neighbors who have treated them with contempt. Then they will know that I am the Lord GOD. Thus says the Lord GOD: When I gather the house of Israel from the peoples among whom they are scattered, and manifest my holiness in them in the sight of the nations, then they shall dwell in their own land that I gave to my servant Jacob . . . They shall dwell securely, when I execute judgments upon all their neighbors who have treated them with contempt. Then they will know that I am the LORD their God." (Ezek. 28:24-26)

One thing is certain: Israel's implacable enemies will soon discover what the seemingly invincible warrior Goliath and the defiant Philistine armies behind him discovered to their great cost in the Valley of Elah. When an indignant shepherd boy armed only with a staff, a sling, and five smooth stones stood before them "in the name of the LORD of hosts, the God of the armies of Israel" (1 Sam. 17:45), he boldly declared that the battle belonged to the Lord. David then confidently announced in the face of Goliath's taunts that the earth was about to learn "that there is a God in Israel" (1 Sam. 17:46).

The Good Shepherd

It is in the book of Ezekiel that we find one of the most profound expressions of God's searching heart. In chapter 34, the revelation of God as shepherd comes into sharp focus both prophetically and pastorally. As noted earlier, the Lord expressed great indignation toward the shepherds or leaders of Israel who had cared so little for His flock. *Dârash* took center stage as the prophetic drama unfolded:

> "My sheep were scattered over all the face of the earth, with none to search [*dârash*] or seek for them... As I live, declares the Lord GOD, surely because my sheep have become a prey... since there was no shepherd, and because my shepherds have not searched [*dârash*] for my sheep, but the shepherds have fed themselves, and have not fed my sheep, Thus says the Lord GOD, Behold, I am against the shepherds, and I will require [*dârash*] my sheep at their hand and put a stop to their feeding the sheep... For thus says the Lord GOD: Behold, I, I myself will search [*dârash*] for my sheep and will seek them out. As a shepherd seeks out his flock when he is among his sheep that have been scattered, so will I seek out my sheep, and I will rescue them from all places where they have been scattered on a day of clouds and thick darkness ... And I will set up over them one shepherd, my servant David, and He shall feed them: He shall feed them and be their shepherd. And I, the LORD, will be their God, and my servant David shall be prince among them. I am the LORD; I have spoken." (Ezek. 34:6-24)

I believe the reference to "David" here is unmistakably Messianic, the prophecy pointing to the time when Jesus would visit His own people. When He did, they were "harassed and helpless, like sheep without a shepherd" (Mt. 9:36). As Jesus said of Himself on one notable occasion,

> "Truly, truly, I say to you, I am the door of the sheep. All who came before me are thieves and robbers, but the sheep did not listen to them. I am the door. If anyone enters by me, he will be saved and will go in and out and find pasture... I am the good shepherd. The good shepherd lays down His life for the sheep. He who is a hired hand and not a shepherd, who does not own the sheep, sees the wolf coming and leaves the sheep and flees, and the wolf snatches them and scatters them... I am the good shepherd. I know my own and my own know me, just as the Father knows me and I know the Father; and I lay down my life for the sheep. And I have other sheep that are not of

this fold. I must bring them also, and they will listen to my voice. So there will be one flock, one shepherd." (Jn. 10:7-16)

Luke records in his Gospel how Jesus came "to seek and to save the lost" (Lk. 19:10). Luke was referring in the first instance to "the lost sheep of the house of Israel" (Mt. 10:6; 15:24; cf. Rom. 1:16). The Greek word for "seek" in Luke 19 is *zēteō*, which is the word used in the Septuagint for *dârash* in Ezekiel 34 verses 6, 8, 10, and 11, as indicated in the aforementioned quote. Ezekiel 34 has special meaning for me personally because it very much epitomized the pastoral and prophetic ministry of my late pastor, Andrew Robinson. The shepherd-sheep metaphor is how Andrew understood the practical, day-to-day outworking of the Lord's loving care for His church, and it defined his own ministry at Hazel Grove Full Gospel Church in Stockport, England.

Jesus the Messiah is revealed in the New Testament as the good, great, and chief Shepherd of God's flock and the Shepherd and Overseer of our souls.[9] He has entrusted the care of His beloved church to His under-shepherds, or "pastor-teachers" as Paul defined them (Eph. 4:11). When the Lord restored and recommissioned Simon Peter by the Sea of Galilee, three times He asked him: "Do you love me?" Simon was given a threefold instruction that was to characterize his future apostolic ministry: "Feed my lambs," "Tend my sheep," "Feed my sheep" (Jn. 21:15-19). It is my personal conviction that the ministry of pastor-teacher is the highest, costliest, most neglected, and most underappreciated calling in the church. I believe it is a ministry that, more than any other, reflects the heart of Jesus for His flock. The gravity of such a call was highlighted by Peter himself in his first letter, when he wrote:

> I exhort the elders among you, as a fellow elder and a witness of the sufferings of Messiah, as well as a partaker in the glory that is going to be revealed: shepherd the flock of God that is among you, exercising oversight, not under compulsion, but willingly, as God would have you; not for shameful gain, but eagerly; not domineering over those in your charge, but being examples to the flock. And when the chief Shepherd appears, you will receive the unfading crown of glory. (1 Pet. 5:1-4)

---

[9] Jn. 10:1-18; Heb. 13:20; 1 Pet. 5:4; 2:25.

Likewise, in his impassioned farewell at Miletus, Paul implored the Ephesian elders to exercise the greatest care by shepherding God's people:

> Pay careful attention to yourselves and to all the flock, in which the Holy Spirit has made you overseers, to care for the church of God, which He obtained with His own blood. I know that after my departure fierce wolves will come in among you, not sparing the flock; and from among your own selves will arise men speaking twisted things, to draw away the disciples after them. Therefore be alert, remembering that for three years I did not cease night or day to admonish every one with tears. (Acts 20:28-31)

Conclusion

When Israel as a remnant nation finally turns to the Messiah Jesus during the tribulation period, the people will realize the extent to which He had sought them out, like a shepherd seeking his lost sheep. We began this chapter by visiting an old, neglected burial plot in a London cemetery. Today, that plot bears witness to William Hechler, who devoted much of his life to serving the Jewish people. It also bears witness to Jerry Klinger, the man who diligently searched out Hechler's grave in order to honor his legacy. But the witness goes far beyond that of a Christian minister or a Jewish historian. It bears the greatest and most enduring testimony to another man: the Son of Man, the Son of God, who came to this earth to seek out and save the lost sheep of the house of Israel and to shine the light of God's redemptive love into the darkened soul of the Gentile world. This man, like Hechler, also died, but unlike Hechler, He has no gravestone for "He has risen, just as He said" (Mt. 28:6, NIV). Even now He is seeking out the lost sheep of Israel, and His arm "is not too short to save" (Isa. 59:1, NIV).

Inscribed at the foot of Hechler's memorial stone are the words of a most solemn and enduring question that I believe the Lord Jesus has been asking His church for the last two thousand years: "Has God Rejected His People?" (Rom. 11:1). Paul's own answer was emphatic: "God forbid!" Sadly, this question has proved a stumbling block to so many professing Christians. Nevertheless, when the glory of the Lord finally rises upon Israel (Isa. 60:1-2), the nation that will have been completely forsaken by all but God Himself will be elevated to a place of highest honor. Furthermore, the city so often conquered, divided, and fought over will be given a new name, as Isaiah prophesied:

> The nations shall see your righteousness, and all the kings your glory, and you shall be called by a new name that the mouth of the LORD will give. You shall be a crown of beauty in the hand of the LORD, and a royal diadem in the hand of your God. You shall no more be termed Forsaken, and your land shall no more be termed Desolate, but you shall be called My Delight Is in Her [*Hephzibah*], and your land Married [*Beulah*]; for the LORD delights in you, and your land shall be married . . . Behold, the LORD has proclaimed to the end of the earth: Say to the daughter of Zion, "Behold, your salvation comes; behold, His reward is with Him, and His recompense before Him." And they shall be called The Holy People, The Redeemed of the LORD; and you shall be called Sought Out [*Dârash*], A City Not Forsaken. (Isa. 62:2-12)

Chapter 8:

Pleading Israel's Cause

And [Moses] said, "If now I have found favor in your sight, O Lord, please let the Lord go in the midst of us, for it is a stiff-necked people, and pardon our iniquity and our sin, and take us for your inheritance [*nâchal*]." (Ex. 34:9)

Remember your congregation, which you have purchased of old, which you have redeemed to be the tribe of your heritage [*nachălâh*]! (Ps. 74:2)

Between the vestibule and the altar let the priests, the ministers of the LORD, weep and say, "Spare your people, O LORD, and make not your heritage [*nachălâh*] a reproach, a byword among the nations." (Joel 2:17)

Bible translators may not always do justice to the original Hebrew text. However, God has ensured that there is sufficient scope within the world's vocabularies to convey the meaning and significance of *nachălâh*. The temptation whenever we study Bible prophecy is to skip over what I would call the more intimate texts and focus on names, places, dates, events, and timelines. Study of the latter may be more tangible and concrete, and with so many resources at our disposal today, it is not too difficult a task. But surely the ultimate goal of Bible prophecy, including the study of Israel, is a closer walk with God. If our minds are engaged but our hearts left untouched, then something is wrong.

Furthermore, with all that the Jewish people have endured throughout the ages, I am convinced that believers cannot *fully* engage with Israel unless they have experienced some degree of suffering in their own lives. How can I, as a believer, really comprehend what it means to be a despised, persecuted, forsaken, afflicted, and chastened people if I have never been through trials that caused me to cry out to God for mercy, forgiveness, healing, protection, deliverance, vindication, or restoration? As a believer, I could readily immerse myself in blogs, websites, newsletters, magazines, documentaries, sermons, and books—and even study tours to Israel—and yet be left unmoved in my heart toward the Jewish people and brought no closer to Jesus.

The Heart of the Matter

In His extraordinary humility, the Lord employed metaphor, simile, idiom, and anthropomorphisms[1] to express the depth of His love for Israel, "stooping down to the level of our comprehension in His endeavor to communicate to us His infinite thoughts, and the feelings of His heart."[2] The scriptures below are just a representative sample to illustrate what covenant relationship looks like from God's heavenly perspective:

> "Because you are precious in my eyes, and honored, and I love you, I give men in return for you, peoples in exchange for your life." (Isa. 43:4)

> "Can a woman forget her nursing child, that she should have no compassion on the son of her womb? Even these may forget, yet I will not forget you. Behold, I have engraved you on the palms of my hands; your walls are continually before me." (Isa. 49:15-16)

> "For your Maker is your husband, the LORD of hosts is His name . . . For the Lord has called you like a wife deserted and grieved in spirit, like a wife of youth when she is cast off, says your God. For a brief moment I deserted you, but with great compassion I will gather you. In overflowing anger for a moment I hid my face from you, but with everlasting love I will have compassion on you," says the LORD, your Redeemer. (Isa. 54:5-8)

> "Is Ephraim my dear son? Is he my darling child? For as often as I speak against him, I do remember him still. Therefore my heart yearns for him; I will surely have mercy on him, declares the LORD." (Jer. 31:20)

> "Therefore, behold, I will allure her, and bring her into the wilderness, and speak tenderly to her . . . And in that day, declares the LORD, you will call me 'My Husband,' and no longer will you call me 'My Baal' . . . And I will betroth you to me forever. I will betroth you to me in righteousness and in justice, in

---

[1] A literary device used to attribute human traits and emotions to non-humans to aid understanding.

[2] David Baron, *Israel in the Plan of God* (Grand Rapids, MI: Kregel Publications, 1983), p. 93.

steadfast love and in mercy. I will betroth you to me in faithfulness. And you shall know the LORD." (Hos. 2:14-20)

"When Israel was a child, I loved him, and out of Egypt I called my son. The more they were called, the more they went away . . . Yet it was I who taught Ephraim to walk; I took them up by their arms, but they did not know that I healed them. I led them with cords of kindness, with the bands of love, and I became to them as one who eases the yoke on their jaws, and I bent down to them and fed them." (Hos. 11:1-4)

These precious scriptures are some of the more intimate texts I was alluding to that are full of paternal and marital imagery. What a privilege God has given us that we should have a window like this into His heart! In many ways, these verses bypass the intellect because they appeal, first and foremost, to the heart. We will be paying closer attention to some of these verses in the proceeding chapters.

Over the years, I have had the privilege of researching a number of men in church history whose hearts were moved by God's love for Israel. In turn, they were used by the Lord to stir the hearts of others, including my own. I have included below a few quotations that have blessed me personally. None of these men lived to witness momentous events like the issuing of the Balfour Declaration in November 1917, the conferment of the Palestine Mandate in April 1920, the passing of UN 'Partition' Resolution 181 in November 1947, the establishment of the modern State of Israel in May 1948, the Six-Day War in June 1967, and the Yom Kippur War in October 1973. These men saw Israel's restoration from afar, through the lens of God's Word and the inspiration of God's Spirit. They also yearned for the salvation of the Jews. May you be blessed and inspired as you read these extracts:

> And have you none of the bowels of Christ in you, that you will not run first to them that are in so sad a case? . . . It is like God to care first for the Jews. It is the chief glory and joy of a soul to be like God . . . [T]he whole Bible shows that God has a peculiar affection for Israel . . . Strange, sovereign, most peculiar love! He loved them because He loved them . . . Now the simple question for each of you is, and for our beloved Church, Should we not share with God in His peculiar affection for Israel? If we are filled with the Spirit of God, should we not love as He loves? Should we not grave Israel upon the palms

of our hands, and resolve that through our mercy they also may obtain mercy?[3] — Robert Murray M'Cheyne (1813-1843)

✡ ✡ ✡

O contrast, for a moment, the mind of Christians in past ages, and the mind of Christ. In our mind, what indifference, what neglect, what scorn, what contempt, what insults, what injury! In the mind of Jesus, what patient, self-sacrificing, unwearied, persevering love! The mind of Christ must mark, does mark, his most devoted followers . . . O the emptiness of this world's wisdom, that affects to despise the Jews as of no importance![4] — Edward Bickersteth (1786-1850)

✡ ✡ ✡

Israel is always the people of God . . . Israel cannot cease to be the people of God. "The gifts and calling of God are without repentance," and it is of Israel that this is said. God never ceases to consider Israel as His people . . . Paul insists in Romans 11 upon this point after their rejection of Christ — "I say, then, Hath God cast away his people? God forbid!" . . . And as to the sovereign love and the counsels of God, Israel as a whole are always His people . . . In all times, Israel is His people, according to His counsels, and the thoughts of His love.[5] — John Nelson Darby (1800-1882)

✡ ✡ ✡

Ought we, or ought we not, to resemble Almighty God in the things most near and dear to God himself? . . . Now, I ask, what is at this very moment, God's view of his ancient people, and his feelings toward them? . . . Have we no cause for shame, and sorrow, and contrition, that we have resembled him so little in past times? . . . Surely, if we felt as we ought, the glory of God, as

---

[3] Quoted in Andrew A. Bonar, *Memoir and Remains of Robert Murray M'Cheyne* (Edinburgh: Banner of Truth Trust, 1978), pp. 490-93.

[4] Edward Bickersteth, "The Mind of Christ Respecting the Jews," in *The Restoration of the Jews to their own Land, in Connection with their Future Conversion and the Final Blessedness of our Earth*, 2nd ed. (London: R. B. Seeley and W. Burnside, 1841), p. 42.

[5] John Nelson Darby, "Examination of a few Passages of Scripture, the Force of which has been Questioned in the Discussion on the New Churches; with Remarks on Certain Principles alleged in Support of their Establishment (1850)," in *The Collected Writings of J. N. Darby*, Vol. 4, pp. 254-55.

connected with this subject, should be dear to us, dearer than life itself . . . Can we hope for God's blessing on our own souls, when we have so little regard for the souls of his most dear people, and so little resemblance in ourselves to him respecting them? I say no more. May God speak to all of you with thunder and with love.[6] — Charles Simeon (1759-1836)

✡ ✡ ✡

Now I ask such a man to consider gravely this day, whether he is not under special obligations to the Jews. I ask him to remember that there are peculiar reasons why we should care with more than ordinary care for Israel. 1. To whom do we owe our Bible? . . . The pens which the Holy Ghost guided to put down the word which He inspired, were held by Jewish fingers . . . 2. To whom do we owe the first preaching of the gospel? . . . The men who first turned the world upside down and deprived heathen temples of their worshippers, and put to silence the philosophers of Greece and Rome, and made kings and rulers tremble on their judgment seats, and made the name of the crucified Jesus of Nazareth more influential than the name of Caesar, they were all children of Israel . . . 3. Above all, what shall we say to the great fact that the woman of whom the Saviour was born, when He condescended to come into the world, was a Jewish woman? . . . I am bold to say that Christians owe a peculiar debt to Israel. If there is such a thing as gratitude in the world, every Gentile church on earth is under heavy obligation to the Jews.[7] — J. C. Ryle (1816-1900)

Ministers of the Altar

This chapter opened with a quotation from the book of Joel. The context was Israel's infidelity and God's instruction to the priests to consecrate a fast and call a solemn assembly. The people had strayed so far in their devotion to God that they needed to repent and "lament like a virgin wearing

---

[6] "Rev. C. Simeon's Address to the Undergraduates of Cambridge, at their Meeting, October 31, 1836," in Bickersteth, *The Restoration of the Jews*, pp. 292-93.

[7] "And So All Israel Shall Be Saved," in J.C. Ryle, *Are You Ready for the End of Time? Understanding Future Events from Prophetic Passages of the Bible* (Fearn, Scotland: Christian Focus Publications, 2001), pp. 155-56.

sackcloth for the bridegroom of her youth" (Joel 1:8). The priests themselves were to "pass the night in sackcloth" in the Temple and wail as "ministers of the altar" (Joel 1:13). At a time when the land lay desolate, the harvest had perished, and an invasion was imminent, the Prophet Joel pleaded with his people to cry out to God for mercy. The day of the Lord was at hand and everything looked hopeless, but still God's heart yearned for His people:

> "Yet even now," declares the LORD, "return to me with all your heart, with fasting, with weeping, and with mourning; and rend your hearts and not your garments." Return to the LORD, your God, for He is gracious and merciful, slow to anger, and abounding in steadfast love [*chesed*]; and He relents over disaster . . . Between the vestibule and the altar let the priests, the ministers of the LORD, weep and say, "Spare your people, O LORD, and make not your heritage [*nachălâh*] a reproach, a byword among the nations. Why should they say among the peoples, 'Where is their God?'" (Joel 2:12-17)

What followed was a glorious promise from the Lord that He would spare His people and restore to them "the years that the swarming locust has eaten" (Joel 2:25). God's tender mercy would remedy Israel's calloused infidelity:

> Then the LORD became jealous for His land and had pity on His people. The LORD answered and said to His people, "Behold, I am sending to you grain, wine, and oil, and you will be satisfied; and I will no more make you a reproach among the nations . . . You shall eat in plenty and be satisfied, and praise the name of the LORD your God, who has dealt wondrously with you. And my people shall never again be put to shame. You shall know that I am in the midst of Israel, and that I am the LORD your God and there is none else. And my people shall never again be put to shame." (Joel 2:18-27)

The Lord wanted His people to rend their hearts and not just their garments, to weep in repentance and not just cry with remorse. That way He would know that they had truly appreciated the gravity of the situation.

In the book of Psalms, we are reminded that God hears and answers the cry of His people whenever they plead with Him for mercy:

> The LORD has heard my plea; the LORD accepts my prayer. (Ps. 6:9)

> Hear the voice of my pleas for mercy, when I cry to you for help, when I lift up my hands toward your most holy sanctuary . . . Blessed be the LORD! For He has heard the voice of my pleas for mercy. (Ps. 28:2-6)

I love the LORD, because He has heard my voice and my pleas for mercy. (Ps. 116:1)

With my voice I cry out to the LORD; with my voice I plead for mercy to the LORD. (Ps. 142:1)

Those who were faithful among God's people always pleaded with the Lord for mercy at perilous moments in Israel's history. For example, when the Babylonian exiles returned following the decree of the Persian king Cyrus, many of them intermarried with those who had settled in the land during their absence. Ezra, a descendant of Aaron and "a scribe skilled in the Law of Moses" (Ezra 7:6), was cut to the heart when he heard what his people had done:

> As soon as I heard this, I tore my garment and my cloak and pulled hair from my head and beard and sat appalled . . . and fell upon my knees and spread out my hands to the LORD my God, saying: "O my God, I am ashamed and blush to lift my face to you, my God, for our iniquities have risen higher than our heads, and our guilt has mounted up to the heavens. From the days of our fathers to this day we have been in great guilt . . . O LORD, the God of Israel, you are just, for we are left a remnant that has escaped, as it is today. Behold, we are before you in our guilt, for none can stand before you because of this." (Ezra 9:3-15)

Upon hearing that the wall of Jerusalem was broken down and its gates destroyed by fire, Nehemiah, the cupbearer to the Persian king Artaxerxes, was overcome with grief:

> As soon as I heard these words I sat down and wept and mourned for days, and I continued fasting and praying before the God of heaven. And I said, "O LORD God of heaven, the great and awesome God who keeps covenant and steadfast love [*chesed*] with those who love Him and keep His commandments, let your ear be attentive and your eyes open, to hear the prayer of your servant that I now pray before you day and night for the people of Israel your servants, confessing the sins of the people of Israel, which we have sinned against you. Even I and my father's house have sinned . . . O Lord, let your ear be attentive to the prayer of your servant . . . and give success to your servant today, and grant him mercy in the sight of this man [Artaxerxes]." (Neh. 1:4-11)

After learning of Haman's edict "to destroy, to kill, and to annihilate all Jews . . . in one day" (Est. 3:13), the Jewish exile Mordecai was overcome with grief:

> When Mordecai learned all that had been done, Mordecai tore his clothes and put on sackcloth and ashes, and went out into the midst of the city, and he cried out with a loud and bitter cry. He went up to the entrance of the king's gate, for no one was allowed to enter the king's gate clothed in sackcloth. And in every province, wherever the king's command and his decree reached, there was great mourning among the Jews, with fasting and weeping and lamenting, and many of them lay in sackcloth and ashes. (Est. 4:1-3)

Perceiving that the seventy-year Babylonian judgment was about to end, Daniel turned his face toward Jerusalem and to the Lord, pleading with "fasting and sackcloth and ashes":

> O Lord, the great and awesome God, who keeps covenant and steadfast love [*chesed*] with those who love Him and keep His commandments, we have sinned and done wrong and acted wickedly and rebelled, turning aside from your commandments and rules . . . To you, O Lord, belongs righteousness, but to us open shame . . . Now therefore, O our God, listen to the prayer of your servant and to his pleas for mercy, and for your own sake, O Lord, make your face to shine upon your sanctuary, which is desolate. O my God, incline your ear and hear. Open your eyes and see our desolations, and the city that is called by your name. For we do not present our pleas before you because of our righteousness, but because of your great mercy. O Lord, hear; O Lord, forgive. O Lord, pay attention and act. Delay not, for your own sake, O my God, because your city and your people are called by your name. (Dan. 9:3-19; cf. 6:10)

What was it that drove these righteous men to their knees and prompted such agonizing pleas for mercy? I believe the answer was given in a previous chapter and lies at the heart of Daniel's prayer: "Delay not, for your own sake, O my God, because your city and your people are called by your name" (Dan. 9:19). Daniel clearly understood that his people had been set apart by God to bear His holy name before the nations but that they had profaned God's name through their rebellion. While the prophet was confessing his sin and the sin of his people Israel and was presenting his plea before the Lord his God for the holy hill of his God (Dan. 9:20), the angel Gabriel appeared and gave him insight and understanding about Israel's future. He also told Daniel that it was at the beginning of his pleas for mercy (Dan. 9:23) that God had sent forth His prophetic word concerning the seventy weeks of years ordained for Jerusalem and the Jewish people (Dan. 9:24-27). In Daniel's pleas for mercy, the Lord heard something that clearly resonated with His own heart. His response was to privilege Daniel with a most remarkable and enduring word of prophecy that continues to occupy (and divide) students of Bible prophecy.

These momentous episodes in biblical history show us what can happen when God's people *really* pray with *His* heart and according to *His* Word. It is important to note that in Daniel's case, the prophet did not offer pleas for mercy on behalf of the nation until the seventy-year Babylonian exile was about to conclude. He understood that God's judgment was just and had to run its course, so it would have been futile, even foolish, for him to have prayed for restoration beforehand. I believe this is why Daniel provided the context to his prayer, which is crucial to understanding what, when, and why he prayed the way he did:

> In the first year of Darius the son of Ahasuerus . . . I, Daniel, perceived in the books the number of years that, according to the word of the LORD to Jeremiah the prophet, must pass before the end of the desolations of Jerusalem, namely, seventy years. *Then* I turned my face to the Lord God. (Dan. 9:1-3)

Is there not a lesson here for believers who are earnestly praying for Israel that our prayers must be tempered and tutored by God's Word? So much prayer today is for the blessing of God to be poured out upon the nation as if Israel were standing in right relationship with Him. But Israel is estranged from God, whose judgment has yet to run its course. As unpalatable as it may be to our natural minds, Scripture instructs us in the most solemn and graphic way that the darkest of days still awaits God's chosen nation—the day of the Lord, the day of tribulation, the day of Antichrist. But Israel will be saved out of that day, as Jeremiah prophesied (Jer. 30:7). I believe the urgent need of the hour is for believers to pray that the eyes, ears, and hearts of as many Jewish people as possible will be opened to their Messiah and Savior, the Lord Jesus. Then, and only then, will they escape the wrath to come and be caught up to meet the Lord in the air when He appears for His bride.

The Advocate of Advocates

The Prophet Micah of Moresheth, a contemporary of Isaiah and the man chosen by God to announce the place of Messiah's birth (Mic. 5:2), prophesied during the years preceding the Assyrian exile in 722 B.C. He had many things to say about "the sins of the house of Israel" (Mic. 1:5) and the false prophets who proclaimed peace when judgment was at hand (Mic. 3:5). But Micah also spoke about a glorious future awaiting his chastened people. In the final chapter, we have what appears to be a dialogue between the Lord and His prophet, with Micah prophetically representing penitent Israel submitting to God's judgment. Israel is promised a new season of blessing when she will once again see "marvelous things" (Mic. 7:15). But I wish to highlight three verses in particular that relate to Israel's acknowledgment of both her guilt *and* the justness of God's sentence. Listen to the way in which Micah expressed complete confidence in God's mercy:

> But as for me, I will look to the LORD; I will wait for the God of my salvation; my God will hear me. Rejoice not over me, O my enemy; when I fall, I shall rise; when I sit in darkness, the LORD will be a light to me. I will bear the indignation of the LORD because I have sinned against Him, *until He pleads my cause* and executes judgment for me. He will bring me out to the light; I shall look upon His vindication. (Mic. 7:7-9; cf. Hos. 5:15)

Micah had previously delivered a resounding rebuke to the people, yet he was convinced that Israel would rise again. This is because he understood the character as well as the covenants of God. He knew that as the Divine Judge, God would rightly administer justice against Israel, but as the Divine Advocate, He would plead Israel's cause and turn the tables on her enemies. Many years earlier, when David was on the run from Saul, he had opportunity to take justice into his own hands and kill the king who had wrongly accused and afflicted him. Instead, he entrusted his life and the injustice he was suffering to God. After sparing Saul's life in the cave, David called out to the king:

> After whom has the king of Israel come out? After whom do you pursue? After a dead dog! After a flea! May the LORD therefore be judge and give sentence between me and you, and see to it and *plead my cause* and deliver me from your hand. (1 Sam. 24:14-15)

This emphasis is also found in the book of Isaiah:

> Thus says your Lord, the LORD, *your God who pleads the cause* of His people: "Behold, I have taken from your hand the cup of staggering; the bowl of my wrath you shall drink no more; and I will put it into the hand of your tormentors." (Isa. 51:22-23)

The advocacy of the Lord also features in the book of Jeremiah, in the great prophecy of Babylon's destruction:

> Thus says the LORD of hosts: "The people of Israel are oppressed, and the people of Judah with them. All who took them captive have held them fast; they refuse to let them go. Their Redeemer is strong; the LORD of hosts is His name. *He will surely plead their cause*" ... Therefore thus says the LORD: "Behold, *I will plead your cause* and take vengeance for you ... Babylon must fall for the slain of Israel." (Jer. 50:33-34; 51:36)

What a solemn warning there is here to the nations of the world and to that part of the church that has mercilessly prosecuted Israel in the name of Jesus: God is going to plead Israel's cause!

What the prophets said about the Lord's advocacy of Israel was a glorious foreshadowing of that which was to come, for all true believers know that "we have an advocate with the Father, Messiah Jesus the righteous" (1 Jn. 2:1). During His life on earth, Jesus "offered up prayers and supplications, with loud cries and tears, to Him who was able to save Him from death, and He was heard because of His reverence" (Heb. 5:7). The Lord now "lives to make intercession" for us (Heb. 7:25), defending His followers whenever "the accuser of the brethren" rises against them (Rev. 12:10, RSV). In the words of Paul, "Who shall bring any charge against God's elect? It is God who justifies. Who is to condemn? Messiah Jesus is the one who died — more than that, who was raised — who is at the right hand of God, who indeed is interceding for us" (Rom. 8:33-34).

There will come a day when Israel's accusers will be silenced once and for all. It will happen when a remnant of Israel finally turns to their long-rejected Messiah and Advocate, who will plead their cause before the Father. Micah foretold that day, jubilantly declaring at the end of his prophecy,

> Who is a God like you, pardoning iniquity and passing over transgression for the remnant of His inheritance [*nachălâh*]? He does not retain His anger

forever, because He delights in steadfast love [*chesed*]. He will again have compassion on us; He will tread our iniquities underfoot. You will cast all our sins into the depths of the sea. You will show faithfulness to Jacob and steadfast love [*chesed*] to Abraham, as you have sworn to our fathers from the days of old. (Mic. 7:18-20)

A Remnant Will Be Saved

In his letter to the Romans, Paul emphatically declared, "all Israel will be saved" (Rom. 11:26). But what did he mean? Clearly, he was not referring to every Jew who has ever lived, having previously stated that the gospel is "the power of God for salvation to everyone who believes, to the Jew first and also to the Greek" (Rom. 1:16). As Peter told the Jewish Sanhedrin, salvation is in Yeshua/Jesus alone, "for there is no other name under heaven given among men by which we must be saved" (Acts 4:12; cf. Lk. 24:45-47; Jn. 20:31; 1 Tim. 2:3-6). Hence, Paul could not have been referring to unbelieving Jews who will be left behind at the rapture for they will pass through the tribulation judgments together with all unbelieving Gentiles. Although many Jews and a multitude of Gentiles will turn to Messiah Jesus and be saved during the tribulation (Dan. 12:1-3; Zech. 12:10-13:1; Rev. 7), many more will receive the Antichrist and his mark, forfeiting forever the hope of salvation (Rev. 13:11-18).

Let us keep the spotlight on the tribulation period for a moment. Preparations for a third temple in Jerusalem are well under way, but this is *not* pleasing to God! It is also *not* something any believing friend of Israel should be excited about, except for the fact that it shows that Bible prophecy is being fulfilled and the rapture of the church is imminent. This temple is being prepared by zealous religious Jews who believe they are serving God when in fact they are in rebellion against Him, having rejected the righteousness that comes only through faith in Yeshua/Jesus (Rom. 10:1-4; Phil. 3:2-9; Jn. 16:2-3; Acts 26:9-11). This will be the temple that the Antichrist will enter to proclaim himself as God (Dan. 9:26-27; 11:31-39; Mt. 24:15; 2 Thess. 2:3-8). However, a remnant of Israel will reject this man of lawlessness and flee to the wilderness, where God will protect them (Rev. 12:1-6; Mt. 24:15-22). Quoting the Prophet Isaiah, Paul stated that only a remnant of Israel would be saved in the end times: "Though the number of the sons of Israel be as the sand of the sea, only a remnant of them will be saved, for the Lord will carry out His sentence upon the earth fully and without delay" (Rom. 10:27-29; Isa. 10:20-23).

Zechariah made it even clearer, declaring that the Lord will sift and purge His people until a remnant remains in the land:

> "In the whole land, declares the LORD, two thirds shall be cut off and perish, and one third shall be left alive. And I will put this third into the fire, and refine them as one refines silver, and test them as gold is tested. They will call upon my name, and I will answer them. I will say, 'They are my people'; and they will say, 'The LORD is my God.'" (Zech. 13:8-9; cf. Ezek. 20:33-38; Mal. 3:1-5)

These verses have been foolishly exploited by enemies of Israel within the church. They have also been neglected or misinterpreted by friends of Israel who refuse to conceive of such an end for God's elect nation. Nevertheless, the message delivered by both prophet and apostle alike is clear: Following the rapture of all Jewish and Gentile believers in Jesus,[8] unbelieving Israel will be judged by God in preparation for the nation's final redemption.

Foreknown, but not Predestined

There is one final point to be made that is crucial to understanding *how* this remnant of Israel will be saved. Through Moses, God solemnly warned His people what would happen if they acted corruptly and broke covenant with Him:

> And the LORD will scatter you among the peoples, and you will be left few in number among the nations where the LORD will drive you. And there you will serve gods of wood and stone . . . But from there you will seek the LORD your God and you will find Him, if you search after Him with all your heart and with all your soul. When you are in tribulation, and all these things come upon you in the latter days, you will return to the LORD your God and obey

---

[8] 1 Thess. 4:13-18; Jn. 12:1-4; 1 Cor. 15:50-57; Rev. 3:10. See also: Rom. 13:12; 1 Cor. 1:7; 3:13; 2 Cor. 1:14; Phil. 1:6; 3:20; Col. 3:4; 1 Thess. 1:10; 2:19; 3:13; 5:9, 23; 2 Tim. 1:12; 4:8; Tit. 2:13; Heb. 10:25; 2 Pet. 1:19; 1 Jn. 2:28; 3:2.

His voice. For the LORD your God is a merciful God. He will not leave you or destroy you or forget the covenant with your fathers that He swore to them. (Deut. 4:27-31)

Scriptures like these clearly indicate that Israel's story is unfolding according to the foreknowledge of God. In other words, when God set Israel apart to be His earthly inheritance and chosen people, He *foreknew* all that was going to happen. But what He did not do, contrary to certain defective theologies within the church, is *predetermine* how and when everything would happen. Israel's story is not unfolding like some great cosmic computer program that the Lord impassively set running in ages past. It is happening in real time according to the dynamic nature of covenant relationship—real choices, daily responses, and genuine consequences, both good and bad. That said, certain things *have* been predetermined by God in relation to Israel, which He has framed within their appointed times and seasons.[9] This is in keeping with the testimony of Scripture throughout. Consider the following:

1. God reassured the Babylonian exiles: "For I know the plans I have for you . . . plans for wholeness and not for evil, to give you a future and a hope" (Jer. 29:11).

2. The psalmist petitioned the Lord, "You will arise and have pity on Zion; it is the time to favor her; the appointed time has come" (Ps. 102:13).

3. The angel Gabriel appeared to Daniel to make known "what shall be at the latter end of the indignation, for it refers to the appointed time of the end" (Dan. 8:19).

4. Gabriel later brought Daniel the tribulation prophecy: "Seventy weeks are decreed about your people and your holy city, to finish the transgression, to put an end to sin, and to atone for iniquity, to bring in everlasting righteousness, to seal both vision and prophet, and to anoint a most holy place" (Dan. 9:24).

---

[9] See, for example: Ps. 102:13; Dan. 8:19; 11:35; Hab. 2:3; Gal. 4:4; Eph. 1:10.

5. Jesus told His disciples that the kingdom would be restored to Israel according to "times or seasons that the Father has fixed by His own authority" (Acts 1:7).
6. Jesus Himself was "foreknown before the foundation of the world" and "delivered up according to the definite plan and foreknowledge of God" (1 Pet. 1:20; Acts 2:23).
7. Paul declared that God has "fixed a day on which He will judge the world in righteousness by a man whom He has appointed; and of this He has given assurance to all by raising Him from the dead" (Acts 17:31; cf. 10:42).

God has made many unilateral and unconditional promises to Israel, even swearing an oath in His own name to guarantee their fulfillment (Gen. 22:15-18; Heb. 6:13-18). He also made many conditional promises as well, which were tied to Israel's obedience. The latter were concerned with the nation's *occupation* of Canaan but crucially not with their *ownership* of that land. Many believers have been confused by all of this, usually because their own churches and denominations have lumped all the promises and covenants of God together without making the vital distinction. Scripture, however, makes it very clear that the covenants God made with Abraham and David were unilateral, unconditional, and everlasting. Supremely, the New Covenant, which was promised to "the house of Israel and the house of Judah" (Jer. 31:31) and through which the Gentiles have been ingrafted (Rom. 11:17-24), was also unilateral, unconditional, and everlasting. By contrast, the covenant that God made with Moses and the Israelites at Mount Sinai was bilateral, conditional, and temporary. It is this latter covenant, referred to in Hebrews as the "first covenant," that God has made obsolete—"first" not by chronological time but in contrast with the second or New Covenant (see 2 Cor. 3:7-16; Gal. 3:22-29; Heb. 8:6-13).

At many times, in various ways, and through different prophets, God declared that Israel would be restored, reconciled, and redeemed. This was gloriously confirmed and guaranteed through the life, death, resurrection, and ascension of Jesus the Messiah. It was later preached by Peter in Solomon's Colonnade (Acts 3:12-26) and expounded upon by Paul in his letter to the Romans (Rom. 9-11, 15:8-12). In His foreknowledge, then, God *knows* how and when the day of Israel's salvation will come to pass. However, He has not *predetermined* everything that is going to unfold as if it should happen irrespective of what is going on in the hearts and minds of His people or of the nations. If that were the case, then cries of "Favoritism!" or "Injustice!" might ring out from those whom God will destroy or judge at the end of the tribulation period (see Zech. 12:9; 14:3; Mt. 25:31-46). Scripture is clear: "There is no injustice with the LORD our God, or partiality or taking bribes" (2 Chron. 19:7).[10]

It is my understanding that when Israel passes through the tribulation period, which will succeed the rapture of the church and precede the second coming of Jesus, God will respond to what He finds in the hearts of His people *at that time*. A desperate cry for mercy will ascend to heaven from a remnant of Israel as they suddenly become aware of their guilt and shame for having rejected the Messiah. This cry will coincide with a sense of utter helplessness as the enemies of Israel assemble at Armageddon to launch a devastating assault against Jerusalem.[11] At that point, God will enable His people to cry out to Him with heart-rending supplications, and the mourning in Israel will be great. But God will hear the cry of His afflicted people just as He did in ages past (Ex. 2:23-25; 3:7-9; 6:5; 1 Sam. 9:16; Neh. 9:9). As we read in the end-time prophecy of Zechariah,

> And I will pour out on the house of David and the inhabitants of Jerusalem a spirit of grace and pleas for mercy, so that, when they look on me, on Him whom they have pierced, they shall mourn for Him, as one mourns for an only child, and weep bitterly over Him, as one weeps over a firstborn. On that day the mourning in Jerusalem will be as great as the mourning for Hadad-rimmon in the plain of Megiddo. The land shall mourn, each family by itself: the family of the house of David by itself, and their wives by themselves; the family of the house of Nathan by itself, and their wives by themselves; the family of the house of Levi by itself, and their wives by themselves; the family of the Shimeites by itself, and their wives by themselves; and all the

---

[10] See also: Deut. 10:17; Acts 10:34; Rom. 2:11; Gal. 2:6; Eph. 6:9; 1 Pet. 1:17.

[11] There is to be no "battle of Armageddon" as is so frequently taught. The nations merely assemble at Armageddon in the north of Israel before moving south to attack Jerusalem (Rev. 16:16; Zech. 12:2-9; 14:1-5).

families that are left, each by itself, and their wives by themselves. (Zech. 12:10-14)

Conclusion

The plight of Israel today must not be underestimated. The rapture of the true church is at hand, while the Antichrist's subsequent appearing, the time of Jacob's trouble, and the second coming of Jesus to this earth are fast approaching. On the surface of things, we see a modern nation in the Middle East that is flourishing, but Israel's economic prosperity conceals its spiritual bankruptcy. Its land may be blossoming, but its heart remains desolate. In 2019, Israel was ranked eighth on a list of most powerful nations compiled by the *US News and World Report Spectator Index*. Only the United States, Russia, China, Germany, the UK, France, and Japan placed higher. This ranking was "based on five key elements—military strength, economic impact, political impact, a nation's leader, and worldwide alliances."[12] This is nothing short of remarkable, miraculous even, for a nation that only recently celebrated its seventieth birthday as a modern state and that lives in the most violent region on planet Earth, outnumbered greatly, threatened daily, and attacked relentlessly by its Islamic neighbors. Yet, Israel continues to spurn her Messiah and is therefore destined to pass under the rod of God's judgment (Ezek. 20:37).

When Daniel inquired about the fulfillment of what God had revealed to him, he was told that it would be "for a time, times, and half a time [3½ years/42 months/1,260 days], and that when the shattering of the power of the holy people comes to an end all these things would be finished" (Dan. 12:7). Israel's strength must be broken and the nation's knees bent in humility and pleading repentance before God brings true and lasting *spiritual* revival and prosperity to His people.

In Jeremiah's prophecy of Babylon's destruction, God accused the Babylonians of being "plunderers of my heritage [*nachălâh*]" (Jer. 50:11). They

---

[12] *Behold Israel*, "Israel Ranked 8th Most Powerful Country in the World Throughout 2019," Dec 2, 2019, https://beholdisrael.org/israel-ranked-8th-most-powerful-country-in-the-world-throughout-2019/.

had "proudly defied the LORD, the Holy One of Israel" (Jer. 50:29). God promised that He would take "vengeance for His temple" (Jer. 50:28; 51:11) and execute judgment "for all the evil that they have done in Zion" (Jer. 51:24). But to His people Israel, the Lord spoke tender words of comfort and hope, promising them restoration and peace. It is with these consoling words that we close this chapter:

> My people have been lost sheep. Their shepherds have led them astray, turning them away on the mountains. From mountain to hill they have gone. They have forgotten their fold . . . I will restore Israel to his pasture, and he shall feed on Carmel and in Bashan, and his desire shall be satisfied on the hills of Ephraim and in Gilead . . . For Israel and Judah have not been forsaken by their God, the LORD of hosts, but the land of the Chaldeans is full of guilt against the Holy One of Israel . . . Not like these [Babylonian idols] is He who is the portion of Jacob, for He is the one who formed all things, and Israel is the tribe of His inheritance [*nachălâh*]; the LORD of hosts is His name. (Jer. 50:6, 19; 51:5, 19)

Chapter 9:

The Golden Gateway of God

> Will the LORD spurn forever, and never again be favorable? . . . Are His promises at an end for all time? Has God forgotten to be gracious? Has He in anger shut up His compassion? (Ps. 77:7-9)
>
> Who is a God like you, pardoning iniquity and passing over transgression for the remnant of His inheritance [nachălâh]? . . . He will again have compassion on us; He will tread our iniquities underfoot. (Mic. 7:18-19)

Despite the hypocrisy for which Jesus roundly denounced the scribes and Pharisees, they still held authority as expositors of God's law; they were men who sat on "Moses' seat" (Mt. 23:2). Provided they faithfully expounded the Scriptures and not their own traditions, their *words* were to be followed but not their deeds. Their authority was thus limited to *the role* that they fulfilled, having failed to represent God faithfully to His people, who had been left shepherdless (Mt. 9:37). Centuries earlier, when God gave His law to Moses at Mount Sinai, He had made a very precise and personal declaration: "I am compassionate" (Ex. 22:27). This divine revelation had been ignominiously veiled by the scribes and Pharisees of Israel, but it was to be gloriously incarnated in the Person of God's beloved Son.

Parables and Prodigals

Time and again in the Gospels, we read how Jesus was "moved with pity" or "had compassion" on those whom the religious leaders had neglected, from the multitudes who followed Him (Mt. 14:14, 15:32; Mk. 6:34) to individuals like the leper (Mk. 1:41) and the widow of Nain (Lk. 7:13). The following verses in Matthew's Gospel serve as important markers in identifying one of the great hallmarks of Messiah's ministry:

> When He saw the crowds, He had compassion for them, because they were harassed and helpless, like sheep without a shepherd. (Mt. 9:36)
>
> These twelve Jesus sent out, instructing them, "Go nowhere among the Gentiles and enter no town of the Samaritans, but go rather to the lost sheep of the house of Israel." (Mt. 10:5-6)
>
> He answered, "I was sent only to the lost sheep of the house of Israel." (Mt. 15:24)

In the first of these verses, we find (in the original Greek text) a rather peculiar-looking and peculiar-sounding word: *splanchnizomai* (pronounced *splank-nee-dzo-my*). This word is commonly translated "compassion" or better still, "moved with compassion," since it conveys the idea of being stirred in one's innermost parts or bowels, where the bowels were seen as the seat of human emotion. Thus, a person could not be considered truly compassionate if there was no movement from them toward helping another in need. When a certain lawyer came to question Jesus about inheriting eternal life, the Lord responded by telling him the parable about a good Samaritan. The lesson was clear: Loving God cannot be detached from loving one's neighbor. The Jewish priest and the Levite demonstrated how empty and cold their religion and their hearts were when they encountered the half-dead man on the Jerusalem-Jericho road and "passed by on the other side" (Lk. 10:31-32). The Samaritan, by contrast, came to where the man lay, "and when he saw him, he had compassion [*splanchnizomai*]" (Lk. 10:33). He then treated the man's wounds before taking him to an inn, where he made sure he would be looked after. Of the three, he alone had been the *true* neighbor.

In the parable of the prodigal son, which Jesus told to the murmuring Pharisees who were indignant at the way He was receiving tax collectors and sinners (Lk. 15:1-2), the Messiah highlighted the contrasting responses of the father and the older brother to the prodigal's return. Whereas the older brother was angry and could not see beyond what his sibling had done and deserved, the father beheld his son "a long way off . . . and felt compassion [*splanchnizomai*] and ran and embraced him and kissed him" (Lk. 15:20). The joyous father then lavishly celebrated his son's return with everyone but the older brother, who remained on the outside of what God was doing within that family.

The Messiah's parables vividly contrasted the compassionate heart of God with the calloused heart of Pharisaical Judaism. I believe an application can also be made to the church. Do we not have in the first parable a striking picture of the amillennial Protestant Reformed Church arrayed in her supersessionist robes, walking proudly on by the despised and afflicted Jews of the pre-1948 Diaspora and then by the State of Israel post-1948? Do we not have in the second parable a striking picture of the same church venting her jealous anger as the Jewish people began to return to their ancient homeland during the nineteenth century? For nearly two millennia, this church had kept so many restoration promises under ecclesiastical lock and key in her own theological vault—promises she had stolen from Israel shortly after the apostles graduated to glory. When Israel was reestablished as a sovereign state in 1948, this church fell into a rage that only intensified when she became aware that many in the wider church were returning these promises to their rightful owners.

No love, no mercy, no understanding of the covenants, promises, and prophecies of God, and no engagement with the compassionate heart of God. That *was* Pharisaical Judaism, that *is* Rabbinic Judaism, and that has been Pharisaical Christianity for centuries, with its cold indifference and crooked theology. Like the angry elder son in the parable, many believers in this part of the church have stubbornly refused to enter into what God is doing within His own earthly family. Israel still has a long way to go and a very difficult and painful road ahead of her. Even so, like the father in the parable, every true follower of Jesus should be acknowledging what God has done with Israel and declaring with one voice: "It was fitting to celebrate and be glad" (Lk. 15:32).

A Word of Consolation

Several Hebrew words are used in Scripture to express compassion, including the verb *râcham*, from which is derived the noun *racham*. The limitations of the English language become evident when we consider the translation of this word in our Bibles. The same versions often vary their translation, using "compassion" in one text, "mercy" in another, "pity" in a handful, and "love" once (Ps. 18:1). The fact that other Hebrew words have been translated using these same English words makes the task of interpreting *râcham/racham* even more difficult.

Occurring forty-seven times, *râcham* appears twice in one of the most beautiful and evocative prophecies of the Bible. Most English translations favor "compassion" in this text, "mercy" (KJV) being a weaker alternative, in my opinion. After pronouncing God's judgment on Israel, Isaiah made this astonishing announcement:

> Sing for joy, O heavens, and exult, O earth; break forth, O mountains, into singing! For the LORD has comforted His people and will have compassion [*râcham*] on His afflicted. But Zion said, "The LORD has forsaken me; my Lord has forgotten me." "Can a woman forget her nursing child, that she should have no compassion [*râcham*] on the son of her womb [*behten*]? Even these may forget, yet I will not forget you. Behold, I have engraved you on the palms of my hands; your walls are continually before me." (Isa. 49:13-16)

If there were no other prophecies to guide us in our understanding of Israel from God's perspective, then surely this one would suffice!

The Movement of God's Heart

From the Hebrew verb *râcham* is derived another noun, *rechem*. Sometimes translated "womb,"[1] the noun is typically used in relation to conception or birth. The more common Hebrew word for womb is *behten*, as highlighted in the text above. Whenever the verb *râcham* appears alongside the noun *behten*—"Can a woman forget her nursing child, that she should have no compassion [*râcham*] on the son of her womb [*behten*]?"—the intention is to express the deepest and most tender kind of human emotion that exists, namely that of a mother toward her newborn child.[2] What, then, was God saying to His people in the Isaiah 49 prophecy? Simply this: His compassion is greater than even that of a

---

[1] For example, when God opens the wombs of Leah and Rachel (Gen. 29:31; 30:22; cf. Ex. 13:2, 12, 15).

[2] *The New International Dictionary of Old Testament Theology and Exegesis*, Vol. 3, p. 1093.

mother. We should note in passing that *râcham* is also used to liken God's compassion for those who fear Him to that of a *father* for his children (Ps. 103:13).

Let us consider for a moment the account in 1 Kings 3 of the remarkable testing of Solomon's wisdom. Two harlots were in dispute over the babies they had borne, one of whom had died in the night. The mother of the dead child had replaced him with the other mother's son. When the king gave his judgment that the living child should be cut in half and divided between the two women, the true mother was in such distress that she asked that her son be given to the other woman, who was more than happy to comply. As we read in the biblical account,

> Then the woman whose son was living spoke to the king, for she yearned with compassion [*racham*] for her son; and she said, "O my lord, give her the living child, and by no means kill him!" But the other said, "Let him be neither mine nor yours, but divide him." So the king answered and said, "Give the first woman the living child, and by no means kill him; she is his mother." (1 Kgs. 3:26-27, NKJV)

The KJV prefers the more literal rendering, "her bowels yearned upon her son." Other translations read, "her heart yearned for her son" (RSV, ESV) or that she "was deeply moved out of love for her son" (NIV). Through this extraordinary episode, Solomon's throne was established and God's glory seen, for when all Israel heard the report, "they stood in awe of the king, because they perceived that the wisdom of God was in him to do justice" (1 Kgs. 3:28). God's wisdom and compassion were working in conjunction with each other.

In the Isaiah 49 prophecy, God used the word *râcham* to reassure His people that He had not forsaken them despite their spiritual harlotry. He did so by painting a scenario in their minds that He knew would provoke an immediate and strong reaction in their hearts. He asked them to consider the prospect of one of their own mothers forgetting her nursing child. Since motherhood was and is so sacred to the Jewish people, that possibility would have been unthinkable, even offensive. Could it be that a mother in Israel might fail to show *racham* to the child of her womb? Yes, it was possible. What was *impossible*, however, was for the One who had metaphorically engraved Israel on the palms of His hands to cast His people aside and forget them.

A few chapters on in the book of Isaiah, we read how God gave the same kind of reassurance to Israel but this time from within a marital rather than maternal context:

> "Fear not, for you will not be ashamed; be not confounded, for you will not be disgraced; for you will forget the shame of your youth, and the reproach of your widowhood you will remember no more. For your Maker is your husband, the LORD of hosts is His name; and the Holy One of Israel is your Redeemer, the God of the whole earth He is called. For the LORD has called you like a wife deserted and grieved in spirit, like a wife of youth when she is cast off, says your God. For a brief moment I deserted you, but with great compassion [*racham*] I will gather you. In overflowing anger for a moment I hid my face from you, but with everlasting love I will have compassion [*râcham*] on you, says the LORD, your Redeemer." (Isa. 54:4-8)

The same emphasis is found in the book of Jeremiah. Despite promising to "double repay their iniquity and their sin" for having filled His "inheritance [*nachălâh*] with their abominations" (Jer. 16:18), God could not restrain the compassion of His heart:

> "Is Ephraim my dear son? Is he my darling child? For as often as I speak against him, I do remember him still. Therefore my heart [literally bowels] yearns for him; I will surely have mercy [*râcham*] on him, declares the LORD" (Jer. 31:20; cf. 33:26).

Shortly after, the Lord announced that He was going to make "a new covenant with the house of Israel and the house of Judah." He would write His law on the hearts of His people, forgive their iniquity, and "remember their sin no more" (Jer. 31:31-34).

Forerunner of the Messiah

Throughout Israel's history, God raised up a number of righteous men to foreshadow the Messiah. One of these prophetic forerunners was Joseph, the great-grandson of Abraham and beloved son of Jacob. In the Genesis account of his life, we have one of the most beautiful illustrations of God's compassion.

Despite being wronged by his brothers, who had sold him into slavery, "the LORD was with Joseph" in Egypt (Gen. 39:2, 21). From prison to premiership, Joseph found favor both with God and man, his future being fashioned on the anvil of painful trial. Upon his release, he was made overseer of the rescue mission and second only to Pharaoh since there was no one "so discerning and wise" (Gen. 41:39). On their second visit to buy grain in Egypt, Joseph's brothers, who had not yet recognized him, brought with them their youngest brother, Benjamin. When Joseph saw his brother, he was overcome with *racham* and took his leave of them. This is how Genesis 43:30 reads in our English Bibles:

> Then Joseph hurried out, for his *compassion [râcham] grew warm* for his brother, and he sought a place to weep. And he entered his chamber and wept there. (ESV)
>
> ... *his bowels did yearn* upon his brother ... (KJV)
>
> ... *his bowels burned* for his brother ... (DBY)
>
> ... *his heart yearned* for/over his brother ... (NKJV, RSV, ASV)
>
> ... *he was deeply stirred* over his brother ... (NASB)
>
> ... *Deeply moved* at the sight of his brother ... (NIV)

When Joseph finally revealed his identity to his brothers, "he wept aloud, so that the Egyptians heard it, and the household of Pharaoh heard it." He then "fell upon his brother Benjamin's neck and wept" and "kissed all his brothers and wept upon them" (Gen. 45:2, 14-15). From the pit to the prison to the palace—through rejection, betrayal, false accusation, wrongful imprisonment, and the unseen hand of his sovereign Lord—the heart of Joseph graduated from the school of suffering. There was to be no bitterness, anger, or thirst for vengeance from God's appointed servant. What issued forth from a heart that had been melted in the crucible of affliction was God's *râcham*. The words of Job come to mind: "When He has tried me, I shall come forth as gold" (Job 23:10, RSV).

The Joseph narrative is a powerfully prophetic picture of what Messiah experienced when He came to His own people and they "received Him not" (Jn. 1:11, KJV; cf. Isa. 53:3). It is also a glorious foreshadowing of the day when Jesus will reveal Himself to the hearts of His beloved Jewish brethren during the tribulation period. Then they will weep and mourn for Him and receive Him as their Lord and Savior (Zech. 12:10) and as their Brother!

The Unchanging God

We will mine again from the rich seam of the Joseph narrative in a later chapter. It is highlighted here to repeat a central premise of this book, namely that Israel's future hinges on God's character. As God declared through Malachi, "I the LORD do not change; therefore you, O children of Jacob, are not consumed" (Mal. 3:6). Two of the things that never change with God are expressed in that much-loved lamentation of Jeremiah: "The steadfast love [*chesed*] of the Lord never ceases; His mercies [*rachamim*] never come to an end; they are new every morning; great is your faithfulness" (Lam. 3:22-23). Keeping in mind that this promise was given to Israel in the first instance, the lamentation continues:

> For the LORD will not cast off forever, but, though He cause grief, He will have compassion [*râcham*] according to the abundance of His steadfast love [*chesed*]; for He does not willingly afflict or grieve the children of men. (Lam. 3:31-33)

It is impossible to rightly divide the prophetic scriptures without properly knowing the Person of prophecy. As previously noted, God's self-revelation to Moses in the cleft of the rock was foundational not only to the nation's worship but also to its very existence and survival. Here is that self-revelation again, this time with *râcham* inserted into the text:

> "I myself will make all my goodness pass before you, and will proclaim the name of the LORD before you; and I will be gracious to whom I will be gracious, and will show compassion [*râcham*] on whom I will show compassion [*râcham*]" ... Then the LORD passed by in front of him and proclaimed, "The LORD, the LORD God, compassionate [*rachûwm*] and gracious, slow to anger, and abounding in lovingkindness [*chesed*] and truth; who keeps lovingkindness [*chesed*] for thousands, who forgives iniquity, transgression and sin; yet He will by no means leave the guilty unpunished, visiting the iniquity

of fathers on the children and on the grandchildren to the third and fourth generations." (Ex. 33:19-34:7, NASB)

Moses later warned the children of Israel that if they acted corruptly and broke the covenant with God, then He would scatter them among the nations. But He would never forget them:

> For the LORD your God is a compassionate [*rachûwm*] God; He will not fail you nor destroy you nor forget the covenant with your fathers which He swore to them. (Deut. 4:31, NASB)

Throughout the time of their residence in the Promised Land, the prayers of God's people and the pronouncements of God's prophets centered around the compassion of God's heart:

> For the LORD your God is gracious and compassionate [*rachûwm*], and will not turn His face away from you if you return to Him. (2 Chron. 30:9, NASB)

> But you, LORD, are a compassionate [*rachûwm*] and gracious God, slow to anger, abounding in love [*chesed*] and faithfulness. (Ps. 86:15, NIV)

> Now return to the LORD your God, for He is gracious and compassionate [*rachûwm*], slow to anger, abounding in lovingkindness [*chesed*] and relenting of evil. (Joel 2:13, NASB)

Time and again the children of Israel tested God's patience, but "He, being compassionate [*rachûwm*], atoned for their iniquity and did not destroy them; He restrained His anger often and did not stir up all His wrath" (Ps. 78:38). So desirous was God for restoration that He sent His prophets to call the people back to Himself, but they refused to listen and return. As we read at the close of 2 Chronicles,

> The LORD, the God of their fathers, sent persistently to them by His messengers, because He had compassion[3] on His people and on His dwelling place. But they kept mocking the messengers of God, despising His words and scoffing at His prophets, until the wrath of the LORD rose against His people, until there was no remedy. (2 Chron. 36:15-16)

These solemn words are among the last recorded in the Hebrew arrangement of the Scriptures known as the *Tanakh*. They are so full of pathos that one can almost feel God's heart breaking over His people. The Chronicles text then continues with a summary of the Babylonian invasion of the

---

[3] A different Hebrew word, *châmal*, is used here to convey God's compassion.

southern kingdom of Judah. Here we find a striking reference to God handing His people over to the king of the Chaldeans, who "had no compassion on young man or virgin, old man or aged" (2 Chron. 36:17). Could there have been a more poignant and devastating indictment against God's people? Paul would later write about how men exchanged the glory of God for images and the truth of God for a lie. Three times the apostle stated in his letter how God "gave them up" to what their hearts truly desired, which was the very opposite of what God intended (Rom. 1:24-28).

There will yet be *the* most chilling realization of this pattern, principle, and precedent when many in Israel and throughout the world will be given up by God to the rule of the Antichrist. Having rejected the Son of Man, they will receive the man of sin. But to God's glory and honor, 2 Chronicles does not end with a remediless Israel and a merciless king, and neither will the story of Israel and the world end with the rule of the Antichrist! In the final two verses of 2 Chronicles, we read how God stirred up the spirit of Cyrus, king of Persia, to issue a decree instructing and enabling the Jewish exiles in Babylon to return and rebuild the Temple in Jerusalem (2 Chron. 36:22-23). There was to be a remedy after all, and that remedy was the compassion [*racham*] of God.

The Golden Gate

Located in the eastern wall of the Old City of Jerusalem is arguably the world's most famous gate. Known as "the Golden Gate," it directly faces the Temple Mount and holds eschatological significance for Jews, Christians, and Muslims alike. The gate was first sealed by the Muslims in 810, reopened by the Catholic Crusaders in 1102, sealed again by the Saracen king Saladin in 1187, and reopened by the Ottoman sultan Suleiman the Magnificent when he began rebuilding the walls of Jerusalem in 1535. In 1541, Suleiman resealed the gate, which has remained closed ever since.[4] Why he did so remains uncertain. So, too, does the precise connection between the Golden Gate today and the *ancient* and *future* gates the Prophet

---

[4] Randall Price, *Rose Guide to the Temple* (Torrance, CA: Rose Publishing, Inc., 2012), p. 135.

Ezekiel saw 2,600 years ago. Whether these gates are synonymous is not, in my opinion, of paramount importance. The one thing I believe *is* important is to understand the connection between the prophecies of Ezekiel 40-48 and Zechariah 12-14 and the account of Jesus' ascension in Acts 1. Together, they tell us that Jesus will one day physically and visibly return to Jerusalem and enter through a gate into what is generally referred to as the Millennial Temple.

While serving the Lord in Babylonian exile, Ezekiel was caught up by the Holy Spirit and brought, in visions from God, to Jerusalem. There he was shown all manner of abominations in the Temple. In these visions, he beheld "the glory of the God of Israel" move from the threshold before standing "at the entrance of the east gate of the house of the LORD" (Ezek. 10:18-19). The Spirit then lifted him up and brought him to that gate, where he prophesied against the princes of Jerusalem. Soon after, he witnessed the glory of God ascend the Mount of Olives (Ezek. 11:23), signifying the departure of God's presence from the Temple, from Jerusalem, and from the land. Nearly twenty years later, Ezekiel was again taken in visions to Jerusalem, this time to receive a guided tour of a magnificent new structure. The prophet received the following command from the Lord:

> "As for you, son of man, describe to the house of Israel the temple, that they may be ashamed of their iniquities; and they shall measure the plan. And if they are ashamed of all that they have done, make known to them the design of the temple, its arrangement, its exits and its entrances, that is, its whole design; and make known to them as well all its statutes and its whole design and all its laws, and write it down in their sight, so that they may observe all its laws and all its statutes and carry them out. This is the law of the temple: the whole territory on the top of the mountain all around shall be most holy. Behold, this is the law of the temple." (Ezek. 43:10-12)

The intricate plans Ezekiel was shown and the clear instruction he was given to make the Temple's design known do not allow for any symbolic or spiritual interpretation, especially since no such interpretation was given by the prophet himself. If this were all merely symbolic, then it could mean anything to anyone; each reader could decide for themselves. What Ezekiel saw was the Temple that Messiah Jesus will enter when He returns in glory to reign in Jerusalem. This Temple should not be confused with the one that unbelieving Jews in Israel are currently preparing to build and that the Antichrist will enter during the tribulation period, proclaiming himself to be God.[5]

Upon completing his extraordinary tour, Ezekiel was again taken to the eastern gate from where he saw "the glory of the God of Israel" returning from the East (Ezek. 43:2). I find it more than interesting that the prophet likened "the sound of his coming" to "the sound of many waters" and fell on his face in reverent fear (Ezek. 43:2-3). Seven hundred years later, when John was caught up in the Spirit on the island of Patmos, he saw Jesus in all His majestic glory and likened His voice to "the roar of many waters." In response, the apostle prostrated himself in fear (Rev. 1:15-17). In Ezekiel's case, the prophet not only saw the glory of God depart but he also saw the glory of God return, no doubt descending the Mount of Olives before entering the Temple "by the gate facing east" (Ezek. 43:4). Six centuries later, and forty days after His resurrection, Jesus ascended the Mount of Olives. From there, He who is the glory of God departed the earth, having been rejected by Israel. As the disciples watched Him ascend, two men in white robes told them that Jesus would return in the same way they had seen Him go (Acts 1:9-11). Messiah's return will thus fulfill both Ezekiel's vision and Zechariah's prophecy of the second coming, when "His feet shall stand on the Mount of Olives that lies before Jerusalem on the east . . . And the LORD will be king over all the earth" (Zech. 14:4-9).

As if to emphasize the physicality of the future Temple *and* the second coming, the glory of the God of Israel spoke to Ezekiel from the sanctuary. What the prophet heard was astounding: "Son of man, this is the place of my throne and *the place of the soles of my feet*, where I will dwell in the midst of the people of Israel forever. And the house of Israel shall no more defile my holy name" (Ezek. 43:7). To this remarkable prophecy, let us add the following: "The glory of Lebanon shall come to you, the cypress, the plane, and the pine, to beautify the place of my sanctuary, and I will make *the place of my feet* glorious" (Isa. 60:13). Now let us recall the promise of God to Solomon after the First Temple was dedicated: "I have consecrated this house that you have built, by putting *my name* there forever. *My eyes and my heart* will be there for all time" (1 Kgs. 9:3).

---

[5] See Dan. 9:27; Mt. 24:15; 2 Thess. 2:4.

In a nutshell, the Temple Mount belongs to the God of Israel. Contrary to the scurrilous claims of replacement theologians, He is far from finished with it! In those three sentences from Isaiah 60 and 1 Kings 9, He who created the universe declared that His feet, His eyes, His heart, His name, His dwelling, His sanctuary, and His throne would be there for all time. As if to underline the literalness of His word and ensure that every succeeding generation got the message loud and clear, the Lord declared through Ezekiel that He would dwell and reign "in the midst of the people of Israel forever." This has yet to happen, but it must and it will, for God is true to His Word.

Is it any wonder, then, that the enemy of God and of Israel has made such a concerted effort through Islam, the Arab world, the Palestinian Authority, and the absurdity that is UNESCO[6] to deny Jewish association with the Temple Mount? Is it any wonder, then, that the enemy of God and of Israel has deceived countless Christians over the centuries into believing that these scriptures are merely symbolic and metaphorical, that Jerusalem and the Temple are theologically redundant, and that all of this somehow applies to the church? What arrogance and unbelief! They would do well to consider carefully the reprimand of the Lord as spoken through Zechariah: "The LORD rebuke you, O Satan! The LORD who has chosen Jerusalem rebuke you!" (Zech. 3:2).

When Ezekiel was brought to the eastern gate for a third time, it was closed. He was told that it would remain so because the glory of God had entered through it, as the prophet had witnessed first-hand. The closure of this gate in Ezekiel's vision cannot be directly linked to the Golden Gate in Jerusalem simply because there was no Temple when Suleiman sealed the gate (as there was in the vision) and because the closing of the Eastern Gate happened *after* God's glory had returned to the Temple. This, I believe, will only be fulfilled when Jesus returns and descends the Mount of Olives before entering the Millennial Temple. However, in 1969, James Fleming, a

---

[6] In October 2016, the United Nations Educational, Scientific, and Cultural Organization (UNESCO) passed a resolution that effectively erased the historic Jewish connection to the Temple Mount by using exclusively Arabic terminology in referring to the site.

young American archaeology student, made a fascinating, albeit accidental, discovery that confirms the significance of the Golden Gate. Fleming was photographing the gate, which overlooks a Muslim cemetery, when the ground beneath him suddenly opened up. Falling eight feet into a large hole, he found himself in a mass burial grave among the bones of many skeletons. More importantly, he saw part of another arch in the back wall of the tomb, situated directly beneath the Golden Gate.[7] Whether or not this quarter-arch belonged to the ancient Eastern Gate, I believe the present Golden Gate holds significance for the following reasons:

1. It is certainly located in the vicinity of the ancient gate.
2. The fact that it is a sealed gate in the wall of Jerusalem leading directly to the Temple Mount prompts us to carefully study the Ezekiel visions and all the biblical prophecies concerning the future Temple.
3. It should inspire us to magnify the greatness of God's mercy. The very fact that Ezekiel was shown this new Temple *while in exile* and told to declare it to his people is further evidence that a new day will dawn for Israel and Jerusalem.
4. The Golden Gate has a very interesting Hebrew name, *Sha'ar Harachamim*, which translates as "Gate of Mercy" or "Gate of Compassion." Notice the plural form of *râcham*, the Hebrew word highlighted earlier. To be precise, the Gate of Mercy is the name given to the left-hand or southern portal as we view the Golden Gate face on; the right-hand or northern portal is known as *Sha'ar Hatshuva* or "Gate of Repentance."

The fact that both portals are closed is, to my mind, full of symbolic meaning. The fullness of God's mercy has yet to be poured out upon Israel because the nation has yet to repent and turn to her Messiah. Without God's mercy, there can be no repentance, and without the people's repentance, there can be no mercy. The two are as inseparable as the portals; either both are closed, or both are open. The sealed gate is also a reminder that there is no Temple in which the Jewish people can make sacrifices today

---

[7] Christ in Prophecy, "The Eastern Gate: Interview with Dr. James Fleming," February 1, 2013, www.youtube.com/watch?v=qc8mlSGyNYg.

because Jesus is the *only* sacrifice acceptable to God (see Eph. 5:2; Heb. 9:26; 10:12). Israel will thus continue to be denied access to God's presence until the nation looks to the One who is the Golden Gateway to God's mercy.

Conclusion

God is merciful and full of compassion and has promised that Israel will be fully restored and reconciled to Him. Consider the following verses from Psalm 102 that are headed in the ESV by "A Prayer of One Afflicted, When He is Faint and Pours out His Complaint Before the Lord." This title depicts the psalmist's personal anguish, but I believe it has prophetic application to Israel in the last days, when God will hear and answer the cry of His people:

> You will arise and have pity [*râcham*] on Zion; it is the time to favor her; the appointed time has come. For your servants hold her stones dear and have pity on her dust. Nations will fear the name of the LORD, and all the kings of the earth will fear your glory. For the LORD builds up Zion; He appears in His glory; He regards the prayer of the destitute and does not despise their prayer. (Ps. 102:13-17)

What can we glean from this prophetic psalm? Here are a few thoughts as we draw this chapter to a close:

1. The psalmist prayed confidently in faith and in accordance with God's Word, knowing that the Lord would show mercy to Zion. This is how believers should approach the Lord when praying for Israel's salvation.

2. A time has been appointed when God will rebuild Zion. Let us recall the final question the disciples asked Jesus prior to His ascension: "Lord, will you *at this time* restore the kingdom to Israel?" Jesus replied, "It is not for you to know *times or seasons* that the Father has *fixed* by His own authority" (Acts 1:6,7). The time of Zion's rebuilding has been set.

3. Those in the church who are truly serving God hold the stones of Jerusalem dear because they know how dear they are to Him. This

emphasis is found in David's psalm when he calls for prayer for "the peace of Jerusalem" before adding, "May they be secure who love you!" (Ps. 122:6) Those who downgrade Jerusalem's importance do not stand secure before God.

4. The nations of the world will one day know for certain *who* it is that will have rebuilt Zion, and they will be in fear.

Immediately before Ezekiel was shown the future Millennial Temple, God made a glorious promise that has yet to be fulfilled:

> "Therefore thus says the Lord GOD: Now I will restore the fortunes of Jacob and have mercy [*râcham*] on the whole house of Israel, and I will be jealous for my holy name. They shall forget their shame and all the treachery they have practiced against me, when they dwell securely in their land with none to make them afraid, when I have brought them back from the peoples and gathered them from their enemies' lands, and through them have vindicated my holiness in the sight of many nations. Then they shall know that I am the Lord their God, because I sent them into exile among the nations and then assembled them into their own land. I will leave none of them remaining among the nations anymore. And I will not hide my face anymore from them, when I pour out my Spirit upon the house of Israel, declares the Lord GOD." (Ezek. 39:25-29)

Considering the extent of Israel's apostasy, and we have much more to say about that in the remaining chapters, God not only promised to bring His people back to their ancient homeland, but He also promised to restore them in such a way that it would seem as if He had never judged them in the first place:

> "I will strengthen the house of Judah, and I will save the house of Joseph. I will bring them back because I have compassion [*râcham*] on them, and they shall be as though I had not rejected them, for I am the LORD their God and I will answer them . . . I will whistle for them and gather them in, for I have redeemed them, and they shall be as many as they were before. Though I scattered them among the nations, yet in far countries they shall remember me, and with their children they shall live and return." (Zech. 10:6-9)

In 1963, Charles Deayton (1887-1967), a member of the Plymouth Brethren, wrote a poem titled "The Comfort of Zion." He based it on Isaiah 51 and 52. With the consoling words of this poem, we close this chapter:

The Comfort of Zion

Awake, Awake, O Zion,
Put on thy strength today –
Jerusalem, thy garments
God's glory to display;
Rise up, thou captive daughter,
Be cleansed and purified,
Put on thy beauteous garments,
And be thou glorified!

Thy God Himself awaketh
To bring thee back again,
In His unfailing mercy –
He does not move in vain!
His glorious arm prevaileth
His promise to fulfill,
And all must yield before Him,
Bow to His sovereign will.

Behold upon the mountains,
How beautiful His feet,
Who bringeth thee glad tidings,
Hark to the message sweet!
Zion, thy God still reigneth,
Waste places, lift your voice,
Break forth and sing together,
And in thy God rejoice.

'Tis thy set time, O Zion,
Thy day, Jerusalem,
Put on thy robes of glory,
And wear thy diadem.
Thy walls shall be salvation,
And all thy gates be praise,
Thy God Himself thy glory
Through everlasting days.[8]

---

[8] Deayton, Charles. "'The Comfort of Zion,' A Door of Hope and Other Poems (1963)." *My Brethren - Poetry - A Door of Hope*, Gordon Rainbow, retrieved from www.mybrethren.org/poetry/framdoor.htm.

Chapter 10:

Comfort God's People!

> She [Jerusalem] weeps bitterly in the night, with tears on her cheeks; among all her lovers she has none to comfort her . . . For these things I weep; my eyes flow with tears; for a comforter is far from me . . . Zion stretches out her hands, but there is none to comfort her. (Lam. 1:2-17)

> There is none to guide her among all the sons she has borne; there is none to take her by the hand among all the sons she has brought up. These two things have happened to you — who will console you? — devastation and destruction, famine and sword; who will comfort you? (Isa. 51:18-19)

> "Comfort, comfort my people, says your God. Speak tenderly to Jerusalem, and cry to her that her warfare is ended, that her iniquity is pardoned, that she has received from the LORD's hand double for all her sins." (Isa. 40:1-2)

The opening verses to Isaiah 40 are remarkable for several reasons. Many readers may know that they begin George Frideric Handel's much-loved and wonderfully uplifting oratorio *Messiah*, a personal favorite of mine. More importantly, they begin a section of the book of Isaiah that contains more Gospel references than any other portion of the Old Testament. In fact, Isaiah has often been referred to as "the fifth Gospel" because the prophecies that follow chapter 40 in particular are full of redemptive language and imagery. For the purposes of this chapter, however, it is the double imperative in verse 1 that warrants our attention.

The command itself is perhaps not one we would have expected if we were reading Isaiah for the first time. In the previous chapter, the Lord informed Hezekiah, king of Judah, that there would come a time when his treasure chambers would be plundered and some of his sons taken captive by the Babylonians. This announcement was in keeping with all that the prophet had spoken previously about the nation's apostasy. That is why God's command to *comfort* His people at the start of the very next chapter is so striking.

A Human Touch from Heaven

The Hebrew text of Isaiah 40:1 reads: *nachămû nachămû 'ammî*. The critical word here is *nâcham*, meaning "to comfort" or "to be comforted," depending on the grammatical tense. From this word, personal names such as Nahum, Nehemiah, and Menahem are derived. Its origin "seems to reflect the idea of 'breathing deeply,'"[1] hence the depth of feeling that is usually involved when comfort is given to someone in their affliction. In Psalm 23, for example, David writes: "Even though I walk through the valley of the shadow of death, I will fear no evil, for you are with me; your rod and your staff, they comfort [*nâcham*] me" (Ps. 23:4). In a later psalm, David cries out: "Show me a sign of your favor, that those who hate me may see and be put to shame because you, LORD, have helped me and comforted [*nâcham*] me" (Ps. 86:17). In Psalm 119, the psalmist called out to God in desperation: "My eyes long for your promise; I ask, 'When will you comfort [*nâcham*] me?'" (Ps. 119:82). One thing is clear: God's people need God's comfort. As we shall see, they need God's comforters too, a human touch from a heavenly God.

We are relational beings who were created to be in fellowship with God and our fellow man, but that fellowship was broken because of sin. Through Jesus, men and women can be reconciled to God and brought into the closest possible relationship this side of heaven. Paul tells us that within the body of Messiah, each member is "joined and held together by every joint with which it is equipped" (Eph. 4:16). One of the functions of the body is to help any member that may be afflicted in some way. If a member of a local church, for example, is denied human consolation during times of suffering, then not only will that church have failed to function as God intended, but it will also incur the displeasure of Jesus Himself, the Head of the body. Long before the church was established, God taught Job's three friends this lesson. It was one they would never forget.

---

[1] *Theological Wordbook of the Old Testament*, p. 570.

Miserable Comforters

Job's friends claimed to know God and His Word. Upon hearing about Job's afflictions, they "made an appointment together to come to show him sympathy and comfort [*nâcham*] him" (Job 2:11). It appears that they started out with the best of intentions. When they saw Job in his afflicted state, they wept, tore their robes, sprinkled dust on their heads, and sat with him on the ground in silence for seven days and nights "for they saw that his suffering was very great" (Job 2:13). However, their thoughts soon began to run loose in their minds, and their comfort quickly turned to condemnation. After enduring nothing but accusation and reproof from them, a deeply wounded Job had this to say to his so-called friends:

> I have heard many such things; miserable comforters [*nâcham*] are you all. Shall windy words have an end? Or what provokes you that you answer? I also could speak as you do, if you were in my place; I could join words together against you and shake my head at you . . . I have sewed sackcloth upon my skin and have laid my strength in the dust. My face is red with weeping, and on my eyelids is deep darkness, although there is no violence in my hands, and my prayer is pure . . . My friends scorn me; my eye pours out tears to God. (Job 16:1-4, 15-20)

Job's personal complaint against his "comforters" was nothing compared to the indictment that God, in the end, brought against them. The Silent Listener to every conversation had heard all their injurious denunciations and decided enough was enough. He addressed Eliphaz the Temanite in no uncertain terms:

> "My anger burns against you and against your two friends, for you have not spoken of me what is right, as my servant Job has. Now therefore take seven bulls and seven rams and go to my servant Job and offer up a burnt offering for yourselves. And my servant Job shall pray for you, for I will accept his prayer not to deal with you according to your folly. For you have not spoken of me what is right, as my servant Job has." (Job 42:7-8)

In his New Testament letter, James spotlighted Job's perseverance to encourage believers to patiently endure until the coming of the Lord. He also highlighted the fact that one of the great truths God had revealed through Job's ordeal was that He is "full of compassion and merciful" (James 5:11, NASB). The Greek word translated "full of compassion" is *polusplanchnos* and is unique to this verse. It is directly related to *splanchnizomai*, the peculiar word we looked at in the previous chapter that was used exclusively by Matthew, Mark, and Luke when referring to the compassion of Jesus.

King David, like Job, experienced his fair share of affliction, suffering, and reproach, receiving little comfort at times from his own friends and family (Ps. 27:10). In Psalm 69, he spoke as a man sinking in the mire or drowning in deep waters. In David's anguished cry to God, we hear a piercing echo from the future, his words prophetically anticipating the Son of David's agony on the cross: "Reproaches have broken my heart, so that I am in despair. I looked for pity, but there was none, and for comforters, but I found none. They gave me poison for food, and for my thirst they gave me sour wine to drink" (Ps. 69:20-21).

The examples of Job and David illustrate an important truth: Administering God's comfort and understanding God's character are intertwined. Simply quoting Bible verses or pursuing a qualification in counseling will never be sufficient if a believer is to administer God's comfort to another. The counsel of the Counselor and the comfort of the Comforter are essential. In my opinion, only those who have endured personal suffering themselves and have walked with God through their affliction are qualified to comfort others. In the words of the Scottish pastor, poet, and hymn writer Horatius Bonar (1808-1889),

> Friends can say much to soothe us, but they cannot lay their finger upon the hidden seat of sorrow. They can put their arm around the fainting body, but not around the fainting spirit. To that they have only distant and indirect access. But here the heavenly aid comes in. The Spirit throws around us the everlasting arms, and we are invincibly upheld. We cannot sink, for He sustains, He comforts, He cheers. And who knows so well as He how to sustain, and comfort, and cheer?[2]

With this in mind, let us return to Isaiah 40 and God's command to comfort Israel.

---

[2] Horatius Bonar, *When God's Children Suffer* (Grand Rapids, MI: Kregel Publications, 2017), p. 116.

A Priestly Responsibility

A question that immediately springs to mind at the beginning of Isaiah 40 is this: Whom is God speaking to? The obvious answer would be Isaiah—or maybe Isaiah as representative of all God's prophets, although Jeremiah (once) and Zechariah (once) are the only others who used *nâcham* in a similar context. According to Lancelot Brenton's translation of the Septuagint, the recipients are actually identified: "Speak, ye priests" is how it reads in verse 2. This presents us with a slight problem, for who were the *godly* priests in Isaiah's day who would have been entrusted with such a message? The Septuagint may still help us, however, because I believe the divine command extends far beyond the days of Israel's prophets and priests to a different kind of priesthood entirely. Consider the following benediction and prayer from two of Paul's letters:

> Blessed be the God and Father of our Lord Jesus the Messiah, the Father of mercies and God of all comfort, who comforts us in all our affliction, so that we may be able to comfort those who are in any affliction, with the comfort with which we ourselves are comforted by God. (2 Cor. 1:3-4)

> Now may our Lord Jesus the Messiah Himself, and God our Father, who loved us and gave us eternal comfort and good hope through grace, comfort your hearts and establish them in every good work and word. (2 Thess. 2:16-17)

We learn from Paul's letters that every believer has received "eternal comfort" from God, having been forgiven, cleansed, and reconciled through faith in Jesus the Messiah. However, those who then take up their cross and wholeheartedly follow the Lord are promised trials and tribulations for which other remedial comforts have been prescribed. In their capacity as priests of God, these faithful believers are then expected to mediate to others the comfort that they have received. But before we consider the priesthood of believers in connection with Isaiah 40, let us address another question: Is it possible for God's comfort to be mediated through those among His people who are not walking in His truth or standing in His counsel?

Time and again in Israel's history, false priests and prophets arose proclaiming peace and prosperity in God's name when all the time they were speaking only lies and deceit to the people (Jer. 23:26). The sin-wound of Israel became so grievous in God's sight that it needed exposing and cleansing, not covering up (Jer. 30:12). Sadly, the nation welcomed and heeded the diagnosis and prognosis of the false prophets, which caused the wound to grow more and more infected. Invasive surgery on God's part became necessary and unavoidable for the survival of the nation.

The true prophets of God, by contrast, were persecuted for pronouncing judgment and calamity instead of peace. Elijah, Micaiah, Jeremiah, and Amos were among those who were viewed as troublers of Israel (1 Kgs. 18:17; Jer. 38:1-4; Am. 7:10-13). Before going into battle against the Syrian-controlled city of Ramoth-gilead, Ahab, king of Israel, gathered round him four hundred prophets under the pretense of seeking God's counsel about the proposed battle. Ahab was told what he wanted to hear: "Go up, for the Lord will give it into the hand of the king" (1 Kgs. 22:6). This assembly of false prophets thought nothing of attaching God's name to their own prophecies, and with one accord, they unwittingly set the king on a course that led to his death. Micaiah, on the other hand, being a true prophet, brought the word of the Lord to the king, and it was far from favorable. But what it did was reveal what was going on in the heavenly realms:

> Therefore hear the word of the LORD: I saw the LORD sitting on His throne, and all the host of heaven standing beside Him on His right hand and on His left; and the LORD said, "Who will entice Ahab, that he may go up and fall at Ramoth-gilead?" ... Then a spirit came forward and stood before the LORD, saying, "I will entice him." And the LORD said to him, "By what means?" And he said, "I will go out, and will be a lying spirit in the mouth of all his prophets." And He said, "You are to entice him, and you shall succeed; go out and do so." Now therefore behold, the LORD has put a lying spirit in the mouth of all these your prophets; the LORD has declared disaster for you. (1 Kgs. 22:19-23)

Micaiah was immediately struck on the cheek by one of the false prophets and consigned to prison. His prophesy was fulfilled, however, and the king was fatally wounded in battle.

God had a lot to say about those in Israel who presumed to speak in His Name:

> Thus says the LORD of hosts: "Do not listen to the words of the prophets who prophesy to you, filling you with vain hopes. They speak visions of their own minds, not from the mouth of the LORD. They say continually to those who despise the word of the LORD, 'It shall be well with you'; and to everyone who stubbornly follows his own heart, they say, 'No disaster shall come upon you' ... I did not send the prophets, yet they ran; I did not speak to them, yet they prophesied ... Let the prophet who has a dream tell the dream, but let him who has my word speak my word faithfully ... Behold, I am against those who prophesy lying dreams, declares the LORD, and who tell them and lead my people astray by their lies and their recklessness, when I did not send them or charge them." (Jer. 23:16-32)
>
> "Thus says the Lord GOD, Woe to the foolish prophets who follow their own spirit, and have seen nothing! ... Precisely because they have misled my people, saying, 'Peace,' when there is no peace, and because, when the people build a wall, these prophets smear it with whitewash, say to those who smear it with whitewash that it shall fall!" (Ezek. 13:3-11)

There can be no true comfort without truth and no truth without standing in God's counsel "to see and to hear His word" (Jer. 23:18). As Jeremiah lamented following the destruction of Jerusalem in 586 B.C.,

> What can I liken to you, that I may comfort [*nâcham*] you, O virgin daughter of Zion? ... Your prophets have seen for you false and deceptive visions; they have not exposed your iniquity to restore your fortunes, but have seen for you oracles that are false and misleading. (Lam. 2:13-14)

Has it been any different in the church, especially in these last days? False prophets and teachers abound today, with words of comfort, healing, and prosperity being streamed into millions of homes via satellite. False peace, false consolation, false healing, and false blessings are being promised to believers in the name of Jesus. Something not too dissimilar is happening in relation to Israel, with self-appointed prophets and teachers in the church proclaiming peace and prosperity to the nation while withholding the gospel of Jesus and the warning of the tribulation judgments to come. They believe they are comforting Israel when in fact they are misleading the nation, just as the false prophets of old did.

Jesus and His apostles clearly foretold that this kind of deception would come again to Israel *and* from within the church in the last days:

"Beware of false prophets, who come to you in sheep's clothing but inwardly are ravenous wolves." (Mt. 7:15)

"And many false prophets will arise and lead many astray . . . For false messiahs and false prophets will arise and perform great signs and wonders, so as to lead astray, if possible, even the elect. See, I have told you beforehand." (Mt. 24:11-25)

"While people are saying, 'There is peace and security,' then sudden destruction will come upon them as labor pains come upon a pregnant woman, and they will not escape." (1 Thess. 5:2-3)

"For the time is coming when people will not endure sound teaching, but having itching ears they will accumulate for themselves teachers to suit their own passions, and will turn away from listening to the truth and wander off into myths." (2 Tim. 4:3-4)

"But false prophets also arose among the people, just as there will be false teachers among you." (2 Pet. 2:1)

Beloved, do not believe every spirit, but test the spirits to see whether they are from God, for many false prophets have gone out into the world. (1 Jn. 4:1)

Waiting for Consolation

Without losing sight of Isaiah 40:1-2, let us pay a quick visit to the Jerusalem Temple at the time that Mary and Joseph dedicated Jesus. Present on that occasion was a devout Jewish man by the name of Simeon. We are told that he was "waiting for the consolation of Israel, and the Holy Spirit was upon him" (Lk. 2:25), or as another translation renders it, he was "looking for the comforting of Israel." No sooner had Mary and Joseph entered the Temple than Simeon took the babe in his arms, blessed God, and prayed,

> Lord, now you are letting your servant depart in peace, according to your word; for my eyes have seen your salvation that you have prepared in the presence of all peoples, a light for revelation to the Gentiles, and for glory to your people Israel. (Lk. 2:29-32)

Simeon had beheld the Messiah with his own eyes. The One for whom he had prayerfully waited all of his life had finally come. The following prophecies of Isaiah would no doubt have been very dear to Simeon through those waiting years:

> You will say in that day: "I will give thanks to you, O LORD, for though you were angry with me, your anger turned away, that you might comfort [*nâcham*] me." (Isa. 12:1)

> For the LORD comforts [*nâcham*] Zion; He comforts [*nâcham*] all her waste places and makes her wilderness like Eden, her desert like the garden of the LORD. (Isa. 51:3)

> Break forth together into singing, you waste places of Jerusalem, for the LORD has comforted [*nâcham*] His people; He has redeemed Jerusalem. (Isa. 52:9)

> "I have seen his ways, but I will heal him; I will lead him and restore comfort [*nichûwm*] to him and his mourners, creating the fruit of the lips." (Isa. 57:18)

> "As one whom his mother comforts [*nâcham*], so I will comfort [*nâcham*] you; you shall be comforted [*nâcham*] in Jerusalem." (Isa. 66:13)

How fitting it was that *the* Comforter of Israel, the Lord Jesus, should make Capernaum on the northwest side of the Sea of Galilee His ministry base. Matthew tells us the significance of the Messiah's relocation from Nazareth following the imprisonment of John the Baptist:

> And leaving Nazareth He went and lived in Capernaum by the sea, in the territory of Zebulun and Naphtali, so that what was spoken by the prophet Isaiah might be fulfilled: "The land of Zebulun and the land of Naphtali, the way of the sea, beyond the Jordan, Galilee of the Gentiles — the people dwelling in darkness have seen a great light, and for those dwelling in the region and shadow of death, on them a light has dawned." (Mt. 4:13-16; cf. Isa. 9:1-2)

Those who have ever visited Galilee will almost certainly have passed a road sign for Capernaum, which in Hebrew reads "Kefer-nahum." The name translates as "Village of Nahum," literally the "village of comfort."

Few chapters in the Bible reveal as much about the heart of God toward Israel than Isaiah 54 and Hosea 11. I would encourage the reader to pause here and take time to read through these extraordinary chapters. Consider carefully and prayerfully the language and imagery God used to express His intentions toward His wayward people. Here are two extracts from these prophecies:

> "Fear not, for you will not be ashamed; be not confounded, for you will not be disgraced; for you will forget the shame of your youth, and the reproach of your widowhood you will remember no more. For your Maker is your husband, the LORD of hosts is His name; and the Holy One of Israel is your Redeemer, the God of the whole earth He is called. For the LORD has called you like a wife deserted and grieved in spirit, like a wife of youth when she is cast off, says your God. For a brief moment I deserted you, but with great compassion I will gather you. In overflowing anger for a moment I hid my face from you, but with everlasting love I will have compassion on you," says the LORD, your Redeemer. (Isa. 54:4-8)

> "When Israel was a child, I loved him, and out of Egypt I called my son. The more they were called, the more they went away . . . Yet it was I who taught Ephraim to walk; I took them up by their arms, but they did not know that I healed them. I led them with cords of kindness, with the bands of love, and I became to them as one who eases the yoke on their jaws, and I bent down to them and fed them . . . How can I give you up, O Ephraim? How can I hand you over, O Israel? . . . My heart recoils within me; my compassion grows warm and tender. I will not execute my burning anger; I will not again destroy Ephraim; for I am God and not a man, the Holy One in your midst, and I will not come in wrath." (Hos. 11:1-9)

May we marvel afresh at the way in which God has revealed Himself to be a tender, loving, and compassionate God who forgives, heals, and restores. Yes, the Lord is a consuming fire but also the fountain of living waters; He is transcendent and majestic (*Elohim*) but also immanent and approachable (*Yahweh*); and He is the righteous Judge of all the earth but also the supreme Defender and Advocate of His people.

Comforting the Mourners

The ascension of the Messiah was the climax to His glorious ministry on earth, a ministry that He Himself had announced three years earlier in His hometown synagogue (Lk. 4:16-21). On that occasion, He had stood to read from the Scriptures, according to the custom, before being handed the scroll of Isaiah. He opened the scroll at chapter 61 and read the excerpt below before announcing that He had come to fulfill the prophecy:

> "The Spirit of the Lord GOD is upon me, because the LORD has anointed me to bring good news to the poor; He has sent me to bind up the brokenhearted, to proclaim liberty to the captives, and the opening of the prison to those who are bound; to proclaim the year of the LORD's favor . . ." (Isa. 61:1-2)

The Lord then stopped mid-sentence, deliberately omitting the words which followed:

> ". . . and the day of vengeance of our God; to comfort all who mourn; to grant to those who mourn in Zion — to give them a beautiful headdress instead of ashes, the oil of gladness instead of mourning, the garment of praise instead of a faint spirit; that they may be called oaks of righteousness, the planting of the LORD, that He may be glorified. They shall build up the ancient ruins; they shall raise up the former devastations; they shall repair the ruined cities, the devastations of many generations." (Isa. 61:3-4)

Jesus' earthly ministry was the *year* of the Lord's favor, not the *day* of His vengeance. That *year* may have extended to the present time, but the *day* is still to break. Notice how the promise to "comfort all who mourn" immediately followed the disclosure of the day of vengeance. Throughout His ministry, the Lord brought great comfort to many mourners in Zion, including Mary and Martha (Jn. 11:1-44), the widow of Nain (Lk. 7:11-17), and Jairus the synagogue ruler (Lk. 8:41-56). He has since brought comfort to millions of Gentiles as well through the consoling presence of the Holy Spirit. However, Isaiah's prophecy ultimately relates to Israel *as a nation*, which means that the comforting of "those who mourn in Zion" still awaits a final fulfillment. I believe this will happen during the second half of the seven-year tribulation period to come.

As Zechariah prophesied, "a spirit of grace and pleas for mercy" will be poured out upon the remnant of Israel at the most precarious time in their history, the time of the Antichrist. With all hope seemingly gone, the remnant will "look unto"[3] the One they have pierced and "mourn for Him, as

---

[3] According to the American Standard Version. Most translations read "look upon" or "look on," but that would imply that they will physically see Messiah Jesus *at that*

one mourns for an only child, and weep bitterly over Him, as one weeps over a firstborn" (Zech. 12:3-10). The next couple of verses in the prophecy reveal the extent of the nation's grief that will break out across the land on that "day" before God fully removes the sin and uncleanness of His people (Zech. 13:1) and defeats the nations that will have gathered against them (Zech. 14:1-3).

The Paraclete

Early in his apostolic ministry, Paul visited the synagogue at Antioch in Pisidia (in present-day Turkey). As was noted in chapter 1, the synagogue rulers sent Paul and his companions a message on that occasion: "Brothers, if you have any word of encouragement for the people, say it." The apostle stood to his feet and opened with these words: "Men of Israel and you who fear God, listen. The God of this people Israel . . ." (Acts 13:15-17). I believe these introductory words are critically important.

Notice how Paul immediately identified God with the nation of Israel, using the present tense, not the past tense! He did precisely the same in his letter to the Romans (chapters 9-11). With Paul, there was to be no spiritualizing, allegorizing, or reinterpreting of "Israel" in his message that day or in any of his Spirit-inspired sermons and letters. So, too, with Peter, who made the same *present* identification when he addressed the crowd in Solomon's Colonnade: "Men of Israel . . . You *are* the sons of the prophets and of the covenant that God made with your fathers, saying to Abraham, 'And in your offspring shall all the families of the earth be blessed'" (Acts 3:12, 25). As noted in chapter 3, Matthew and Luke referred to "the God of Israel" (Mt. 15:31) and "the Lord God of Israel" (Lk. 1:68) in their Gospel accounts.

Paul's Pisidian preaching, though direct and uncompromising, was rooted in the knowledge that God had not rejected Israel despite Israel's rejection of His Son (Rom. 11:1). The apostle had been asked to bring a

---

moment and then mourn. I believe this "looking unto" Jesus means that the remnant will suddenly become aware of who He is and fix their attention upon Him, crying out to Him for mercy.

"word of encouragement for the people," and that is precisely what he did—the undiluted, non-seeker-friendly message of Jesus the Messiah. It was delivered with respect and compassion and was underpinned by the truth that God had changed neither course nor character in relation to Israel. The Greek word translated "encouragement" (or "exhortation") in the Acts 13 account is *paráklēsis*. The noun derives from the verb *parakaléō*, meaning "to be summoned for the purpose of strengthening, refreshing, exhorting, encouraging, defending, or comforting." This word was also used by Luke to describe the pastoral ministry of Paul and Barnabas when they returned to the cities where they had previously ministered. There they drew alongside the disciples, "encouraging them to continue in the faith" (Acts 14:22).

The word was frequently used in ancient times in a legal context to denote an advocate or counsel for the defense. This is why John supremely speaks of Jesus as being our *Paráklētos* with the Father (1 Jn. 2:1). If we think back to righteous Simeon for a moment, we recall that he was "waiting for the consolation of Israel" or, as it reads in the Greek, for the *paráklēsis* of Israel. We are further told that "the Holy Spirit was upon him" (Lk. 2:25). During their last Passover supper together, Jesus spoke to His disciples at length about the Person and ministry of the Holy Spirit, whom He described as the *Paráklētos*—variously translated "Comforter," "Helper," or "Counselor" (Jn. 14:26; 15:26; 16:7). In fact, the Messiah referred to the Holy Spirit as being "another" *Paráklētos* (Jn. 14:16), meaning that He would be just like Jesus, representing Him to the disciples by strengthening, refreshing, exhorting, encouraging, defending, and comforting them. Charles Spurgeon expressed it this way: "The Holy Spirit consoles, but Christ is the consolation."[4]

Hallmark of the Messiah

For centuries, it had been the hope and longing of the righteous in Israel for the Holy Spirit to be "poured out" like living waters upon a dry and

---

[4] C.H. Spurgeon, *Morning and Evening*, "October 12—Evening" (McLean, VA: MacDonald Publishing Company, 1973).

thirsty nation. Isaiah, more than any other prophet, spoke about the day when this thirst for God's outpouring would be quenched, when both people and land would be watered and renewed from heaven:

> With joy you will draw water from the wells of salvation [Heb. *yeshuah*]. (Isa. 12:3)
>
> For the palace is forsaken, the populous city deserted . . . until the Spirit is poured upon us from on high, and the wilderness becomes a fruitful field, and the fruitful field is deemed a forest. (Isa. 32:14-15)
>
> For waters break forth in the wilderness, and streams in the desert; the burning sand shall become a pool, and the thirsty ground springs of water. (Isa. 35:6-7)
>
> "When the poor and needy seek water, and there is none, and their tongue is parched with thirst, I the LORD will answer them; I the God of Israel will not forsake them. I will open rivers on the bare heights, and fountains in the midst of the valleys. I will make the wilderness a pool of water, and the dry land springs of water." (Isa. 41:17-18)
>
> "For I will pour water on the thirsty land, and streams on the dry ground; I will pour my Spirit upon your offspring, and my blessing on your descendants. They shall spring up among the grass like willows by flowing streams." (Isa. 44:3-4)
>
> For the LORD comforts [*nâcham*] Zion; He comforts [*nâcham*] all her waste places and makes her wilderness like Eden, her desert like the garden of the LORD. (Isa. 51:3)

The double imperative of Isaiah 40:1 to "comfort, comfort my people" sits in the neighborhood of these life-renewing prophecies, all of which find their glorious fulfillment in and through Messiah Jesus. In John's Gospel, we read about Jesus' attendance in Jerusalem at the Feast of Tabernacles, or *Sukkot*, a requirement of every Jewish male (Ex. 23:14-17; Deut. 16:16). On the last and greatest day of the feast, the Lord stood up in the Temple and cried out, "If anyone thirsts, let him come to me and drink. Whoever believes in me, as the Scripture has said, 'Out of his heart will flow rivers of living water'" (Jn. 7:37-38).

All of the prophetic promises of divine comfort and refreshment were incarnated in the Messiah. Those who truly thirsted for God's presence came to Him and were renewed by the living waters of the Holy Spirit.

Israel's leaders, however, spurned the life-giving Lord and continued to draw from their own "broken cisterns" (Jer. 2:13), leaving the nation desolate. Nevertheless, these same promises had been given to the nation, largely within the context of an end-time fulfillment. The fact that many *individual* Jews received and have continued to receive those life-giving waters from the Messiah does not imply that *the nation* has forever forfeited those promises or that they have somehow been reinterpreted, spiritualized, and reapplied to the church. That line of theological reasoning, which is prevalent in many parts of the church, is unbiblical, damaging, and dishonoring to God.

In the prophetic promises of Isaiah, we see how God committed Himself personally to renewing His desolate people and His barren land. Yet, in the midst of such pronouncements, He issued a command for Israel to be comforted. Why did the Lord choose to involve a third party? Here are a few thoughts:

1. The promises of God had to be communicated not only to the people of Isaiah's day but also to the generations to come, including the one that will pass through the tribulation period. Ever since the Assyrian and Babylonian exiles and especially since the destruction of the Temple by the Romans in A.D. 70, there has never been a time when the people of Israel have not needed to be reminded of God's consoling promises. But in the words of Paul, "How are they to hear without someone preaching? And how are they to preach unless they are sent?" (Rom. 10:14-15).

2. The Prophet Amos tells us that "the Lord GOD does nothing without revealing His secret to His servants the prophets" (Am. 3:7). Furthermore, Jesus told His disciples, "I no longer call you servants, because a servant does not know his master's business. Instead, I have called you friends, for everything that I learned from my Father I have made known to you" (Jn. 15:15). In His triunity, God is relational—Father, Son, and Holy Spirit. He seeks to bring into fellowship with Himself those He has redeemed before employing them in His service.

In this way, then, the appointed comforters were/are enabled to think, feel, and act in a way that reflects and honors God so that He is the One who is ultimately seen, heard, and glorified. Jesus spoke figuratively about the flock of Israel not listening to "the voice of strangers," to the voice of "thieves and robbers" who cared nothing for them. His sheep would only respond to the familiar voice of the Shepherd (Jn. 10:1-16). Following Jesus' ascension, that same voice was to be communicated from Jerusalem to the ends of the earth through His "witnesses" (Acts 1:8). Tragically, today and for centuries past, many in the church have spoken to Israel with the voice of a stranger. The Good Shepherd has not been recognized in their preaching, teaching, writing, campaigning, and pontificating.

The verses that follow the double command of Isaiah 40:1 transport the reader to John the Baptist, *the* messenger of the Messiah who was sent to "prepare the way of the LORD" (Isa. 40:3; Mt. 3:1-3). John's life was uniquely dedicated to heralding the coming of the Comforter. His message consoled the hearts of the humble and contrite and confronted those of the proud and impenitent. We are told that John "went into all the region around the Jordan, proclaiming a baptism of repentance for the forgiveness of sins" (Lk. 3:3) and that "with many other exhortations he preached good news to the people" (Lk. 3:18). The Greek word translated as "exhortations" is derived from the verb *parakaléō*, which was highlighted earlier. John was thus summoned by God to draw alongside Israel and announce to the people that One greater than he was coming, who would baptize them with the *Paráklētos*.

During his relatively short life and ministry, this man of the wilderness, who had been cut from the same prophetic cloth as Elijah, was recognized by many as God's messenger. However, the time of fulfillment for the nation as a whole would have to wait. But it would come, as Simon Peter later told the men of Israel in Solomon's Colonnade. On that occasion, rather than condemning those present, he gave them hope:

> Repent therefore, and turn back, that your sins may be blotted out, that times of refreshing may come from the presence of the Lord, and that He may send the Messiah appointed for you, Jesus, whom heaven must receive until the time for restoring all the things about which God spoke by the mouth of His holy prophets long ago. (Acts 3:19-21)

Why was Peter's message received by so many that day? I believe it was because he bore the hallmark of the Messiah. His heart had been broken in the dark shadows of denial before being lovingly restored by Jesus in the Galilean rays of resurrection. It was now being filled with God's compassion for the people. That day in Jerusalem, the men of Israel were able to hear God's voice in both the Spirit-inspired message and the Spirit-filled messenger, thus preparing the way for the Spirit Himself to move many toward the Messiah.

Conclusion

If the prophet Isaiah had been the only intended messenger of God's comfort to Israel, then the timeframe for heeding the double command would have been limited to his own prophetic ministry. Since Isaiah 40 begins a long series of connected prophecies culminating in the promise of new heavens and a new earth, then the command to comfort Israel must surely extend *far beyond* the immediate historical context. I believe the Greek translation of Isaiah 40:1-2 (we will focus on verse 2 in the next chapter) is instructive here, if not entirely in keeping with our English translations: "Comfort ye, comfort ye my people, saith God. Speak, ye priests, to the heart of Jerusalem; comfort her, for her humiliation is accomplished, her sin is put away." The accuracy of the Septuagint (LXX) is not my *major* concern in this instance. Of prime importance is discerning what the Holy Spirit was *and is* trying to communicate. Yes, we need to know what the text actually says as best as we can, but when the meaning is not immediately obvious, we must look for some helpful pointers. I believe one of those pointers is the LXX translation because it makes us think about *priestly* messengers, those appointed and anointed to mediate on God's behalf. For the same reasons outlined above, the "priests" in Isaiah 40:2 cannot be restricted to Isaiah's day. I believe we need to journey past the time of the prophets until we come to the New Covenant age of the church and those who have been made "priests to His God and Father" (Rev. 1:6; cf. 5:10; 1 Pet. 2:5, 9). This is cemented in my own thinking by the fact that the promises contained within the comfort-command of God are all tied to Jesus and His second coming.

For many believers, God's message to Israel may simply be held and cherished in their hearts and brought before Him in prayer. For others, it may be further expressed through witnessing, evangelism, preaching, teaching, writing, or some form of advocacy on behalf of God's people. The important thing is that every believer bears faithful witness to the Consoler and Consolation of Israel. Any heart that is truly indwelt by the Holy Spirit should be a vessel through which God can reach out to the most despised and afflicted nation on earth, *His* nation. I fervently maintain that any who read the command to comfort God's people are without excuse if they do not willingly and wholeheartedly comply. It may take a young believer time and teaching to understand Israel's place in the purposes of God. However, there is no excusing a mature believer's ignorance, indifference, or even defiance. Those in the church who teach that the name "Israel" has been reinterpreted, redefined, expanded, or fulfilled; those in the church who claim that biblical Israel and the modern State of Israel are unrelated; and those in the church who question whether the Jews in the land today are really the descendants of Abraham, Isaac, and Jacob are "miserable comforters"—all of them. Furthermore, God has not sent them, for they have not stood in His counsel and therefore cannot speak with His voice!

One man who got it right and paid dearly for it was John the Baptist. Jesus testified that "among those born of women there has arisen no one greater than John the Baptist" (Mt. 11:11). The following verses help explain why that was so and give us a wonderful example to follow as we pray for the salvation of the Jews and the consolation of Israel:

> Jesus went away again across the Jordan to the place where John had been baptizing at first, and there He remained. And many came to Him. And they said, "John did no sign, but everything that John said about this man was true." And many believed in Him there. (Jn. 10:40-42)

When the message spoken about the Messiah is true and bears His hallmark, then the Holy Spirit will use both the message and the messenger to touch the lives of those He loves.

I close with a devotional message from Charles Spurgeon, which I believe is pertinent to this chapter. I also pray that it might be used to bring a measure of God's comfort to those who may be passing through a particular trial of their own right now:

> There are times when all the promises and doctrines of the Bible are of no avail, unless a gracious hand shall apply them to us. We are thirsty, but too

faint to crawl to the water-brook. When a soldier is wounded in battle it is of little use for him to know that there are those at the hospital who can bind up his wounds, and medicines there to ease all the pains which he now suffers: what he needs is to be carried there, and to have the remedies applied. It is thus with our souls, and to meet this need there is one, even the Spirit of truth, who takes of the things of Jesus, and applies them to us . . . Oh Christian, if you are tonight labouring under deep distresses, your Father does not give you promises and then leave you to draw them up from the Word like buckets from a well, but the promises He has written in the Word He will write anew on your heart. He will manifest His love to you, and by His blessed Spirit, dispel your cares and troubles.

Be it known unto you, Oh mourner, that it is God's prerogative to wipe every tear from the eye of His people. The good Samaritan did not say, "Here is the wine, and here is the oil for you;" he actually poured in the oil and the wine. So Jesus not only gives you the sweet wine of the promise, but holds the golden chalice to your lips, and pours the life-blood into your mouth. The poor, sick, way-worn pilgrim is not merely strengthened to walk, but he is borne on eagles' wings. Glorious gospel! which provides everything for the helpless, which draws near to us when we cannot reach after it — brings us grace before we seek for grace! Here is as much glory in the giving as in the gift. Happy people who have the Holy Spirit to bring Jesus to them.[5]

---

[5] Spurgeon, *Morning and Evening*, "October 22—Evening."

Chapter 11:

Speak to the Heart

> Ah, sinful nation, a people laden with iniquity, offspring of evildoers, children who deal corruptly!... Why will you still be struck down? Why will you continue to rebel? The whole head is sick, and the whole heart faint... "Come now, let us reason together, says the LORD: though your sins are like scarlet, they shall be as white as snow; though they are red like crimson, they shall become like wool." (Isa. 1:4-5, 18)

> "Speak tenderly to Jerusalem, and cry to her that her warfare is ended, that her iniquity is pardoned, that she has received from the LORD's hand double for all her sins." (Isa. 40:2)

In the previous chapter, we considered God's double command to comfort His people. We looked at the Hebrew word *nâcham* and tried to identify the recipients of the command. Although many of the Jewish people received Jesus as their Messiah, the promised comfort *to the nation* was postponed because the leaders rejected Him. I proposed that, for the past two millennia, it has been the responsibility of the New Covenant "priests" of God to carry His consolation to Israel in their hearts, convey it with their lips, and confirm it through their actions. I believe the double command is one of the most pressing obligations the Lord ever placed upon His church. In this chapter, we will consider *the way* in which God intended His comfort to be ministered to His people. Our primary focus will be verse 2 of Isaiah 40 and the Lord's instruction to "speak tenderly to Jerusalem."

The Heart of the Matter

It is no surprise that when God speaks, the words He uses are rich with meaning; nothing is ever mundane or superfluous. In our key verse, Bible translations render the Hebrew words slightly differently:

"Speak ye comfortably to Jerusalem" (Geneva 1560, KJV, RV, ASV)

"Speak tenderly to Jerusalem" (ESV, RSV, NIV, NLT)

"Speak comfort to Jerusalem" (NKJV)

"Speak kindly to Jerusalem" (NASB, NET)

These versions are all helpful and should be combined, but what they give us is an *interpretation* and not a literal translation. Among the very few versions that do provide a literal rendering are the fourteenth century Wycliffe Bible, Robert Young's Literal Translation (YLT, 1862), and John Nelson Darby's New Translation, otherwise known as The Darby Bible (DBY, 1890)—not exactly mainstream. These all read as follows: "Speak (ye) to the heart of Jerusalem." We can also add to our short list the Septuagint, which gives us a very interesting and I believe illuminating translation as was noted in the previous chapter: "Speak, ye priests, to the heart of Jerusalem." The word *lêb*, which appears in the original Hebrew, literally means "the heart" as an internal organ. However, it is rarely used in Scripture in its literal sense. It is also highly unlikely that anyone reading this verse would have a literal heart in mind, especially when its figurative meaning is used throughout the Bible to denote the human will, understanding, or seat of emotion. But the actual wording of Isaiah 40:2 also reveals a Hebrew idiom that can only be found in a handful of verses in the Old Testament: Genesis 34:3; 50:21; Ruth 2:13; 2 Samuel 19:7; 2 Chronicles 30:22; 32:6; Hosea 2:14. Three of these verses are particularly instructive and tie in beautifully with our main verse:

1. Through the Prophet Hosea, God accused Israel of having "played the whore" and having "loved a prostitute's wages" (Hos. 9:1). Yet, in an outpouring of amazing grace, He made this startling announcement: "Therefore behold, I will allure her, and bring her into the wilderness, and *speak to her heart*... and I will betroth thee unto me in righteousness, and in judgment, and in lovingkindness [*chesed*], and in mercies [*rachamim*]" (Hos. 2:14-19, DBY).

2. Upon meeting Boaz for the first time while gleaning in his field, the Moabite widow Ruth responded to his kindness with words of endearing humility: "Let me find grace in thine eyes, my lord, because thou hast comforted me [*nâcham*], and because thou hast *spoken*

unto the heart of thy maidservant, and I — I am not as one of thy maidservants" (Ruth 2:13, YLT).

In the Hosea passage, no sooner had God condemned Israel for her spiritual harlotry and moral decay than He spoke "tenderly/kindly/comfortably/to the heart" of His estranged and wayward wife, Israel. In the book of Ruth, we hear the kinsman-redeemer Boaz speaking "to the heart" of Ruth in a way that so beautifully foreshadowed *the* Kinsman-Redeemer of Israel, Jesus the Messiah. However, there is another occurrence of this Hebrew idiom—its first in the Bible—that incorporates such a precious and prophetic illustration of God's mercy and comfort. It is here that we return to the Joseph narrative.

Balm, not Blame

When the patriarch Jacob died, his sons feared retribution from their brother for having sold him into slavery. Overwhelmed with guilt and remorse, they were unable to fully accept that Joseph had long since forgiven them and that God had sovereignly used their wicked deed to accomplish a great good. As we read in the Genesis account, the brothers pleaded with Joseph for mercy:

> So they sent a message to Joseph, saying, "Your father gave this command before he died: 'Say to Joseph, Please forgive the transgression of your brothers and their sin, because they did evil to you.' And now, please forgive the transgression of the servants of the God of your father." Joseph wept when they spoke to him. His brothers also came and fell down before him and said, "Behold, we are your servants." But Joseph said to them, "Do not fear, for am I in the place of God? As for you, you meant evil against me, but God meant it for good, to bring it about that many people should be kept alive, as they are today. So do not fear; I will provide for you and your little ones." Thus he comforted them and spoke kindly to them [speaketh unto their heart, YLT]. (Gen. 50:16-21)

What the brothers received from Joseph was consolation, not condemnation; reconciliation, not retribution; balm, not blame—an outpouring of divine love through the brokenness of a man whose heart had resided in heaven while his feet were being held in fetters.[1] Joseph had spoken to their hearts.

We read in the Psalms that God "does not deal with us according to our sins, nor repay us according to our iniquities" (Ps. 103:10). When Joseph's brothers were overcome with fear and alarm, what they were shown was not what they feared or expected. They were the undeserving recipients of God's *chesed* (loyal love), *nâcham* (comfort), and *racham* (compassion) through a man whose brokenness had not made him bitter, but better. Joseph had been molded into a vessel of great honor in God's redemptive plan for His people. We are told that he even wept when he realized the extent of his brothers' anguish and fear. Falling down at his feet, they offered themselves as his servants—one final fulfillment, at least in their own lifetimes, of the dreams Joseph had received from God as a young man (Gen. 37:5-11). In spite of all that they had done to him, Joseph was not about to punish his brothers; he was going to bless them.

What a moving and gloriously prophetic picture this is of Jesus, the Jewish Messiah who was despised, rejected, betrayed, and sold into the hands of a foreign power by His own brethren. The foreshadowing, or typology, is all too evident in this remarkable narrative. On that future "day" of greatest tribulation for Israel, when all hope seems lost, Jesus will reveal Himself to the hearts of His people, not as their accuser but as their Advocate; not as their destroyer but as their Defender; not as their contender but as their Comforter. Tribulation will ultimately lead to triumph for Israel, but the glory will be the Messiah's. In those momentous words spoken by God through Isaiah, "I will divide Him [the Messiah] a portion with the great, and He shall divide the spoil with the strong; because He poured out His soul to death, and was numbered with the transgressors; yet He bore the sin of many, and made intercession for the transgressors" (Isa. 53:12).

God's Workmanship

Based in Netanya, Israel, *One For Israel* is a ministry of born-again Israeli Jews and Arabs who understand that the only true and lasting way to bless

---

[1] Ps. 105:16-22.

the Jewish people is to share with them the good news of Messiah. In one of the many inspiring Jewish testimonies of salvation posted on their website, Scott Schwartz, who was raised in a devout Jewish home, speaks of his search for peace after finding himself homeless, alone, and addicted.

Scott was treated at four rehab clinics, two halfway houses, and a psychiatric hospital, but "none of them worked." Doctors, psychologists, and psychiatrists had all tried to "fix" him but without success.[2] In desperation, he "stumbled into a church" looking for food, despite having been warned all his life to avoid Christians. There he received unconditional love. As Scott continued his search for God and for peace in his life, he acquired a copy of the New Testament and was shocked to discover how Jewish it was. This is how his testimony continues in the video:

> Every word that I read on the pages of the New Testament *spoke right to my heart*. It was almost like God could see into my heart and could see how fearful I was and was speaking right to my fear, right to my anxiety. And I remember saying to myself, "Why didn't somebody tell me this sooner?" Jesus never studied psychology in university, but His very words spoke to me better than any doctor has ever spoken to me. *His words spoke right to my heart.*[3]

In the previous chapter, we looked at the way in which God's messengers were/are required not only to *convey* a message but also to *carry* it in their hearts. They need to be in such close communion with God that through their words and deeds the people for whom His comfort is intended will recognize His voice. When Peter and John stood boldly and strongly before the Jewish council, their interrogators "recognized that they had been with Jesus" (Acts 4:13). They did not have to *do* anything or find the right words to say. Who they were as faithful followers of Jesus enabled the Holy Spirit to speak through them.

The principle has never changed. The closeness of a believer's walk with Jesus is what ultimately counts, whether that believer is trying to reach out

---

[2] In Luke's Gospel, we read about a woman who had suffered from a hemorrhage for twelve years and "spent all her living on physicians," but "could not be healed by anyone" but by Jesus (Lk. 8:43-48).

[3] One For Israel, "Scott Schwartz – (I Met Messiah)," www.oneforisrael.org/bible-based-teaching-from-israel/video/jewish-testimonies-i-met-messiah/scott-schwartz-how-i-met-messiah/.

to individuals like Scott Schwartz or speak to the heart of Jerusalem and administer God's comfort to Israel. I believe this is all encapsulated in the following scriptures:

> Now there are varieties of gifts, but the same Spirit. And there are varieties of ministries, and the same Lord. There are varieties of effects, but the same God *who works all things in all persons*. (1 Cor. 12:4-6, NASB)
>
> For we are *His workmanship*, created in Messiah Jesus for good works, which God prepared beforehand, that we should walk in them. (Eph. 2:10)
>
> And I am sure of this, that He who began *a good work in you* will bring it to completion at the day of Jesus the Messiah. (Phil. 1:6)
>
> Therefore . . . work out your own salvation with fear and trembling, for it is God who *works in you*, both to will and to work for His good pleasure. (Phil. 2:13)
>
> Now may the God of peace . . . equip you with everything good that you may do His will, *working in us* that which is pleasing in His sight, through Jesus the Messiah, to whom be glory forever and ever. Amen. (Heb. 13:20-21)

Furthermore, Paul described himself and his companions as ambassadors for Messiah, as though God were pleading *through them* (2 Cor. 5:20, NKJV). Whereas an ambassador of the world serves in the absence of the ruler or government he or she is representing, an ambassador of Jesus always serves in His presence. It is the Lord Himself who works through His representative. As ambassadors, then, believers have no authority of their own and no liberty to say anything other than what the One who sent them has said. The psalmist expressed it well when he wrote, "Let me hear what God the LORD will speak" (Ps. 85:8). Remember what Jesus said about His own ministry: "I proceeded and came forth from God; I came not of my own accord, but He sent me . . . For I have not spoken on my own authority; the Father who sent me has Himself given me commandment what to say and what to speak" (Jn. 8:42; 12:49, RSV).

When the Messiah was urged by some of the Pharisees to flee Jerusalem because of Herod's death threats, He stood firm, unmoved from the course appointed for Him. His reply was resolute: "Go and tell that fox, 'Behold, I cast out demons and perform cures today and tomorrow, and the third day I finish my course'" (Lk. 13:32). As on every other occasion, He went on to speak not only the Father's word but also from the Father's heart:

> "O Jerusalem, Jerusalem, the city that kills the prophets and stones those who are sent to it! How often would I have gathered your children together as a hen gathers her brood under her wings, and you were not willing! Behold, your house is forsaken. And I tell you, you will not see me until you say, 'Blessed is He who comes in the name of the Lord!'" (Lk. 13:34-35)

During His far-from-triumphal entry into Jerusalem, the Lord descended the Mount of Olives and wept over the city, uttering this loud lament:

> "Would that you, even you, had known on this day the things that make for peace! But now they are hidden from your eyes. For the days will come upon you, when your enemies will set up a barricade around you and surround you and hem you in on every side and tear you down to the ground, you and your children within you. And they will not leave one stone upon another in you, because you did not know the time of your visitation." (Lk. 19:42-44)

It was more than a tear that Jesus shed for Jerusalem that day. The crowds may have been triumphant, but Messiah was broken as the shadow of the cross fell upon His brow and the vision of Jerusalem's destruction pierced His heart. For generations the Lord, in His pre-incarnate state, had longed to ingather His people (Isa. 65:1-2), but they had stiffened their necks, turned a stubborn shoulder, stopped their ears, made their hearts diamond-hard, and broken loose.[4] The only way the Son of God could break this pattern of destructive behavior was to be broken Himself.

It is clear that Paul experienced some degree of the Messiah's pain. He spoke of having "great sorrow and unceasing anguish" in his heart to the point that he could have wished himself accursed if it would have saved his people (Rom. 9:2-3). If the Lord's ambassadors today are to speak as tenderly to the heart of Jerusalem as Paul did, then they must experience at least some measure of the brokenness he experienced: the brokenness of the Lord.

---

[4] See, for example, Ex. 32:9, 25; 33:3; 34:9; Deut. 9:6, 13; 2 Chron. 36:13; Jer. 7:26; 16:12; 19:15; Ezek. 3:7; Zech. 7:11-12; Acts 7:51.

The Whole Truth, and Nothing but the Truth, to Israel!

Believers have no mandate from God to "pick 'n' mix" from His Word. That applies as much to those who stand with Israel as it does to those who stand against her. Within the command to comfort God's people is the reality that Israel's sin and transgression must be dealt with, and there is no greater sin than spurning the Son of God. There is coming a day when the church will no longer have the opportunity to speak to the heart of Jerusalem. Once the rapture has occurred, the Antichrist will step forward onto the world stage and confirm a seven-year covenant with Israel and other nations (Dan. 9:27). This will signal the start of the seven-year tribulation period, otherwise known as "the time of Jacob's trouble" (Jer. 30:7, NKJV). According to the book of Daniel, this will be "a time of trouble, such as never has been since there was a nation till that time" (Dan. 12:1). In the words of Zephaniah, it will be "a day of wrath . . . a day of distress and anguish, a day of ruin and devastation, a day of darkness and gloom, a day of clouds and thick darkness, a day of trumpet blast and battle cry" (Zeph. 1:15-16).

Messiah Jesus referred specifically to Daniel's prophecies when He declared that there would come a time of "great tribulation, such as has not been from the beginning of the world until now, no, and never will be" (Mt. 24:21). This part of God's message to Israel is being withheld by many believers who stand with God's people but who refuse to accept that the nation is yet to endure its darkest hour. It is certainly an understandable position to take when we consider the unspeakable horrors of the Holocaust, but it is not biblical. Jeremiah's prophecy concerning Jacob's trouble begins with a promise of restoration and return before proceeding immediately to the time when "a cry of panic, of terror, and no peace" will be heard among the people (Jer. 30:1-7). The Lord then speaks comfort to His people by assuring them that He will save them out of it and make "a full end of all the nations" to which they were scattered (Jer. 30:8-11). But God did not finish there, adding these solemn words, which we considered in a previous chapter:

"I will discipline you in just measure, and I will by no means leave you unpunished. For thus says the LORD: Your hurt is incurable, and your wound is grievous. There is none to uphold your cause, no medicine for your wound, no healing for you." (Jer. 30:11-12)

The Lord informed His people that He had dealt them "the blow of an enemy, the punishment of a merciless foe" because their guilt was "great" and their sins "flagrant" (Jer. 30:14). But just when everything seemed hopeless, He promised to show mercy and heal them (Jer. 30:18-20). Thus, we see how God's message of comfort to His people has never glossed over their sin, which means that if believers are going to speak to the heart of Jerusalem, then they must testify to—not tamper with—the truth. As Paul declared in his farewell address to the Ephesian elders, "I did not shrink from declaring to you the *whole* counsel of God" (Acts 20:27).

The truth hurts, but it does not have to be hurtful. Here is another of Jeremiah's prophecies that is full of comfort and hope but with a solemn reminder that God still has a controversy with His people:

"But fear not, O Jacob my servant, nor be dismayed, O Israel, for behold, I will save you from far away, and your offspring from the land of their captivity. Jacob shall return and have quiet and ease, and none shall make him afraid. Fear not, O Jacob my servant, declares the LORD, for I am with you. I will make a full end of all the nations to which I have driven you, but of you I will not make a full end. I will discipline you in just measure, and I will by no means leave you unpunished." (Jer. 46:27-28)

For Zion's Sake

When Jeremiah was commissioned as a prophet, the Lord told him: "Behold, I have put *my words* in your mouth . . . say to them everything that I command you. Do not be dismayed by them, lest I dismay you before them" (Jer. 1:9, 17; cf. 5:14). Likewise, Ezekiel was told, "Son of man, go to the house of Israel and speak with *my words* to them . . . Son of man, *all my words* that I shall speak to you receive in your heart, and hear with your ears" (Ezek. 3:4, 10). Peter made it clear that "no prophecy of Scripture comes from someone's own interpretation. For no prophecy was ever produced by the will of man, but men *spoke from God* as they were carried along by the Holy Spirit" (2 Pet. 1:20-21). We saw in chapter 2 how infuriated Balak was at the way Balaam consistently blessed Israel, but as Balaam explained to the Moabite king, "Must I not take care to speak what the LORD puts in my mouth?" (Num. 23:12). Interestingly, the Hebrew word translated "take care" in this verse is *shâmar*, meaning "to be watchful," "to guard," "to keep," "to pay special attention to," or "to protect." The essence of this word comes to the fore in one of the great restoration prophecies of Isaiah:

> "For Zion's sake I will not keep silent, and for Jerusalem's sake I will not be quiet, until her righteousness goes forth as brightness, and her salvation as a burning torch. The nations shall see your righteousness, and all the kings your glory, and you shall be called by a new name that the mouth of the LORD will give. You shall be a crown of beauty in the hand of the LORD, and a royal diadem in the hand of your God. You shall no more be termed Forsaken, and your land shall no more be termed Desolate, but you shall be called My Delight Is in Her, and your land Married; for the LORD delights in you, and your land shall be married. For as a young man marries a young woman, so shall your sons marry you, and as the bridegroom rejoices over the bride, so shall your God rejoice over you." (Isa. 62:1-5)

To have received such a prophecy from the Lord must have been like balm to Isaiah's burdened soul after all the judgments he had pronounced. But who spoke these words? Who declared that they would not remain silent? Was it Isaiah, God, or maybe the Messiah? I believe the answer is all three, with another voice joining the prophetic chorus centuries later: that of the church. In the very next verse, a vivid illustration is used that was taken from one of the customs of the day, and it is here that we find our Hebrew word *shâmar*:

> "On your walls, O Jerusalem, I have set watchmen [*shômerim*]; all the day and all the night they shall never be silent. You who put the LORD in remembrance, take no rest, and give Him no rest until He establishes Jerusalem and makes it a praise in the earth." (Isa. 62:6-7)

But when did Jerusalem *ever* become a praise in the earth *after* this promise was made? For centuries, the city, land, and people of Israel have been "a byword of cursing among the nations" (Zech. 8:13)—anything but a praise. But God inspired this prophetic promise, and since we know that His word never returns to Him void (Isa. 55:10-11), it must and will be fulfilled. As we read in one of Balaam's oracles, "God is not man, that He should lie, or a son of man, that He should change His mind. Has He said, and will He not do it? Or has He spoken, and will He not fulfill it?" (Num. 23:19). So what about these watchmen or *shomerim*? Who were they, and more to the point, do they still exist?

In one of Isaiah's earlier prophecies, we read the following: "One is calling to me from Seir, 'Watchman, what time of the night? Watchman, what time of the night?' The watchman says: 'Morning comes, and also the night. If you will inquire, inquire; come back again'" (Isa. 21:11-12). In ancient times, watchmen were appointed to keep constant vigil over a city. We have quite a unique example of this in Nehemiah, when the walls of Jerusalem were being rebuilt and Israel's enemies were trying to halt the work. Nehemiah wrote:

> Nevertheless we made our prayer to our God, and because of them we set a watch against them day and night... At the same time I also said to the people, "Let each man and his servant stay at night in Jerusalem, that they may be our guard by night and a working party by day." So neither I, my brethren, my servants, nor the men of the guard who followed me took off our clothes, except that everyone took them off for washing. (Neh. 4:9, 22-23, NKJV)

The task of the watchman was demanding and somewhat thankless but crucial to the protection and welfare of a city. He was responsible for looking out for messengers of good or bad tidings and for the approach of friend or foe. God accused Israel's leaders of being blind, slumbering, silent watchmen who had failed in their duty (Isa. 56:10; cf. 42:18-20). His response was to set true, *spiritual* watchmen over His people who would be preoccupied day and night with listening for and proclaiming the word of God to them. This was a solemn and formidable responsibility. Habakkuk declared, "I will take my stand at my watchpost and station myself on the tower, and look out to see what He will say to me" (Hab. 2:1). As we have seen, the prophets were not at liberty to speak of their own accord but only as God prompted them. However, if they remained silent after God had given fair warning, then they themselves would reap the consequences. There was no prophetic immunity. This was made very clear to Ezekiel:

> "Son of man, I have made you a watchman for the house of Israel. Whenever you hear a word from my mouth, you shall give them warning from me. If I

say to the wicked, 'You shall surely die,' and you give him no warning, nor speak to warn the wicked from his wicked way, in order to save his life, that wicked person shall die for his iniquity, but his blood I will require at your hand... So you, son of man, I have made a watchman for the house of Israel. Whenever you hear a word from my mouth, you shall give them warning from me." (Ezek. 3:17-18; 33:7)

The prophets did not shrink back, and it cost them dearly. But the more the watchmen called to the people, the more the people closed their ears. This was the Lord's indictment:

"I set watchmen over you, saying, 'Pay attention to the sound of the trumpet!' But they said, 'We will not pay attention.'" (Jer. 6:17)

"I have sent to you all my servants the prophets, sending them persistently, saying, 'Turn now every one of you from his evil way, and amend your deeds, and do not go after other gods to serve them, and then you shall dwell in the land that I gave to you and your fathers.' But you did not incline your ear or listen to me." (Jer. 35:15; cf. 7:25; 25:4; 29:19; 44:4)

"Say to them, 'As I live, declares the Lord GOD, I have no pleasure in the death of the wicked, but that the wicked turn from his way and live; turn back, turn back from your evil ways, for why will you die, O house of Israel?' ... Yet your people say, 'The way of the Lord is not just,' when it is their own way that is not just ... O house of Israel, I will judge each of you according to his ways." (Ezek. 33:11-20)

What a joy it must have been, then, for prophets like Isaiah to behold from their prophetic watchtowers "the feet of Him who brings good news, who publishes peace, who brings good news of happiness, who publishes salvation, who says to Zion, 'Your God reigns'" (Isa. 52:7; cf. Nah. 1:15; Rom. 10:15). These were the "feet" of the Messiah. As this prophecy continues:

The voice of your watchmen — they lift up their voice; together they sing for joy; for eye to eye they see the return of the LORD to Zion. Break forth together into singing, you waste places of Jerusalem, for the LORD has comforted [nâcham] His people; He has redeemed Jerusalem. (Isa. 52:8-9; cf. 33:17; 51:3, 11; Zech. 8:3)

How could they not rejoice! The watchmen were not simply fulfilling a duty; their hearts were engaged, their lives were on the line, and in the case of Ezekiel and Hosea, they had to endure tremendous personal heartache (Ezek. 24:15-18; Hos. 1:2-3; 3:1-3). But notice the reference in the Isaiah 52 prophecy to the watchmen seeing "eye to eye" the Lord returning to Zion. What did Isaiah mean?

In 1859, William McClure Thomson (1806-1894), an American evangelical Presbyterian missionary, who for many years resided in the Land of Israel (Palestine as it was known then), published an account of his experiences. Entitled *The Land and the Book*, it proved to be so popular in the United States that for the next forty years it was outsold only by Harriet Beecher Stowe's anti-slavery novel *Uncle Tom's Cabin* (1852). On his travels through God's land, Thomson witnessed firsthand the watchmen on the walls of Jerusalem and gave the following account:

> If you conceive of Zion as a city defended by walls and towers, and guarded by soldiers, the illustration is natural and striking, particularly in time of war. Then, as I myself have seen at Jerusalem, these watchmen are multiplied, and so stationed that every yard of the wall falls under their surveillance, and thus *they literally see eye to eye*. They never remit their watchfulness, nor do they keep silence, especially at night. When danger is apprehended they are obliged to call to one another and to respond every few minutes. The guard on the look-out at the Tower of David, for instance, lifts up his voice in a long call, the one next south of him takes up the note and repeats it, and thus it runs quite round the circuit of the walls. At Sidon the custom-house guards stationed around the city are required to keep one another awake and alert in the same way, particularly when there is danger of smuggling.[5]

For the past two thousand years, every true disciple of Jesus should have stationed themselves, metaphorically speaking, on the walls of Jerusalem. Seeing one another "eye to eye," they should have proclaimed with one voice all that God has spoken concerning Israel. Rightly interpreting the signs of the times, they should have recognized what (and more importantly, Who) is on the horizon and fast-approaching the city.

In Psalm 130, we find a beautiful expression of hope for God's people, which draws upon the watchman analogy:

> I wait for the LORD, my soul waits, and in His word I hope; my soul waits for the Lord more than watchmen for the morning, more than watchmen for

---

[5] William McClure Thomson, *The Land and the Book. Or, Biblical Illustrations Drawn from the Manners and Customs, the Scenes and Scenery of the Holy Land* (London: T. Nelson and Sons, 1858), p. 598 (emphasis added).

the morning. O Israel, hope in the LORD! For with the LORD there is steadfast love [*chesed*], and with Him is plentiful redemption. And He will redeem Israel from all his iniquities. (Ps. 130:5-8)

When all is said and done, one thing is clear: "Unless the LORD watches over the city, the watchman stays awake in vain" (Ps. 127:1). That applies to the life of an individual believer, to the ministry of a local fellowship or church denomination, and to the survival of Israel as a nation. Where Israel is concerned, the watchfulness of believers as spiritual watchmen on the walls of Jerusalem will not be in vain. Scripture is clear:

- ✡ God Himself watches over Jerusalem: "My eyes and my heart will be there for all time" (1 Kgs. 9:3).
- ✡ He Himself watches over His land: "The eyes of the LORD your God are always upon it" (Deut. 11:11).
- ✡ He Himself watches over His people: "Behold, He who keeps Israel will neither slumber nor sleep" (Ps. 121:4).

This begs the question: Why are there so many vacant posts along the "walls" of Jerusalem today?

A Vow of Non-Silence . . . and Praise

I believe the command to comfort God's people and speak to the heart of Jerusalem reaches its glorious climax in the "For Zion's sake" prophecy of Isaiah 62. The Holy One of Israel has invested so much in Zion that He cannot hold His peace. He will establish Jerusalem and make it "a praise in the earth" (Isa. 62:7). But what does this mean?

We know from God's Word that the Lord has commanded all nations to praise Him for His mighty works. Jerusalem's redemption will be among the mightiest! Here is what the psalmists declared as they called upon the nations to extol the Lord for His wondrous deeds:

Shout for joy to God, all the earth; sing the glory of His name; give to Him glorious praise! Say to God, "How awesome are your deeds! . . . All the earth worships you and sings praises to you; they sing praises to your name." (Ps. 66:1-4)

Let the peoples praise you, O God; let all the peoples praise you! Let the nations be glad and sing for joy, for you judge the peoples with equity and guide the nations upon earth. Let the peoples praise you, O God; let all the peoples praise you! (Ps. 67:3-5)

Oh sing to the LORD a new song; sing to the LORD, all the earth! ... Ascribe to the LORD, O families of the peoples, ascribe to the LORD glory and strength! Ascribe to the LORD the glory due His name ... The LORD reigns, let the earth rejoice; let the many coastlands be glad! ... Make a joyful noise to the LORD, all the earth; break forth into joyous song and sing praises! ... Make a joyful noise to the LORD, all the earth! (Ps. 96:1-8; 97:1; 98:4; 100:1)

A number of Hebrew words are used in the Old Testament for praising God. When we read in Isaiah 62:7 of Jerusalem becoming "a praise in the earth," the noun is *tehillâh*. The plural is *tehillîm*, which is the Hebrew name for the book of Psalms. The noun derives from the Hebrew verb *hâlal* meaning "to praise," "to glory," or "to boast." From this verb comes the more familiar word "hallelujah." Moses had once told the Israelites that it was God's intention to set them "in praise [*tehillâh*] and in fame and in honor high above all nations that He has made" (Deut. 26:19). Centuries later, God lamented through the Prophet Jeremiah: "I made the whole house of Israel and the whole house of Judah cling to me ... that they might be for me a people, a name, a praise [*tehillâh*], and a glory, but they would not listen" (Jer. 13:11). Therefore, if Jerusalem is to become "a praise in the earth," then all nations must one day praise God for all that He will have done for the city and His people.

Jerusalem has been repeatedly conquered during its long and tempestuous history. It was even renamed Aelia Capitolina in A.D. 135 in honor of Roman Emperor Hadrian partly as an attempt to sever the Jewish connection with the city. Emperor Constantine restored its name in A.D. 324. Supremely, of course, Jerusalem is the city where Jesus was betrayed, tried, crucified, and resurrected. It was from there that the Lord returned to heaven, and it is to the city that He will return in power and glory. Only then will Jerusalem become a praise in the earth. Through the prophecies of Isaiah, Jeremiah, and Zephaniah, the Lord has spoken so passionately and emphatically about how this will happen:

And nations shall come to your light, and kings to the brightness of your rising ... A multitude of camels shall cover you, the young camels of Midian and Ephah; all those from Sheba shall come. They shall bring gold and frankincense, and shall proclaim the praise [*t^ehillâh*] of the LORD . . . Your gates shall be open continually . . . that men may bring to you the wealth of the nations, with their kings led in procession . . . [T]hey shall call you the City of the LORD, the Zion of the Holy One of Israel . . . Violence shall no more be heard in your land, devastation or destruction within your borders; you shall call your walls Salvation, and your gates Praise [*t^ehillâh*]. (Isa. 60:3-18, RSV)

"Behold, I will bring to it [Jerusalem] health and healing, and I will heal them and reveal to them abundance of prosperity and security. I will restore the fortunes of Judah and the fortunes of Israel, and rebuild them as they were at first . . . And this city shall be to me a name of joy, a praise [*t^ehillâh*] and a glory before all the nations of the earth who shall hear of all the good that I do for them. They shall fear and tremble because of all the good and all the prosperity I provide for it." (Jer. 33:6-9)

"And I will save the lame and gather the outcast, and I will change their shame into praise [*t^ehillâh*] and renown in all the earth. At that time I will bring you in, at the time when I gather you together; for I will make you renowned and praised [*t^ehillâh*] among all the peoples of the earth, when I restore your fortunes before your eyes, says the LORD." (Zeph. 3:19-20)

With the rapture of the church imminent, the prophesied invasion of Gog and Magog fast approaching, and the Antichrist waiting in the wings to usher in Satan's new world order, who else but the true believer is going to speak tenderly to the heart of Jerusalem or rejoice at the prospect of what God is about to do with His *nachălâh*? If further incentive were needed for believers to station themselves on their appointed watchtowers and speak to the heart of Jerusalem, then consider three of the most extraordinary restoration prophecies found in the Old Testament:

For as a young man marries a young woman, so shall your sons marry you, and as the bridegroom rejoices over the bride, so shall your God rejoice over you. (Isa. 62:5)

"I will rejoice in doing them good, and I will plant them in this land in faithfulness, with all my heart and all my soul." (Jer. 32:41)

Sing aloud, O daughter of Zion; shout, O Israel! Rejoice and exult with all your heart, O daughter of Jerusalem! The LORD has taken away the judgments against you; He has cleared away your enemies. The King of Israel, the

LORD, is in your midst; you shall never again fear evil. On that day it shall be said to Jerusalem: "Fear not, O Zion; let not your hands grow weak. The LORD your God is in your midst, a mighty one who will save; He will rejoice over you with gladness; He will quiet you by His love; He will exult over you with loud singing." (Zeph. 3:14-17)

Did we hear that? The Creator of the universe and the Most High God has declared that He will one day rejoice—even sing—over His people. How great is our God, the God of Israel!

Conclusion

When the Ark of the Covenant was being brought up to Jerusalem, King David could be seen "leaping and dancing before the LORD" with "all his might" (2 Sam. 6:14-16). This evoked strong displeasure from his wife Michal, who was left barren for having despised the joy of the Lord in her husband's heart. How full the church is today of Michals who despise those who are rejoicing in the *nâcham* (comfort), *racham* (compassion), and *chesed* (loyal covenant love) of God toward His people. How spiritually barren the church is where love for Israel is absent.

As we have seen, believers are at liberty to speak only what God has spoken, but they must speak. In the words of Amos, "The Lord GOD has spoken; who can but prophesy?" (Am. 3:8). Consider the following as we draw this chapter to a close:

✥ If God has *not* spoken in His Word about replacing, fulfilling, retelling, enlarging, redefining, nullifying, reconstituting, universalizing, reinterpreting, incorporating, renewing, or even "Christifying" Israel, then how dare the church speak this way![6]

---

[6] For a comprehensive survey and analysis of replacement theology and its various manifestations, see: Robinson, *Israel Betrayed, Volume 1: The History of Replacement Theology*; Wilkinson, *Israel Betrayed, Volume 2: The Rise of Christian Palestinianism*.

- If God has *not* spoken about boycotting, divesting from, and sanctioning Israel, then how dare the church actively endorse the demonically driven B.D.S. campaign, which seeks to do these hateful things!
- If God has *not* spoken about joining forces with the godless nations and false religions of the world to denounce Israel, then how dare the church do so!
- If God has *not* spoken about the church being Israel's censor, judge, jury, police, and probation officer, then how dare the church assume these roles!
- **BUT** if God *has* spoken about the need to share the gospel with the Jewish people first, then how dare the church withhold from them the good news of Jesus!
- If God *has* spoken about salvation being in no other name but Jesus, then how dare the church suggest that Israel is saved through God's covenant with Abraham!
- If God *has* spoken about a future Temple and the tribulation horrors that await the nation of Israel, then how dare the church deny this and remain silent!
- **AND** if God *has* spoken so profoundly about the regathering, restoring, rebuilding, and rejoicing of Israel, then how can the church hold her peace?

We close this chapter with a poem written by James George Deck entitled "The Watchman's Cry." It is based on the words of Isaiah 21:11-12. Deck applied these verses to the church, which he believed was slumbering in the dark instead of looking, longing, and watching in the light for her heavenly Bridegroom:

The Watchman's Cry

"WATCHMAN, what of the night?"
It is gloomy, and thick, and dark:
Alas! wherever I turn my sight,
And seek for a faithful watcher's light,

I can scarcely discern a spark.
I hear the drunken reveler's cry,
The mocker's taunt, and the skeptic's lie;
But few believe that the Lord is nigh:
All is gloomy, and sad, and dark."

"Watchman, what of the night?"
"It is murky, and chill, and drear:
The lamps erst burning so clear and bright;
The hearts once glowing with warm delight,
At the hope that the Lord was near:
Many are quenched to burn no more;
Few are trimmed, and their luster pour:
Alas! the days of first-love are o'er;
All is murky, and chill, and drear."

"Watchman, what of the night?"
"Oh, list!—'tis the midnight cry!
It fills the sleepers with joy, or fright;
These cheeks grow pale, and those eyes grow bright!
The Bridegroom, He draweth nigh!
The slumbering virgins from sleep awake;
The wise their lamps fresh-trimmed all take;
The knees of the foolish with terror quake,
At the sound of the midnight cry."

"Watchman, what of the night?"
"The night is fast passing away;
The Morning-star, with effulgence bright,
Shall shortly burst on our raptured sight,
And usher the longed-for day.
He cometh! He cometh! awake! arise!
Behold! the Day-star illumines the skies;
Ye slumbering virgins, unveil your eyes,
The night is just passing away."

"Watchman, what of the night?" . . .
The work of the watchman is o'er:
"The morning's come, and also the night,"
Eternity's darkness—eternity's light.
'Inquire ye, . . . inquire ye no more.'
His word is ended, and work is done;

The marriage-supper is now begun;
The conflict over, the victory won:
The work of the watchman is o'er.[7]

---

[7] Deck, *Hymns and Sacred Poems*, pp. 183-84.

Chapter 12:

Jealous for Zion

For they provoked Him to anger with their high places; they moved Him to jealousy with their idols. When God heard, He was full of wrath, and He utterly rejected Israel. He forsook His dwelling at Shiloh, the tent where He dwelt among mankind . . . He gave His people over to the sword and vented His wrath on His heritage [*nachălâh*]. (Ps. 78:58-62)

Again the word of the LORD of hosts came, saying, "Thus says the LORD of hosts: 'I am zealous for Zion with great zeal; with great fervor I am zealous for her.' Thus says the LORD: 'I will return to Zion, and dwell in the midst of Jerusalem. Jerusalem shall be called the City of Truth, The Mountain of the LORD of hosts, The Holy Mountain.'" (Zech. 8:1-3, NKJV)

God is loving, God is merciful, God is gracious, God is compassionate, God is longsuffering, and God is faithful. This list could run on and on, to God's eternal glory. Such divine attributes are not only biblical, they are also beautiful and ever praiseworthy. No true believer will dispute their veracity. However, if we insert "God is jealous" into the list, then I suspect some of us may start to feel a little awkward, uneasy, or cautious, especially if we have ever experienced or been confronted with jealousy in our own lives. But this particular quality of God's nature cannot be separated from any of His other attributes. It is entirely in keeping with the rest and just as praiseworthy.

Revelation at Sinai

The first specific reference to God's jealousy is found in the Ten Commandments. The second commandment, as written by the finger of God, reads as follows:

"You shall not bow down to them or serve them, for I the LORD your God am a jealous God, visiting the iniquity of the fathers on the children to the third and the fourth generation of those who hate me, but showing steadfast love [*chesed*] to thousands of those who love me and keep my commandments." (Ex. 20:5-6; cf. Deut. 5:9)

The Hebrew word translated "jealous" is the adjective *qannâ'*, which is derived from the verb *qânâ'*, meaning "to be envious, jealous, or zealous," depending on the context. Whereas the verb occurs thirty-three times in Scripture, the adjective appears only six times and always in connection with God. The fact that *qannâ'* was first used on Mount Sinai by the Lord Himself is extremely significant, for it was at the foot of the mountain that God entered into what was effectively a marriage covenant with Israel. Furthermore, the use of such a word illustrates how the Ten Commandments were intended to be far more than just a series of laws or directives. They contained the self-revelation of God. This was to be foundational not only to God's covenant relationship with Israel but also with the church.

The second occurrence of *qannâ'* is in the account of the golden calf, when "Moses' anger burned hot" against the children of Israel (Ex. 32:19). On that infamous occasion, Moses broke the stone tablets at the foot of the mountain before later re-ascending to receive the commandments on a second set of tablets. He also received a grave warning from the Lord for the people:

> "Do not worship any other god, for the LORD, whose name is Jealous [*qannâ'*], is a jealous [*qannâ'*] God. Be careful not to make a treaty with those who live in the land; for when they prostitute themselves to their gods and sacrifice to them, they will invite you and you will eat their sacrifices. And when you choose some of their daughters as wives for your sons and those daughters prostitute themselves to their gods, they will lead your sons to do the same." (Ex. 34:14-16, NIV)

God's warning would go unheeded, and Israel would reap the whirlwind. But what we learn from this solemn declaration is one of the fundamental truths of the Bible: Not only is God a jealous God, but His very name is "Jealous." It is *who* He is! In Deuteronomy, with the Israelites about to cross into the Promised Land, Moses continued to warn the people not to forget the One who had brought them to Himself:

> Take care, lest you forget the covenant of the LORD your God . . . For the LORD your God is a consuming fire, a jealous [*qannâ'*] God. (Deut. 4:24; cf. Heb. 12:29)

> You shall not go after other gods, the gods of the peoples who are around you, for the LORD your God in your midst is a jealous [*qannâ'*] God, lest the anger of the LORD your God be kindled against you, and He destroy you from off the face of the earth. (Deut. 6:14-15)

Many years later, Joshua had no doubt that the people would ultimately provoke God's jealousy and cause His wrath to be kindled against them. When the tribes of Israel were assembled at Shechem to renew the covenant with God, Joshua declared:

> You are not able to serve the LORD, for He is a holy God. He is a jealous [*qannôw'*] God; He will not forgive your transgressions or your sins. If you forsake the LORD and serve foreign gods, then He will turn and do you harm and consume you, after having done you good. (Josh. 24:19-20)

An almost identical Hebrew adjective, *qannôw'*, is used here. Its only other occurrence is in the second verse of the book of Nahum, which reads:

> The LORD is a jealous [*qannôw'*] and avenging God; the LORD is avenging and wrathful; the LORD takes vengeance on His adversaries and keeps wrath for His enemies. (Nah. 1:2)

Whenever God acts, He does so with the utmost precision and dedication until His purpose is accomplished, and always in keeping with His character. It is sometimes said of a person who has behaved inappropriately that their behavior was "out of character," but this can never be said of the Lord. In one of the great restoration prophecies, God was at pains to underscore His dedication and dependability when He made this promise to His exiled people: "I will rejoice in doing them good, and I will plant them in this land in faithfulness, *with all my heart and all my soul*" (Jer. 32:41). God's commitment to fulfilling His promises, no matter how great the obstacles may be or how impossible their fulfillment may appear, is unwavering. Isaiah prophesied:

> Of the increase of His government and peace there shall be no end, upon the throne of David, and upon his kingdom, to order it, and to establish it with judgment and with justice from henceforth even for ever. The zeal of the LORD of hosts will perform this. (Isa. 9:7, KJV)

An immediate question arises: When was this section of the prophecy ever fulfilled? When did we ever see the One of whom the prophet spoke reign on David's throne (in Jerusalem) and over his kingdom (Israel), establishing it forever (as long as this earth endures)? Amillennialists in the church have caused untold damage by tampering with God's Word, claiming that Jesus is reigning now on David's throne in heaven! This claim is preposterous and makes a mockery of the text, for the language, context, and geography of the entire prophecy is centered around Jerusalem, the land of Israel, and the Jewish people.

Let us turn now to one of our opening scriptures and take a closer look at Zechariah 8. I would encourage you to read through the whole chapter before continuing because it is one of those "hand-over-the-mouth-in-awe-and-wonder" passages that speaks on so many levels about Israel's glorious future.

Burning with Jealousy

The reason I quoted Zechariah 8:1-3 from the New King James Version at the beginning of this chapter was to highlight the ardency in the Lord's voice: "I am zealous for Zion with great zeal; with great fervor I am zealous for her." If we compare this with other translations, then another important perspective emerges:

"I was jealous for Zion with great jealousy, and I was jealous for her with great fury." (KJV)

"I am jealous for Zion with great jealousy, and I am jealous for her with great fury." (DBY)

"I am jealous for Zion with great jealousy, and I am jealous for her with great wrath." (RSV, ASV, ESV)

"I am exceedingly jealous for Zion; yes, with great wrath I am jealous for her." (NASB)

"I am very jealous for Zion; I am burning with jealousy for her." (NIV)

All of the above translations are consistent in emphasizing that what God has felt and feels toward Zion is above and beyond zeal. He is *extremely jealous*! It is possible to be zealous without being jealous but not vice versa. One can be zealous about something without having any personal attachment to it, but jealousy implies a pre-existing association or relationship.

Here in Zechariah 8:2, God was restating what He had already declared in Zechariah 1:14 when the angel of the Lord told the prophet to cry out:

"I am jealous for Jerusalem and for Zion with a great jealousy." (KJV, ASV, DBY)

"I am zealous for Jerusalem and for Zion with great zeal." (NKJV)

"I am exceedingly jealous for Jerusalem and [for] Zion." (NASB, RSV, ESV)

"I am very jealous for Jerusalem and Zion." (NIV)

The repetition in Zechariah 1 and 8 and the use of adverbs like "exceedingly" and nouns like "fury" and "wrath" paint a very dramatic portrait of God's relationship with Zion, where "Zion" encompasses His land, His city, and His people. The name itself first occurs in 2 Samuel when David and his men captured "the stronghold of Zion" from the Jebusites in Jerusalem and renamed it "the city of David" (2 Sam. 5:7; 1 Chron. 11:5). Supremely, it became known as the city of God, the place where the Ark of the Covenant would finally come to rest and from where God would reign in the midst of His people. In David's time, God decreed that Zion would be the mountain from which His beloved Son and Messiah would one day rule over the nations with a rod of iron. The book of Psalms in particular is replete with references to Zion and the honor that God has bestowed upon it:

Then He will speak to them in His wrath, and terrify them in His fury, saying, "As for me, I have set my King on Zion, my holy hill." (Ps. 2:5-6)

Great is the LORD and greatly to be praised in the city of our God! His holy mountain, beautiful in elevation, is the joy of all the earth, Mount Zion, in the far north, the city of the great King. (Ps. 48:1-2)

Out of Zion, the perfection of beauty, God shines forth. (Ps. 50:2)

His abode has been established in Salem, His dwelling place in Zion. (Ps. 76:2)

He rejected the tent of Joseph; He did not choose the tribe of Ephraim, but He chose the tribe of Judah, Mount Zion, which He loves. (Ps. 78:67-68)

On the holy mount stands the city He founded; the LORD loves the gates of Zion more than all the dwelling places of Jacob. Glorious things of you are spoken, O city of God. (Ps. 87:1-3)

For the LORD has chosen Zion; He has desired it for His dwelling place: "This is my resting place forever; here I will dwell, for I have desired it." (Ps. 132:13-14)

The Hebrew verb translated "jealous" or "zealous" in Zechariah 1:14 is *qânâ'*. It is used elsewhere to describe barren Rachel's response to her sister Leah, who was able to conceive (Gen. 30:1), and the reaction of Jacob's sons toward their brother Joseph after he had revealed to them his dreams to them (Gen. 37:11). Integral to the meaning of this word is a pre-existing relationship between the subject who is jealous (e.g., Rachel) and the object of that jealousy (e.g. Leah). The object possesses something (the ability to bear children) that provokes an animated response from the subject (envy).[1] In Zechariah 8:2, the Hebrew word translated "jealousy" or "zeal" (KJV/NKJV) is *qin'âh* and is used to emphasize the passionate or fervent nature of *qânâ'*, a passion that provokes decisive action. If we insert the adverb *gādôwl* ("great") alongside *qin'âh*, then the expression is strengthened. If we then put the Hebrew noun *chêmâh* in the mix, which is typically translated "fury" or "wrath," then the emotion is intensified even further. If we now insert all these words into the KJV rendering of Zechariah 8:2, this is what we are left with: "I was jealous [*qânâ'*] for Zion with great [*gādôwl*] jealousy [*qin'âh*], and I was jealous [*qânâ'*] for her with great [*gādôwl*] fury [*chêmâh*]." The noun *chêmâh* is interesting because it stems from the verb *yâcham*, meaning "to be/become hot." Young's Literal Translation of this verse reads, "With great heat I have been zealous for her." The noun is used elsewhere to describe Esau's murderous intent after he had sold his birthright to his brother Jacob, before being cheated out of his father's blessing (Gen. 27:44). It was used to express the wrath of the Persian king Ahasuerus toward Haman after Esther had exposed his plot to annihilate the Jews (Est. 7:7). It was also used by Moses to depict the "hot displeasure" of the Lord when He was about to destroy the Israelites (Deut. 9:19) and by God Himself when He warned the remnant of Judah not to flee to Egypt following Jerusalem's destruction (Jer. 42:18). So, with *gādôwl* ("great") and *chêmâh* ("fury") alongside *qin'âh* ("jealousy") in Zechariah 8:2, God has left us with a most vivid and dramatic impression: **He is burning with furious jealousy for Zion!** That same jealousy also keeps the

---

[1] *Theological Wordbook of the Old Testament*, p. 802.

other nations in God's sights, for He is constantly assessing the way they relate to His people. As He declared through His prophets,

> "Surely in the fire of my jealousy [*qin'âh*] I have spoken against the rest of the nations, and against all Edom, who appropriated my land for themselves as a possession... Behold, I have spoken in my jealousy [*qin'âh*] and in my wrath [*chêmâh*] because you have endured the insults of the nations. Therefore thus says the Lord GOD, I have sworn that surely the nations which are around you will themselves endure their insults." (Ezek. 36:5-7, NASB)

> "I am exceedingly angry with the nations that are at ease; for while I was angry but a little, they furthered the disaster. Therefore, thus says the LORD, I have returned to Jerusalem with mercy; my house shall be built in it, declares the LORD of hosts, and the measuring line shall be stretched out over Jerusalem." (Zech. 1:15-16)

One nation or empire that was at ease was the Assyrian Empire. Nineveh, its capital and the city so mercifully spared in the days of Jonah, felt the full force of God's jealous wrath in 612 B.C. when it was conquered by the Babylonians. Nahum was the prophet who announced to the Ninevites that their time was up:

> God is jealous [*qannôw'*], and the LORD avenges; the LORD avenges and is furious [*chêmâh*]. The LORD will take vengeance on His adversaries, and He reserves wrath for His enemies; the LORD is slow to anger and great in power, and will not at all acquit the wicked. (Nah. 1:2-3, NKJV)

When we consider the heat of God's jealousy for Israel, is it any wonder that Satan has ignited fires of hatred among the nations? In his diabolical genius, he has even managed to incite a similar kind of hatred from within the church! The devil hates everything that is precious to God. On November 10, 1975, the United Nations General Assembly passed Resolution 3379, which legitimized anti-Semitism by declaring Zionism to be a form of racism. Many churchmen shamefully supported the resolution and have even continued to endorse it despite the UN's revocation in 1991. On that infamous occasion in 1975, the Israeli ambassador to the UN, Chaim Herzog (1918-1997), publicly condemned what he termed the "wicked resolution." With great indignation, he warned that the UN was "on its way to becoming the world center of anti-Semitism," suggesting that "Hitler would have felt at home . . . listening to the proceedings in this forum, and above all to the proceedings during the debate on Zionism."[2]

Great is Thy Faithfulness

The Hebrew verb *qânâ'* ("jealous/zealous") occurs most frequently within the context of marriage. In the Torah, for example, we see it used in the test for adultery. If an Israelite man became jealous of his wife and suspected her of unfaithfulness and she was found to be guilty, then the penalty was death (Num. 5:14; Lev. 20:10; Deut. 22:22). This was carried through to the marriage covenant that God made with Israel at Mount Sinai. There the Lord took to Himself a nation of redeemed slaves, promising to love, honor, and protect them provided they remained faithful. As God reminded the Israelites, "I bore you on eagles' wings and brought you to myself" (Ex. 19:4). The consequences of betraying and spurning the Lord would be grave: "Now therefore, if you will indeed obey my voice and keep my covenant, you shall be my treasured possession among all peoples, for all the earth is mine; and you shall be to me a kingdom of priests and a holy nation" (Ex. 19:5-6). After Moses had declared God's intentions, the people replied with one voice, "All that the LORD has spoken we will do" (Ex. 19:8). When the day came, the Lord descended on the mountain in fire, accompanied by thunder, lightning, a thick cloud, and a very loud trumpet blast that made the people tremble. Moses, like the father of the bride, "brought the people out of the camp to meet God, and they took their stand at the foot of the mountain" (Ex. 19:17). The terms of the marriage contract were later written by the finger of God on two stone tablets and given to Moses, the first of which made one thing very clear: "I the LORD your God am a jealous [*qannâ'*] God" (Ex. 20:5).

One of my favorite Christian hymns is "Great is Thy Faithfulness," which was written by Thomas Chisholm in 1923 and was based on the

---

[2] "Zionism Is Not Racism: A Speech 40 Years Ago," *Jerusalem Post*, November 9, 2015, www.jpost.com/Israel-News/Politics-And-Diplomacy/Zionism-is-not-racism-A-speech-40-years-ago-432506.

words of Lamentations 3:23. Our English word "faithfulness" in this lament is translated from the Hebrew word *'ĕmûwnâh*, which conveys the basic idea of firmness, steadiness, and certainty. It is used in its literal sense in the book of Exodus to describe the steadying of Moses' hands by Aaron and Hur during Israel's battle with the Amalekites (Ex. 17:12). Thus, when God took Israel to Himself at Sinai, He assured them of His unwavering devotion and loyalty. At the end of his life, in his prophetic song to Israel, Moses exalted the Lord with these words: "The Rock, His work is perfect, for all His ways are justice. A God of faithfulness [*'ĕmûwnâh*] and without iniquity, just and upright is He" (Deut. 32:4). Thus, the Lord had every right to expect fidelity from His people and warned them in no uncertain terms of the consequences of breaking their marriage vows. It was utterly inconceivable that His people would shame Him by committing spiritual adultery, but shame Him they did—and in the sight of the nations!

Idolatrous and Adulterous Israel

When we think of the word "jealousy" from a purely human perspective, it is difficult to pull away from its negative and destructive connotations. It is not a good attribute to have, as anyone who has ever struggled with jealousy will testify. In the words of James, "For where jealousy and selfish ambition exist, there will be disorder and every vile practice" (James 3:16; cf. 1 Cor. 3:3). King Solomon explained in Proverbs 6:34, "For jealousy [*qin'âh*] makes a man furious, and he will not spare when he takes revenge." In Proverbs 27:4, he added, "Wrath is cruel, anger is overwhelming, but who can stand before jealousy [*qin'âh*]?" This is how God sees jealousy in us: more damaging and potentially more dangerous than even wrath or anger. Perhaps this is because jealousy tends to be more hidden, it is more difficult to detect, it can fester for years before showing itself, and it can manifest itself in such a variety of ways that the person harboring it may be completely oblivious. With God, however, the opposite is true.

Since we know that there is nothing intrinsically dark, cruel, manipulative, or out of control with the Lord, His jealousy has to be understood and expressed differently from man's. The jealousy of God is inherently protective and reassuring, even though the consequences of provoking it are extremely serious indeed. When the people of Israel were faithful, there was peace, prosperity, and security. Their armies were victorious, their enemies were fearful, their harvests were abundant, their flocks and herds multiplied, and their women were fruitful in the womb—just as God had promised (Lev. 26:3-13; Deut. 28:1-14). During the high point of Solomon's reign, every man from Dan to Beersheba lived in peace and security, dwelling "under his vine and under his fig tree" (1 Kgs. 4:25). As noted previously, when the Queen of Sheba visited Solomon and witnessed the nation's prosperity, "there was no more spirit in her" (1 Kgs. 10:5, RSV). Her response must have delighted not only the king but also the Lord Himself, whom she publicly honored with this benediction: "Blessed be the LORD your God, who has delighted in you and set you on the throne of Israel! Because the LORD loved Israel forever, He has made you king, that you may execute justice and righteousness" (1 Kgs. 10:9).

Tragically, for all his great wisdom, Solomon foolishly entered into forbidden marriages and allowed his wives to steal away his heart from the Lord. God's jealousy was provoked, the nation was divided, and the history of God's people was thereafter riddled with idolatry and infidelity. Yet, for all their waywardness, God repeatedly called His people to return and renew their vows. The Hebrew word *shâkam*, which literally means "to rise early to work," was used by the Lord to express His persistence in appealing to faithless Israel. As we read in the book of Jeremiah,

> "And now, because you have done all these works," says the LORD, "and I spoke to you, rising up early [*shâkam*] and speaking, but you did not hear, and I called you, but you did not answer, therefore I will do to the house which is called by my name, in which you trust, and to this place which I gave to you and your fathers, as I have done to Shiloh... For this city has been to me a provocation of my anger and my fury from the day that they built it, even to this day... And they have turned to me the back, and not the face; though I taught them, rising up early [*shâkam*] and teaching them, yet they have not listened to receive instruction." (Jer. 7:13-14; 32:30-33; cf. 7:25; 11:7; 26:5; 29:19; 35:15, NKJV)

In 2 Chronicles 36, which concludes the *Tanakh* (the Hebrew arrangement of the Scriptures), the same expression is used with a palpable sense of melancholy:

And the LORD God of their fathers sent warnings to them by His messengers, rising up early [*shâkam*] and sending them ... But they mocked the messengers of God, despised His words, and scoffed at His prophets, until the wrath of the LORD arose against His people, till there was no remedy. (2 Chron. 36:15-16, NKJV)

God was so offended by His people's infidelity that He used the most explicit language to chasten them. He accused Israel of adultery, harlotry, wantonness, prostitution, and whoredom and told His people that not even righteous Noah, Daniel, and Job would have been able to turn away His judgments (Ezek. 14:12-23; cf. Hos. 4:10-5:4). Such was the nature and extent of Israel's unfaithfulness that the Lord's only recourse was to send her away with a certificate of divorce (Isa. 50:1; Jer. 3:8; cf. Hos. 2:2). The Lord expressed not only indignation as the forsaken God of Israel but also anguish as the betrayed "Husband." We can sense His emotion in the way He cross-examined His wayward "wife":

"O Israel, if you would but listen to me! ... But my people did not listen to my voice; Israel would not submit to me ... Oh, that my people would listen to me, that Israel would walk in my ways!" (Ps. 81:8-13)

"What more was there to do for my vineyard, that I have not done in it? When I looked for it to yield grapes, why did it yield wild grapes?" (Isa. 5:4)

"What wrong did your fathers find in me that they went far from me, and went after worthlessness, and became worthless?" (Jer. 2:5)

"O my people, what have I done to you? How have I wearied you? Answer me!" (Mic. 6:3)

Israel forsook the Lord by turning to impotent idols, false gods that could not see, hear, speak, smell, walk, deliver, or tell the future.[3] Carpenters, ironsmiths, silversmiths, and goldsmiths had fashioned these worthless idols and had become worthless themselves. Blind to the utter futility and stupidity of worshiping a piece of wood, metal, or stone, the people were shamed by the Lord. As He put it to them,

"What profit is an idol when its maker has shaped it, a metal image, a teacher of lies? For its maker trusts in his own creation when he makes speechless idols! Woe to him who says to a wooden thing, Awake; to a silent stone,

---

[3] See Isa. 41:21-29; 44:9-20; 46:5-7; Ps. 115:4-7.

Arise! Can this teach? Behold, it is overlaid with gold and silver, and there is no breath at all in it. But the LORD is in His holy temple; let all the earth keep silence before Him." (Hab. 2:18-20)

A Cup of Fury . . . and of Comfort

Jerusalem was to bear the brunt of God's jealous wrath. He had placed her in the midst of the nations and at the center of the earth to be a light to the Gentiles, a torch that would burn brightly with His holiness and truth (Ezek. 5:5; cf. 38:12). On account of her vile abominations, which even exceeded those of the surrounding nations, God likened "the bloody city" to an "adulterous wife" and "a brazen prostitute" who had "multiplied [her] whoring" (Ezek. 22:2; 24:6-9; 16:20-36). Ezekiel was shown these abominations in a vision and saw in the Temple "the seat of the image of jealousy [*qin'âh*], which provokes to jealousy [*qânâ'*]" (Ezek. 8:3-5). In a chilling fulfillment of Moses' prophetic song, God's people had "stirred Him to jealousy [*qânâ'*] with strange gods; with abominations they provoked Him to anger" (Deut. 32:16; cf. Ps.78:58). The land was "full of adulterers" (Jer. 23:10), and the inhabitants of God's city had become like Sodom and Gomorrah (Jer. 23:14; cf. Isa. 1:10; Ezek. 16:44-58). Now they would drink from the cup of God's wrath as Isaiah had foretold:

> Wake yourself, wake yourself, stand up, O Jerusalem, you who have drunk from the hand of the LORD the cup of His wrath [*chêmâh*], who have drunk to the dregs the bowl, the cup of staggering . . . These two things have happened to you—who will console you?—devastation and destruction, famine and sword; who will comfort [*nâcham*] you? (Isa. 51:17-19)

Few chapters gauge the temperature of God's jealousy as profoundly as Ezekiel 5 and the pronouncement of God's sentence upon His people:

> "And because of all your abominations I will do with you what I have never yet done, and the like of which I will never do again . . . My eye will not spare, and I will have no pity . . . Thus shall my anger spend itself, and I will vent my fury [*chêmâh*] upon them and satisfy myself [*nâcham*]. And they shall know that I am the LORD — that I have spoken in my jealousy [*qin'âh*] — when I spend my fury [*chêmâh*] upon them . . . You shall be a reproach and a taunt, a warning and a horror, to the nations all around you, when I execute

judgments on you in anger and fury [*chêmâh*], and with furious [*chêmâh*] rebukes — I am the LORD; I have spoken." (Ezek. 5:9-15)

The number of references in these verses to "fury" (*chêmâh*) illustrates how utterly offensive Israel's behavior had become. However, the way in which God spoke about the effect Jerusalem's judgment would have *upon Himself* opens for us yet another window into His heart.

The Lord declared that by venting His fury, He would "satisfy" Himself (RSV, ESV) or be "avenged" (NKJV, NIV), "appeased" (NASB, NET), or "comforted" (KJV, ASV, RV, YLT). It may have surprised the reader to see the Hebrew word *nâcham* in this text, having looked at this word in some detail in chapter 10. Our focus then was on God's consolation of Israel, but here we are told that *God Himself* would be comforted or satisfied/avenged/appeased. The emphasis is even stronger in Darby's New Translation (DBY): "I will comfort myself." Without this disclosure, we might have considered Ezekiel 5 to have been merely a judicial sentence that was executed by God to satisfy His justice. No doubt this was an important aspect of what happened, for as the Lord later declared, "So will I satisfy my wrath [*chêmâh*] on you, and my jealousy [*qin'âh*] shall depart from you" (Ezek. 16:42), and "I also will clap my hands, and I will satisfy my fury" (Ezek. 21:17). However, the use of *nâcham* in Ezekiel 5 suggests to my mind that something more was going on than just appeasement, vengeance, or the satisfaction of justice.

The Brokenness of God

As a general rule, it is worth comparing different Bible versions when studying Scripture, for they all have their strengths and weaknesses. A look at some of the earliest English Bibles will often yield additional insights. In the case of Ezekiel 5:13, it is interesting to note that the first English translation, known as the Wycliffe Bible ("Later Version," 1395), along with the immensely popular Geneva Bible (1560), the Bishops' Bible (1568), and the King James Version (1611), all used the word "comforted" when translating *nâcham* in this verse. Those responsible for the New King James Version clearly thought they had good reason to change "comforted" to "avenged," and that would certainly appear to have been more in keeping with the rest of the verse and the chapter as a whole. I am neither a Bible translator nor a Hebrew scholar, but the broader context of the prophetic scriptures and the self-revelation of God throughout suggests to me that an important perspective may have been lost in translation. I also wonder whether it is simply beyond the scope of the English language to do justice to *nâcham* in this particular context.

Let us recall that the root meaning of *nâcham* reflects the idea of breathing deeply, thereby signifying deep emotion. In Ezekiel 5, words like "fury," "wrath," "anger," "destruction," "jealousy," "pestilence," "famine," "sword," "blood," and "judgment" unmistakably reveal the depth of feeling on God's part toward Jerusalem on account of her abominations. Moreover, when we hear God say, "And they shall know that I am the LORD — that I have spoken in my jealousy" (Ezek. 5:13), I believe we are hearing God speak in a predominantly marital context as the betrayed Husband. The Lord continued to speak in the same vein for the next few chapters, scrutinizing His people's behavior and promising a thorough purge. However, early in chapter 6, a ray of hope suddenly breaks through the dark clouds of divine judgment as God makes a promise: "I will leave some of you alive" (Ezek. 6:8; cf. 14:22-23). Yet, the privileged survivors would "be loathsome in their own sight for the evils that they have committed, for all their abominations" (Ezek. 6:9; cf. 16:54, 61-63) But what is particularly striking about this text is the way in which God speaks about the injury that His people had inflicted upon Him:

> "When you have among the nations some who escape the sword, and when you are scattered through the countries, then those of you who escape will remember me among the nations where they are carried captive, how I have been broken over their whoring heart that has departed from me and over their eyes that go whoring after their idols." (Ezek. 6:9)

Another translation has God saying, "because I was crushed by their adulterous heart" (NKJV). The Hebrew word God used here is the verb *shâbar*, which in different contexts can mean to "break," "break in pieces," "break down," "destroy," "smash," "shatter," or "crush." It is used, for example, of Moses when he broke the stone tablets at the foot of Mount Sinai (Ex. 32:19). The word is used most frequently in the book of Jeremiah, notably when God instructed His prophet to purchase and then break a potter's earthenware flask in the sight of the elders of Jerusalem. This was to symbolize the way in which God was going to "break this people and this city, as one breaks a potter's vessel, so that it can never be mended" (Jer. 19:11; cf. Isa. 30:14). Elsewhere God promised to break the yoke of those who had oppressed His people, especially Egypt, Assyria, and Babylon.[4] However, in Ezekiel 6 we have a unique use of the verb. Instead of describing what God has done to His people, *shâbar* is used by God Himself to describe what His people have done to Him: They have broken His heart; they have crushed Him.[5] Why tell such an adulterous people that they had broken His heart? Why use such language if this was merely a case of divine justice being satisfied?

We should note once again that in His divine *foreknowledge*, God knew that His people would betray Him. As He told Moses,

> "Behold, you are about to lie down with your fathers. Then this people will rise and whore after the foreign gods among them in the land that they are entering, and they will forsake me and break my covenant that I have made with them." (Deut. 31:16)

Centuries later the Lord addressed His people through the Prophet Isaiah: "For I knew that you would surely deal treacherously, and that from before birth you were called a rebel" (Isa. 48:8).

This makes the language in Ezekiel 6 all the more remarkable: God foreknew what would happen, yet when it did it broke His heart. Who among us can possibly comprehend what it was that the Lord experienced in His heart when He foretold Israel's betrayal and when it came to pass? Even so, there may be some reading this right now who have endured great personal heartache on account of their children's rebellion or even the betrayal of a spouse. I believe they will be able to identify more closely with God's anguish. The Lord is gracious and does not disclose everything that lies ahead for us in this life so that we can live out our days in faith, not fear. Yet, the Lord Himself willingly chose to bear the pain and sorrow of being

---

[4] Isa. 14:25; 21:9; Jer. 28:2-11; 30:8; 43:13; 48:4-38; 49:35; 50:23; 51:8-30; 52:17; Ezek. 30:8-24; 31:12; 32:28; 34:27; Am. 1:5; Nah. 1:13.

[5] Jeremiah, who is known as "the weeping prophet," uses the same word to describe the brokenness he felt on account of his people (Jer. 8:21; 23:9; Lam. 3:4).

spurned by His beloved people. This is a reminder to us that wherever we turn in Scripture, we are never too far from the cross!

When we reflect on the extent to which God has long suffered with His people, well might we declare with Moses, "Who is like you, O LORD, among the gods?" (Ex. 15:11), or with the psalmist, "Your thoughts are very deep!" (Ps. 92:5). We might also declare with Micah, "Who is a God like you, pardoning iniquity and passing over transgression for the remnant of His inheritance [*nachălâh*]?" (Mic. 7:18). In His jealousy, God opened His heart. In His justice, He punished. In His righteousness, He purged. In His holiness, He withdrew. Yet, in His compassion, He yearned. In His grace, He promised. In His mercy, He made a way. In His love, He sent forth His Son to be a sacrifice for His people. In His appointed time, He will "hasten" the resurrection of Israel (Isa. 60:22; cf. Ezek. 37:11-14; Rom. 11:15). Glory to God!

In summary, when we read in certain translations of Ezekiel 5:13 words like "appease," "avenge," or "satisfy," I believe something vitally important is missing. Yes, God's justice was satisfied, His name vindicated, His fury quenched, His betrayers punished, and His house of prayer cleansed. But when we insert the word "comfort" into our thinking, then I believe we are given greater scope to appreciate more fully the depth of God's love for and anguish over His people Israel.

Just because God may be speaking in His wrath and acting punitively toward His people does not negate the fact that He is love and full of grace. Just because He may be delivering a devastating blow to His own people—even destroying His own city and Temple—does not alter the fact that He is merciful, forgiving, and always seeking to restore. Just because He is a jealous God who will not entertain rivals does not downgrade Him to our human level, for *His* jealousy is pure, holy, and good. Just because He promises death and desolation does not mean there is no room for resurrection and renewal. Just because Israel was judged in full measure and exiled does not mean that God changed His mind and started over with a new people, thereby committing adultery Himself! Just because the name "Israel" appears in the New Testament does not give the church any warrant for redefining and reinterpreting that sacred name or the promises associated with those who rightly bear it.

God's Honor Killing

From the outset, the nation of Israel was diligently schooled in the jealousy of God. While the people faithfully kept covenant, the nation was held secure in a blessed state of supernatural protection and bountiful provision. When the covenant was broken, God's jealousy became a burdensome yoke and a threat to Israel's existence. In Numbers 25, another aspect of divine jealousy comes to the fore in a very dramatic and shocking manner. Enter Phinehas.

Having bidden farewell to Balaam and the curse-conspiring king of Moab, we find the men of Israel whoring with the daughters of Moab and worshiping their gods (Num. 25:1-3; Ps. 106:28). They had yoked themselves to the Baal of Peor, committing spiritual adultery in full view of the Moabites. Those culpable were executed and ignominiously hung up in the sun as a warning from God that such behavior would not be tolerated. However, while justice was being served and the people were weeping before the Tabernacle, an Israelite man (Zimri) brought a Midianite woman (Cozbi) into the camp in full view of Moses, the people, and God. As soon as Aaron's grandson, Phinehas, saw what was happening, he "stood up and intervened" (Ps. 106:30) and executed the offending couple with his spear.

Twenty-four thousand Israelites died as a result of God's judgment.[6] Had Phinehas not intervened when he did *and* in the manner in which he did, the number would have been considerably higher. Had he simply acted in anger and taken justice into his own hands, then he himself would have been put to death. However, God revealed to Moses the motivation of Phinehas' heart and honored him accordingly:

"Phinehas the son of Eleazar, son of Aaron the priest, has turned back my wrath [*chêmâh*] from the people of Israel, in that he was jealous [*qânâ'*] with my jealousy [*qin'âh*] among them, so that I did not consume the people of Israel in my jealousy [*qin'âh*]. Therefore say, 'Behold, I give to him my covenant of peace, and it shall be to him and to his descendants after him the

---

[6] Probably one thousand by execution and twenty-three thousand by plague (cf. 1 Cor. 10:8).

covenant of a perpetual priesthood, because he was jealous [*qânâ'*] for his God and made atonement for the people of Israel.'" (Num. 25:11-13)

Phinehas was so consumed with holy zeal for God's honor that he could not bear to see a fellow Israelite defy Him in such a brazen manner. What he did "was counted to him as righteousness from generation to generation forever" (Ps. 106:31). For God to make such an example of Phinehas reveals how much He delights in seeing His own character imprinted on the hearts and minds of His people. But there was to be another man whose jealousy for God's honor would far surpass that of Phinehas, a man who would be forever singled out and esteemed by God as the One in whom He was "well pleased."[7]

The Jealousy of Jesus

During his absence from the Corinthian church, Paul's ministry was undermined by the work of false apostles whom he labeled "deceitful workmen" and servants of Satan (2 Cor. 11:13-15). Compelled by the Holy Spirit to write, he admonished the Corinthians with these words:

> For I am jealous for you with a godly jealousy; for I betrothed you to one husband, so that to Messiah I might present you as a pure virgin. But I am afraid that, as the serpent deceived Eve by his craftiness, your minds will be led astray from the simplicity and purity of devotion to Messiah. (2 Cor. 11:2-3)

Paul's jealousy for the Corinthians and for all the churches under his care emanated from the heart of Jesus Himself. This is perhaps best captured by the RSV and ESV translations, which read: "I feel a divine jealousy for you." Many times in his letters, the apostle expressed deep love for his brethren. He yearned for the Philippians "with the affection of Messiah Jesus" (Phil. 1:8), he was "affectionately desirous" of the Thessalonians "like a nursing mother taking care of her own children" (1 Thess. 2:7-8), and he held the Corinthians in his heart "to die together and to live together" (2 Cor. 7:3). James referred to the same kind of jealousy when he wrote: "Do

---

[7] Mt. 3:17; 12:18; 17:5; Mk. 1:11; Lk. 3:22; 2 Pet. 1:17.

you suppose it is to no purpose that the Scripture says, 'He yearns jealously over the spirit that he has made to dwell in us'?" (James 4:5).

The Greek word translated "jealousy" in 2 Corinthians 11:2 is *zēlos*, from which we get our English words "zeal," "zealous," and "zealot." It is the word used in the Greek translation (LXX) of the Phinehas text in Numbers 25 and all of the primary Old Testament verses we have considered in this chapter. The noun comes from the verb *zēō*, meaning "to boil" or "to glow with heat." Figuratively, then, it conveys the idea of burning or boiling over with zeal. By using the word *zēlos* in his letter, Paul was expressing a concern that transcended the human realm. He had established the church in Corinth through his gospel preaching and apostolic ministry and, in that sense, had become their "father" (1 Cor. 4:15). However, from a heavenly perspective, he had betrothed the Corinthian believers to the Savior. They had become part of Jesus' bride.[8] It was Paul's responsibility to keep them in a state of perpetual readiness for the day when the Bridegroom receives the bride to Himself,[9] takes her to the Father's house,[10] and celebrates the marriage supper of the Lamb.[11]

Paul also used the verb *zēō* to exhort the believers in Rome to be "fervent in spirit" for the things of God (Rom. 12:11; cf. 2 Cor. 9:2). Before his Damascus-road encounter with the risen Lord, Saul—as he was known then—had been "extremely zealous [*zēlōtēs*]" for the law of Moses and the traditions of his fathers to such an extent that he had tried to destroy the church (Gal. 1:14; cf. Acts 22:3; Phil. 3:6). Like so many of his fellow Jews both then and now, his zeal had not been based on knowledge, having been "ignorant of the righteousness that comes from God" through faith in Jesus (Rom. 10:1-4). Following his life-changing encounter with the Lord, Paul did his utmost to edify the church by exhorting every believer to be fervent in their devotion. As he wrote in his pastoral letter to Titus:

> For the grace of God has appeared, bringing salvation for all people, training us to renounce ungodliness and worldly passions, and to live self-controlled,

---

[8] Mt. 9:15; 25:1-10; Jn. 3:29; Eph. 5:22-33; Rev. 19:7; 21:9; 22:17.

[9] 1 Thess. 4:13-18; 1 Cor. 15:50-57; Jn. 14:3.

[10] Jn. 14:2-4.

[11] Rev. 19:6-9; cf. Mt. 22:1-14; 25:1-13.

upright, and godly lives in the present age, waiting for our blessed hope, the appearing of the glory of our great God and Saviour Jesus the Messiah, who gave Himself for us to redeem us from all lawlessness and to purify for Himself a people for His own possession who are zealous [*zēlōtēs*] for good works. (Titus 2:11-14)

The only person who is actually labeled *zēlōtēs* in the New Testament is Simon the Zealot, one of the original twelve disciples of Jesus (Mt. 10:4; Mk. 3:18; Acts 1:13). Simon had previously belonged to a militant sect of Judaism known as the Zealots, who would later revolt against Rome. Interestingly, one of the great heroes of this sect and of the earlier Maccabean movement was "Phinehas the Zealot," as he is referred to in the apocryphal book 4 Maccabees. In the Gospel accounts, it is Luke who uses the word *zēlōtēs* to identify Simon (Lk. 6:15; cf. Acts 1:13). Matthew and Mark use the word *Kananaios*, which has been translated in our English Bibles as "Cananaean," "Cananite," "Canaanite" (not to be confused with "Canaanite" in the Old Testament), and "Zealot" (Mt. 10:4; Mk. 3:18). This Greek word *Kananaios* may sound familiar to the reader, for it is derived from the Hebrew/Aramaic word *qannâ'*, which, as we have observed in this chapter, means "jealous." Thus, Simon had been a jealous patriot of Israel before his jealousy was sanctified by the Lord.

Although the Messianic ministry of Jesus was supremely characterized by divine jealousy, the only occurrence of the Greek word *zēlos* in the Gospels is found in John's account of the cleansing of the Temple. After Jesus had driven out the sellers and money-changers, "His disciples remembered that it was written, 'Zeal for your house will consume me'" (Jn. 2:17; cf. Ps. 69:9). The Lord's whole life was characterized by His devotion and obedience to the Father. At the age of twelve, He famously stayed behind in Jerusalem after His traveling party from Nazareth had departed following the Feast of Passover. When Mary and Joseph, who had searched for Him for three days, eventually found Jesus, they were astonished to hear Him ask, "Did you not know that I must be in my Father's house?" or, as other translations read, "Did you not know that I must be about my Father's business?" (Lk. 2:49). Years later, Jesus told His disciples, "My food is to do the will of Him who sent me and to accomplish His work" (Jn. 4:34). During the last Passover supper that He ate with them, He made it very clear why He had to finish His work at the cross: "I do as the Father has commanded me, so that the world may know that I love the Father" (Jn. 14:31). In the words of Charles Spurgeon, one of the most zealous preachers the world has known,

> Zeal for God is so little understood by men of the world, that it always draws down opposition upon those who are inspired with it; they are sure to be accused of sinister motives, or of hypocrisy, or of being out of their senses. When zeal eats us up, ungodly men seek to eat us up too, and this was pre-eminently the case with our Lord, because his holy jealousy was pre-eminent. With more than a seraph's fire he glowed, and consumed himself with his fervor.[12]

Conclusion

The jealousy of God is to be feared by the faithless but cherished by the faithful. It can be all-consuming yet all-embracing. We have considered in this chapter some of the most devastating pronouncements that God ever made to Israel and that appeared to sound the death knell for the nation. But Israel lives! The jealousy of God has, at times, burned fiercely against His people, but it has ultimately preserved them, for God's name is upon Israel. It is this same jealousy that will ultimately consume those who have despised the Lord and tried to destroy His precious *nachălâh*. Contrast the respective outcomes for the nations and for Israel according to Ezekiel 38, the fulfillment of which is now imminent:

> "But on that day, the day that Gog shall come against the land of Israel, declares the Lord GOD, my wrath [*chêmâh*] will be roused in my anger. For in my jealousy [*qin'ah*] and in my blazing wrath I declare, On that day there shall be a great earthquake in the land of Israel... With pestilence and bloodshed I will enter into judgment with him [Gog], and I will rain upon him and his hordes and the many peoples who are with him torrential rains and hailstones, fire and sulphur. So I will show my greatness and my holiness and make myself known in the eyes of many nations. Then they will know that I am the LORD." (Ezek. 38:18-23)

> "Now I will restore the fortunes of Jacob and have mercy on the whole house of Israel, and I will be jealous [*qânâ'*] for my holy name. They shall forget

---

[12] Spurgeon, *The Treasury of David, Vol. II*, pp. 178-79.

their shame and all the treachery they have practiced against me, when they dwell securely in their land with none to make them afraid, when I have brought them back from the peoples and gathered them from their enemies' lands, and through them have vindicated my holiness in the sight of many nations . . . I will leave none of them remaining among the nations anymore. And I will not hide my face anymore from them, when I pour out my Spirit upon the house of Israel, declares the Lord GOD." (Ezek. 39:25-29; cf. Joel 2:18)

The God of restoration and retribution is also the God of reversal. This theme is prominent throughout the prophetic scriptures, teaching us that no sentence is ever complete until God has finished speaking:

"For thus says the LORD: Just as I have brought all this great disaster upon this people, so I will bring upon them all the good that I promise them." (Jer. 32:42)

"As you rejoiced over the inheritance of the house of Israel, because it was desolate, so I will deal with you; you shall be desolate, Mount Seir, and all Edom, all of it." (Ezek. 35:15)

"As I purposed to bring disaster to you when your fathers provoked me to wrath, and I did not relent, says the LORD of hosts, so again have I purposed in these days to bring good to Jerusalem and to the house of Judah; fear not." (Zech. 8:14-15)

In the final reckoning, Israel's story is not about *the nation* of Israel but about *the God* of Israel! Since May 14, 1948, the nations of the earth have been confronted every day with the reality of Israel's existence as a sovereign state, but instead of blessing Israel, they have cursed her. The clamor of contempt toward God's earthly inheritance is rising to a crescendo, but He hears and records every note and sound. Many Palestinian Arabs mistakenly and malevolently claim God's inheritance as their own while powerful nations like Russia look on, poised to plunder a piece of Israel's pie and "seize great spoil" (Ezek. 38:10-13). Many nations are indifferent and much of the church is ignorant, but God is indignant!

When we stop and reflect upon the greatness and goodness of God, whose compassion eclipses His condemnation, how can we not cry out with David, "Such knowledge is too wonderful for me; it is high; I cannot attain it" (Ps. 139:6). How can we not exclaim with Paul, "Oh, the depth of the riches and wisdom and knowledge of God! How unsearchable are His judgments and how inscrutable His ways!" (Rom. 11:33). May those in the church who have cast Israel aside and adopted, either in ignorance or in arrogance, a theology that the Bible knows nothing of, humbly confess with Job, "I have uttered what I did not understand, things too wonderful for me, which I did not know" (Job 42:3). Charles Spurgeon, who understood the promises of God concerning Israel's physical and spiritual restoration,[13] wrote in his commentary on Psalm 139 words that I would like to apply to the theme and thrust of this chapter:

> Mount as I may, this truth is too lofty for my mind. It seems to be always above me, even when I soar into the loftiest regions of spiritual thought. Is it not so with every attribute of God? Can we attain to any idea of his power, his wisdom, his holiness? Our mind has no line with which to measure the Infinite. Do we therefore question? Say, rather, that we therefore believe and adore. We are not surprised that the Most Glorious God should in his knowledge be high above all the knowledge to which we can attain: it must of necessity be so, since we are such poor limited beings; and when we stand a-tip-toe we cannot reach to the lowest step of the throne of the Eternal.[14]

The final Hebrew word of the Old Testament, according to the arrangement of books in our English Bibles, is *chêrem*, which is usually translated "destruction" or "curse." But God had not finished speaking about Israel when the Prophet Malachi fell silent. In the very next sentence of God's Word, in the first verse of the New Testament, we read these momentous words: "The book of the genealogy of Jesus the Messiah, the son of David,

---

[13] In the sermon he preached on Ezekiel 37 at his Metropolitan Tabernacle in London in 1864, Spurgeon declared, "The meaning of our text, as opened up by the context, is most evidently, if words mean anything, first, that there shall be a political restoration of the Jews to their own land and to their own nationality; and then, secondly, there is in the text, and in the context, a most plain declaration, that there shall be a spiritual restoration, a conversion in fact, of the tribes of Israel . . . There will be a native government again; there will again be the form of a body politic; a state shall be incorporated, and a king shall reign . . . I wish never to learn the art of tearing God's meaning out of His own words . . . Let this be settled . . . that if there be meaning in words, Israel is yet to be restored." (Charles Haddon Spurgeon, *The Restoration and Conversion of the Jews: A Sermon Preached on Thursday Evening, June 16th, 1864 . . . at the Metropolitan Tabernacle, Newington, in Aid of the Funds of the British Society for the Propagation of the Gospel amongst the Jews* [Pasadena, TX: Pilgrim Publications, n.d.], pp. 428-29).

[14] Spurgeon, *The Treasury of David, Vol. III*, p. 260.

the son of Abraham" (Mt. 1:1). In that opening announcement, God declared to the world that all His promises to the nation of Israel were about to be confirmed through one Man! Hope was to be rekindled and faith fortified by news that the King of all comfort was coming.

Chapter 13:

The King of Israel

> Blessed be the LORD! for He has heard the voice of my supplications... The LORD is the strength of His people, He is the saving refuge of His anointed. O save thy people, and bless thy heritage [*nachălâh*]; be thou their shepherd, and carry them for ever. (Ps. 28:6-9, RSV)
>
> The LORD has taken away the judgments against you; He has cleared away your enemies. The King of Israel, the LORD, is in your midst; you shall never again fear evil. (Zeph. 3:15)

Two thousand years ago the signs could not have been clearer—to those who were watching and waiting—that Messiah's coming was imminent. There were righteous Simeon and the faithful prophetess Anna, who both were looking for "the consolation of Israel" (Lk. 2:25) and "the redemption of Jerusalem" (Lk. 2:38). There were Zechariah the priest and his wife, Elizabeth, in the hill country of Judah. There were a young Jewish virgin named Miriam ("Mary") and Joseph (her betrothed) in the northern town of Nazareth. There were Simon son of Jonah and his brother Andrew in the Galilean fishing village of Bethsaida, and there were those throughout the Land of Israel who were soon to become followers of the Messiah. The angelic announcements that were made to Mary and Joseph, like the prophecy given to Isaiah seven centuries earlier, revealed a startling truth: In and through this child, God was about to visit His people—by becoming one of them!

> "And behold, you will conceive in your womb and bear a son, and you shall call His name Jesus. He will be great and will be called the Son of the Most High. And the Lord God will give to Him the throne of His father David, and He will reign over the house of Jacob forever, and of His kingdom there will be no end." (Lk. 1:31-33)
>
> "Joseph, son of David, do not fear to take Mary as your wife, for that which is conceived in her is from the Holy Spirit. She will bear a son, and you shall

call His name Jesus, for He will save His people from their sins." All this took place to fulfill what the Lord had spoken by the prophet: "Behold, the virgin shall conceive and bear a son, and they shall call His name Immanuel" (which means, God with us). (Mt. 1:20-23)

For to us a child is born, to us a son is given; and the government shall be upon His shoulder, and His name shall be called Wonderful Counsellor, Mighty God, Everlasting Father, Prince of Peace. Of the increase of His government and of peace there will be no end, on the throne of David and over his kingdom, to establish it and to uphold it with justice and with righteousness from this time forth and forevermore. (Isa. 9:6-7)

Thus, through the angelic and prophetic word of God, the kingship of Jesus prophetically shone like a golden constellation against the backdrop of Israel's long, dark night. Upon arriving in Jerusalem for the first time, Magi from the East, who had discerned from the appearance of a star that a king was to be born in Judea, made the following inquiry: "Where is He who has been born King of the Jews? For we saw His star in the east and have come to worship Him" (Mt. 2:2, NASB). Only the humble and wise worship the King of the Jews.

God is King!

As noted throughout this book, the prophetic scriptures are far more than a guide to the future; they reveal God's character. In the previous chapter, we saw how the Lord made sure that His people never forgot *who* it was they had forsaken and *whose* covenant they had violated. Whenever God expressed indignation toward Israel, He invariably highlighted one or more of His names/titles, one of which was "King." In Psalm 22, David declared that "kingship belongs to the LORD, and He rules over the nations" (Ps. 22:28). Let us consider the following pronouncements God made to His people when He asserted His kingship:

"I am the LORD, your Holy One, the Creator of Israel, your King." (Isa. 43:15)

Thus says the LORD, the King of Israel and His Redeemer, the LORD of hosts: "I am the first and I am the last; besides me there is no god." (Isa. 44:6)

But the LORD is the true God; He is the living God and the everlasting King. (Jer. 10:10)

> The King of Israel, the LORD, is in your midst; you shall never again fear evil. (Zeph. 3:15)
>
> "For I am a great King, says the LORD of hosts, and my name will be feared among the nations." (Mal. 1:14)

The kingship of God was a source of great comfort, strength, and joy to Israel when the nation walked in obedience, for the people knew that He would protect them, fight for them, and deliver them from their enemies. It became a central theme of the nation's worship, as summed up in the book of Psalms:

> The LORD is king forever and ever . . . For the LORD, the Most High, is to be feared, a great king over all the earth . . . He chose our heritage [*nachălâh*] for us, the pride of Jacob whom He loves . . . Sing praises to our King, sing praises! For God is the King of all the earth . . . God reigns over the nations; God sits on His holy throne . . . For the LORD is a great God, and a great King above all gods . . . With trumpets and the sound of the horn make a joyful noise before the King, the LORD! . . . Let Israel be glad in his Maker; let the children of Zion rejoice in their King! (Ps. 10:16; 47:2-8; 95:3; 98:6; 149:2; cf. 44:4; 48:2; 74:12)

Among the great declarations of God's kingship in the Bible are those that were made by pagan kings. After Daniel had interpreted Nebuchadnezzar's dream, the king of Babylon declared, "Truly, your God is God of gods and Lord of kings" (Dan. 2:47). God later humbled Nebuchadnezzar on account of his pride, driving him out from among men to live with the beasts of the field until he acknowledged that "the Most High rules the kingdom of men and gives it to whom He will" (Dan. 4:25). After Nebuchadnezzar had been restored by God, the king honored the One whose kingdom and dominion are from everlasting to everlasting. He departed the pages of biblical history with these memorable words: "Now I, Nebuchadnezzar, praise and extol and honor the King of heaven, for all His works are right and His ways are just; and those who walk in pride He is able to humble" (Dan. 4:37).

To Nebuchadnezzar's proclamation we may add three more (not in chronological order). We begin with the decree of Cyrus, king of Persia, whose spirit the Lord stirred up to allow the first wave of Jewish exiles in Babylon to return and rebuild the Temple:

> "The LORD, the God of heaven, has given me all the kingdoms of the earth, and He has charged me to build Him a house at Jerusalem, which is in Judah. Whoever is among you of all His people, may the LORD his God be with him. Let him go up" (2 Chron. 36:23; cf. Ezra 1:2-4).

In his letter to Ezra, Artaxerxes, king of Persia, made the following statement in permitting the priest to lead a second wave of exiles back to Jerusalem:

> "Whatever is decreed by the God of heaven, let it be done in full for the house of the God of heaven, lest His wrath be against the realm of the king and his sons" (Ezra 7:23).

Finally, we have the decree of Darius the Mede. After God had delivered Daniel from the den of lions, Darius wrote to every people and nation on earth:

> I make a decree, that in all my royal dominion people are to tremble and fear before the God of Daniel, for He is the living God, enduring forever; His kingdom shall never be destroyed, and His dominion shall be to the end. He delivers and rescues; He works signs and wonders in heaven and on earth, He who has saved Daniel from the power of the lions. (Dan. 6:25-27)

The King is Coming!

Not only did God frequently portray Himself as King, but He also announced the coming of an Anointed One, a Messiah, who would arise from among His own people and reign on His behalf. Here are some of the great Messianic prophecies of the Bible that pointed God's people to the day of His appearing:

> The scepter shall not depart from Judah, nor the ruler's staff from between His feet, until Shiloh comes, and to Him shall be the obedience of the peoples. (Gen. 49:10, NASB)

> I see Him, but not now; I behold Him, but not near: a star shall come out of Jacob, and a scepter shall rise out of Israel. (Num. 24:17)

> The LORD will judge the ends of the earth; He will give strength to His king and exalt the power of His anointed. (1 Sam. 2:10)

> "As for me, I have set my King on Zion, my holy hill." (Ps. 2:6)

Your throne, O God, is forever and ever. The scepter of your kingdom is a scepter of uprightness; you have loved righteousness and hated wickedness. Therefore God, your God, has anointed you with the oil of gladness beyond your companions. (Ps. 45:6-7; Heb. 1:8-9)

The LORD says to my Lord: "Sit at my right hand, until I make your enemies your footstool." The LORD sends forth from Zion your mighty scepter. Rule in the midst of your enemies! (Ps. 110:1-2)

Of the increase of His government and of peace there will be no end, on the throne of David and over his kingdom to establish it and to uphold it with justice and with righteousness from this time forth and forevermore. (Isa. 9:7)

Then the moon will be confounded and the sun ashamed, for the LORD of hosts reigns on Mount Zion and in Jerusalem, and His glory will be before His elders. (Isa. 24:23)

Your eyes will behold the king in His beauty; they will see a land that stretches afar . . . For the LORD is our judge; the LORD is our lawgiver; the LORD is our king; He will save us. (Isa. 33:17-22)

"Behold, the days are coming, declares the LORD, when I will raise up for David a righteous Branch, and He shall reign as king and deal wisely, and shall execute justice and righteousness in the land." (Jer. 23:5)

And in the days of those kings the God of heaven will set up a kingdom that shall never be destroyed, nor shall the kingdom be left to another people. It shall break in pieces all these kingdoms and bring them to an end, and it shall stand forever. (Dan. 2:44)

And to Him was given dominion and glory and a kingdom, that all peoples, nations, and languages should serve Him; His dominion is an everlasting dominion, which shall not pass away, and His kingdom one that shall not be destroyed. (Dan. 7:14)

Afterward the children of Israel shall return and seek the LORD their God, and David their king, and they shall come in fear to the LORD and to His goodness in the latter days. (Hos. 3:15)

"But you, O Bethlehem Ephrathah, who are too little to be among the clans of Judah, from you shall come forth for me one who is to be ruler in Israel, whose coming forth is from of old, from ancient days." (Mic. 5:2)

Rejoice greatly, O daughter of Zion! Shout aloud, O daughter of Jerusalem! Behold, your king is coming to you; righteous and having salvation is He, humble and mounted on a donkey, on a colt, the foal of a donkey. (Zech. 9:9)

And the LORD will be king over all the earth. On that day the LORD will be one and His name one. (Zech. 14:9)

Then everyone who survives of all the nations that have come against Jerusalem shall go up year after year to worship the King, the LORD of hosts, and to keep the Feast of Booths. And if any of the families of the earth do not go up to Jerusalem to worship the King, the LORD of hosts, there will be no rain on them. (Zech. 14:16-17)

He will be great and will be called the Son of the Most High. And the Lord God will give to Him the throne of His father David, and He will reign over the house of Jacob forever, and of His kingdom there will be no end. (Lk. 1:32-33)

Then the seventh angel blew his trumpet, and there were loud voices in heaven, saying, "The kingdom of the world has become the kingdom of our Lord and of His Messiah, and He shall reign forever and ever." (Rev. 11:15)

They will make war on the Lamb, and the Lamb will conquer them, for He is Lord of lords and King of kings, and those with Him are called and chosen and faithful. (Rev. 17:14)

From His mouth comes a sharp sword with which to strike down the nations, and He will rule them with a rod of iron. He will tread the winepress of the fury of the wrath of God the Almighty. On His robe and on His thigh He has a name written, King of kings and Lord of lords. (Rev. 19:15-16; cf. 12:5)

Palm Sunday

"Who is Jesus?" Surely, this is *the* question of the ages. It is one that every man, woman, and child of accountability will be confronted with at some point in their lives and one that demands an answer. It is the question Jesus Himself put to His disciples as they arrived in the district of Caesarea Philippi. At first, the Lord asked them, "Who do people say that the Son of Man is?" The answers He received included John the Baptist, Elijah, Jeremiah, and one of the prophets. Jesus then asked them directly, "But who do *you* say that I am?" to which Simon Peter famously replied, "You are the Messiah, the Son of the living God!" Jesus declared that answer to have been not only a revelation from the Father but also the foundation upon which He would build His church (Mt. 16:13-20).

Upon meeting Jesus of Nazareth for the first time and before hearing any of His teaching or witnessing any of His miracles, Nathanael of Galilee made a declaration that thrills me every time I read it: "Rabbi, you are the Son of God! You are the King of Israel!" (Jn. 1:49). Jesus responded with this astounding promise: "Truly, truly, I say to you, you will see heaven opened, and the angels of God ascending and descending on the Son of Man" (Jn. 1:51). Three years later, cries and cheers of jubilation greeted the Messiah as He rode into Jerusalem on the foal of a donkey, with many in the crowd triumphantly declaring, "Blessed is He who comes in the name of the Lord, even the King of Israel!" (Jn. 12:13). But let us consider how Matthew, in particular, recorded that momentous and prophetic Palm Sunday when the Lord's entrance into Jerusalem set in motion a chain of events that culminated in His exodus from the earth:

> And the crowds that went before Him and that followed Him were shouting, "Hosanna to the Son of David! Blessed is He who comes in the name of the Lord! Hosanna in the highest!" And when He entered Jerusalem, the whole city was stirred up, saying, "Who is this?" And the crowds said, "This is the prophet Jesus, from Nazareth of Galilee." (Mt. 21:9-11)

At this point, I believe we need to rewind the clock several centuries and join the Levitical choir in Psalm 24. This psalm was probably written by David to commemorate the day when he danced before the Lord while the Ark of the Covenant was being brought up to Jerusalem (2 Sam. 6:12-19). By carrying the ark toward Zion, the Levites had symbolically escorted the triumphant King of glory into His holy city, His resting place. As the procession of worshipers approached the walls of Jerusalem, half of the choir shouted out as if to the keepers of the gates, "Lift up your heads, O gates! And be lifted up, O ancient doors, that the King of glory may come in." The other half of the choir, acting out the role of the gatekeepers, responded, "Who is this King of glory?" The other Levites then identified their King and repeated the command: "The Lord, strong and mighty, the Lord, mighty in battle! Lift up your heads, O gates! And lift them up, O ancient doors, that the King of glory may come in." For a second time the question came back: "Who is this King of glory?" The final declaration was now made, prompting the gatekeepers to lift up the heads of the gates and open the doors: "The LORD of hosts, He is the King of glory!" (Ps. 24:7-10). The King of glory, as represented by the Ark of the Covenant, now assumed His rightful place in the midst of His people.

On that momentous Sunday two thousand years ago, I believe Psalm 24 was prophetically played out before the eyes of everyone in Jerusalem as Jesus, *the* Ark of God's presence, entered "the city of the great King" (Ps. 48:2; Mt. 5:35). As Jesus humbly made His way into the city, the crowd that went before Him and those that followed cried out, "Blessed is He who comes in the name of the Lord, even the King of Israel!" (Jn. 12:13). But of all the Gospel writers, I believe that Matthew made the clearest connection to Psalm 24:

> And when He entered Jerusalem, the whole city was stirred up, saying, "Who is this?" And the crowds said, "This is the prophet Jesus, from Nazareth of Galilee." And Jesus entered the Temple. (Mt. 21:10-12)

Tragically, as events unfolded that week, it was heaven and not Jerusalem that was to receive the King of glory (Heb. 9:24; 1 Pet. 3:22). As Spurgeon beautifully wrote in his commentary on Psalm 24:

> Jehovah of hosts, LORD of men and angels, LORD of the universe, LORD of the worlds, is the King of glory. All true glory is concentrated upon the true God, for all other glory is but a passing pageant, the painted pomp of an hour. The ascended Saviour is here declared to be the Head and Crown of the universe, the King of Glory. Our Immanuel is hymned in sublimest strains. Jesus of Nazareth is Jehovah Sabaoth.[1]

The King Is Crucified!

The kingship of Jesus was to be a focal point of His trial and execution. When the Jewish council brought Him before the Roman procurator Pontius Pilate, they laid false accusations of sedition against Him: "We found this man misleading our nation and forbidding us to give tribute to Caesar, and saying that He Himself is Messiah, a king" (Lk. 23:2). When Jesus stood before the procurator, this question dominated the proceedings:

---

[1] Spurgeon, *The Treasury of David, Vol. I*, p. 378.

So Pilate entered his headquarters again and called Jesus and said to Him, "Are you the King of the Jews?" Jesus answered, "Do you say this of your own accord, or did others say it to you about me?" Pilate answered, "Am I a Jew? Your own nation and the chief priests have delivered you over to me. What have you done?" Jesus answered, "My kingdom is not of this world. If my kingdom were of this world, my servants would have been fighting, that I might not be delivered over to the Jews. But my kingdom is not from the world." Then Pilate said to him, "So you are a king?" Jesus answered, "You say that I am a king. For this purpose I was born and for this purpose I have come into the world — to bear witness to the truth. Everyone who is of the truth listens to my voice." (Jn. 18:33-37)

When Pilate subsequently addressed the crowd that the chief priests of Israel had incited against the Lord, he persisted in referring to Jesus as their King. According to two of the Gospel accounts, Pilate asked:

Do you want me to release for you the King of the Jews? . . . Then what shall I do with the man you call the King of the Jews? (Mk. 15:9-12)

Behold your King! . . . Shall I crucify your King? (Jn. 19:14-15)

Pilate sought to release Jesus, having declared Him innocent, but his efforts proved in vain. Scourged, beaten, robed in purple, and crowned with thorns, the King of glory stood before His people one last time, after being hailed "King of the Jews!" by the soldiers of Rome (Mt. 27:29). The chief priests scuppered any possibility of release by appealing to Caesar and in so doing made a shocking confession that must have cut deep into the Lord's heart: "If you release this man, you are not Caesar's friend. Everyone who makes himself a king opposes Caesar . . . We have no king but Caesar" (Jn. 19:12-15).

Some time prior to His crucifixion, the Lord had indicted the religious authorities with these prophetic words: "I have come in my Father's name, and you do not receive me. If another comes in his own name, you will receive him" (Jn. 5:43). Many false messiahs have come and gone in their own name since Jesus spoke these words. They include Shimon bar Kokhba (d. A.D. 135), who led the final Jewish revolt against Rome. He features in one of the reliefs on the giant bronze Menorah opposite the Israeli Knesset in Jerusalem. Jesus' words will find their ultimate fulfillment when *the* false messiah, the Antichrist, is received by the world *and* by many in Israel.[2] According to some scholars, the books of Daniel and Revelation suggest that this man of lawlessness will arise from within a reconstituted European Union, which will effectively be a *spiritual* revival of the old Roman Empire. If this is so, then the appeal of the chief priests to Caesar was a chilling portent of things to come. It was also a solemn reminder of what God had once said to Samuel when Israel committed a great "evil" by demanding a king so they could be like the other nations: "Obey the voice of the people in all that they say to you, for they have not rejected you, but they have rejected me from being king over them" (1 Sam. 8:7; cf. 10:19; 12:12-19).

While Jesus was enduring unspeakable agony on the cross, the Roman soldiers ruthlessly reviled Him: "If you are the King of the Jews, save yourself!" (Lk. 23:37). They were joined by the chief priests and scribes of Israel, who mercilessly mocked God's beloved Son: "Let the Messiah, the King of Israel, come down now from the cross that we may see and believe" (Mk. 15:32). Written in Aramaic, Latin, and Greek on a placard affixed to the cross was the alleged crime for which the Messiah was crucified: "Jesus of Nazareth, the King of the Jews" (Jn. 19:19).[3] Officially, the Roman charge was sedition. Unofficially, and for the sake of his own retributive pleasure, Pontius Pilate was publicly humiliating the chief priests for interfering with Roman justice. When the chief priests read Pilate's inscription, they were outraged and told him, "Do not write, 'The King of the Jews,' but rather, 'This man said, I am King of the Jews.'" Pilate was unmoved: "What I have written I have written" (Jn. 19:21-22).

I believe God the Father sovereignly ensured that this inscription would be nailed above the head of His beloved Son for all of Israel and the world to see. The King of glory was being crucified in their place, the Judge of all men was being judged by man, the Innocent One was being condemned

---

[2] During the second century B.C., the Seleucid king, Antiochus Epiphanes IV, a forerunner of the Antichrist who desecrated the Temple in his endeavor to suppress Judaism, was received by apostate Jews. This gave rise to the Maccabean revolt, the cleansing and rededication of the Temple, and the inauguration of the Jewish festival of Hanukkah.

[3] The fact that Pilate had the inscription written in these three languages probably accounts for the slightly different translations in the Gospels.

by the guilty many, and the Author of life was being put to death by those who were dead in their trespasses and sins. Pilate was merely the human scribe who unwittingly found himself serving an authority far greater than Caesar.

Who Killed Jesus?

One of the perennial pitfalls in loving the Jewish people and standing with Israel is emotionalism. I believe it is critically important that a believer's love for Israel is deeply rooted in the full counsel of God's Word and divinely regulated by the Holy Spirit. In previous chapters, we have looked at the uncompromising and often explicit language God used in His prophetic indictments against His people, language that may have caused some of us to gasp and wince at its severity and earthiness. I have contended in this book that it is not for the church to act as judge and jury over Israel. That right belongs to God. Equally, it is not for the church to exonerate or absolve the Jewish people of their crimes against God and His Messiah. That, again, is God's prerogative.

Jesus told the Samaritan woman at Jacob's well that "true worshipers will worship the Father in spirit and truth, for the Father is seeking such people to worship Him" (Jn. 4:23). If our love for Israel is not informed by a sober reading of God's Word but driven by our emotions, then we will find ourselves at the mercy of our flesh and perhaps even more powerful forces. This can happen, for example, out of a misguided sense of collective guilt for crimes committed against the Jewish people in the name of Jesus/the church; or as a reaction to the anti-Semitism we see escalating all around the world *and* in the church; or because of an unhealthy fascination with all things Jewish, which can at best distract and at worst deceive. One of the emotional claims I have heard some Christians make over the years is that the Jewish people *did not* kill Jesus. It is important to address that claim for the sake of balance and truth. What does God's Word say?

Let us begin with the prophecy of Zechariah, which friends of Israel always quote because of the glorious promise it contains:

"And I will pour out on the house of David and the inhabitants of Jerusalem a spirit of grace and pleas for mercy, so that, when they look on me, on Him whom *they have pierced*, they shall mourn for Him, as one mourns for an only child, and weep bitterly over Him, as one weeps over a firstborn." (Zech. 12:10; cf. Jn. 19:37; Rev. 1:7)

Now let us join the two despondent disciples on the road to Emmaus when the risen Lord met them but kept His identity hidden for a time. The Lord asked Cleopas and his fellow disciple what it was that had made them so downcast. They replied:

> Concerning Jesus of Nazareth, a man who was a prophet mighty in deed and word before God and all the people, and how *our chief priests and rulers* delivered Him up to be condemned to death, and *crucified Him*. But we had hoped that He was the one to redeem Israel. (Lk. 24:19-21)

Now let us fast-forward fifty days to Pentecost when Peter, "filled with the Holy Spirit" (Acts 2:4), made the following proclamation:

> Men of Israel, hear these words: Jesus of Nazareth, a man attested to you by God with mighty works and wonders and signs that God did through Him in your midst, as you yourselves know — this Jesus, delivered up according to the definite plan and foreknowledge of God, *you crucified and killed* by the hands of lawless men . . . Let all the house of Israel therefore know for certain that God has made Him both Lord and Messiah, this Jesus whom *you crucified*. (Acts 2:22-23,36)

Peter later made a similar declaration in Solomon's Colonnade:

> Men of Israel . . . The God of Abraham, the God of Isaac, and the God of Jacob, the God of our fathers, glorified His servant Jesus, whom you delivered over and denied in the presence of Pilate, when he had decided to release Him. But you denied the Holy and Righteous One, and asked for a murderer to be granted to you, and *you killed* the Author of life, whom God raised from the dead. To this we are witnesses. (Acts 3:12-15)

While standing with the Apostle John before the Jewish Sanhedrin, Peter was again "filled with the Holy Spirit" (Acts 4:8). On that occasion, he boldly declared:

> Rulers of the people and elders . . . let it be known to all of you and to all the people of Israel that by the name of Jesus the Messiah of Nazareth, whom *you crucified*, whom God raised from the dead — by Him this man is standing before you well. (Acts 4:10)

On another occasion, while standing with his fellow apostles before the Sanhedrin, Peter made this statement:

> The God of our fathers raised Jesus, whom *you killed* by hanging Him on a tree. God exalted Him at His right hand as Leader and Savior, to give repentance to Israel and forgiveness of sins. And we are witnesses to these things, and so is the Holy Spirit, whom God has given to those who obey Him. (Acts 5:30-32)

When Stephen was brought before the Sanhedrin and falsely accused, he concluded his defense by bringing the following indictment against them, before being stoned to death:

> "You stiff-necked people, uncircumcised in heart and ears, you always resist the Holy Spirit. As your fathers did, so do you. Which of the prophets did your fathers not persecute? And they killed those who announced beforehand the coming of the Righteous One, *whom you have now betrayed and murdered*, you who received the law as delivered by angels and did not keep it." (Acts 7:51-53)

In the home of the God-fearing Roman centurion Cornelius, Peter explained the good news of Jesus and His mission to Israel:

> And we are witnesses of all that He [Jesus] did both in the country of the Jews and in Jerusalem. *They put Him to death* by hanging Him on a tree, but God raised Him on the third day. (Acts 10:39)

Finally, let us consider the words penned by Paul in his first letter to the Thessalonians:

> For you, brothers, became imitators of the churches of God in Messiah Jesus that are in Judea. For you suffered the same things from your own countrymen as they did from *the Jews, who killed* both the Lord Jesus and the prophets, and drove us out, and displease God and oppose all mankind by hindering us from speaking to the Gentiles that they might be saved — so as always to fill up the measure of their sins. (1 Thess. 2:14-16)

Let us be clear: It was because "God so loved the world that He gave His only begotten Son . . . that the world might be saved through Him" (Jn. 3:16-17, NASB). When John the Baptist saw Jesus approaching, he declared, "Behold, the Lamb of God, who takes away the sin of the world!" (Jn. 1:29). In his letter to the Romans, Paul explained that "all, both Jews and Greeks, are under sin," that "none is righteous, no, not one," and that "all have sinned and fall short of the glory of God" (Rom. 3:9-23). In his first letter, the Apostle John wrote about Jesus being "the propitiation for our sins, and not for ours only but also for the sins of the whole world" (1 Jn. 2:2). In other words, before any consideration is given to Israel's specific role and responsibility as far as the crucifixion is concerned, it needs to be established that *the whole world* stood guilty and condemned before God on account of its sin. Ultimately, we were *all* responsible for what happened two thousand years ago.

Jesus told His disciples that the religious leaders of Israel were going to "condemn Him to death and deliver Him over to the Gentiles to be mocked and flogged and crucified" (Mt. 20:17-19). Then, during the last supper, He told them, "The Son of Man goes as it is written of Him" (Mt. 26:24). The events that unfolded during that momentous Passover feast in Jerusalem were foreknown by God and in full compliance with His sovereign will, both for Israel and for the world. Furthermore, Israel's leaders could not have handed Jesus over to the Gentiles nor could the Gentiles have perpetrated the act of crucifixion itself had the Lord not first laid down His life in submission to the Father's will (Jn. 10:18; Mt. 26:39-44) and had the Father not given His authority for such a sentence to be carried out against His Son (Jn. 19:11).

In the book of Acts, I believe we have the definitive answer to the question, "Who killed Jesus?" In his Spirit-filled address at Pentecost, Peter declared, "Men of Israel . . . this Jesus, delivered up according to the definite plan and foreknowledge of God, you crucified and killed by the hands of lawless men" (Acts 2:23). Later in Acts, we read how the friends of Peter and John prayed together following the release of the two apostles from custody. In their prayer, they spoke of the Lord's crucifixion in the context of Psalm 2 and David's words about *the nations* conspiring against God and His Messiah. They mentioned how "Herod and Pontius Pilate, along with the Gentiles and the peoples of Israel" had "gathered together" against Jesus but in so doing had only fulfilled what God had ordained (Acts 4:24-28; cf. 13:27-30). The fingerprint of both Jew and Gentile would be found at the scene of the greatest crime in human history. Yet, in the final reckoning, "it was the will of the LORD to bruise Him" (Isa. 53:10, RSV).

I believe we can conclude by saying that from *God's perspective* according to His Word, Israel did indeed kill Jesus—by the hands of the Gentiles and in accordance with His will.

"Thy Kingdom Come!"

Let us revisit Palm Sunday one last time and listen to one of the many "Hosannas" that rang out from the jubilant crowd that day: "Blessed is the coming kingdom of our father David!" (Mk. 11:10). The crowd understood from the Scriptures that when Messiah came, He would establish His kingdom on earth. What they failed to understand was that the Messiah had to suffer first and be enthroned in the hearts of men before He could ascend the throne in Jerusalem and reign over the earth. But ascend that throne He must and will.

Six days before He was transfigured on the mountain, Jesus made the following statement: "Truly, I say to you, there are some standing here who will not taste death until they see the Son of Man coming in His kingdom" (Mt. 16:28; cf. Mk. 9:1; Lk. 9:27). For a few unforgettable moments, Peter, James, and John were privileged to see the Son of God manifest His heavenly majesty. They beheld the King of glory and the glory of the kingdom to come.

While Jesus was suffering on the cross, one of the two criminals who were crucified with Him suddenly became acutely aware of his own sin and of the Lord's innocence. The shocking reality of *who* it was dying next to him pierced his heart. What followed was one of the most glorious confessions and promises ever exchanged between the Savior and a sinner:

> And [the criminal] said, "Jesus, remember me when you come into your kingdom." And He said to him, "Truly, I say to you, today you will be with me in Paradise." (Lk. 23:42-43)

Immediately prior to His ascension, the disciples asked the risen Lord one final question, a question which has sadly divided the church for nearly two thousand years:

> So when they had come together, they asked Him, "Lord, will you at this time restore the kingdom to Israel?" He said to them, "It is not for you to know

times or seasons that the Father has fixed by His own authority. But you will receive power when the Holy Spirit has come upon you, and you will be my witnesses in Jerusalem and in all Judea and Samaria, and to the end of the earth." (Acts 1:6-8)

The disciples had understandably asked the Messiah, who for forty days had taught them extensively "about the kingdom of God" (Acts 1:3), whether He was now going to take up the throne of David and reign as King over Israel. How the enemy has twisted this dialogue in the minds of many! I have documented elsewhere the scurrilous misuse and abuse of this text by churchmen who have fallen foul of the devil's theological wiles and arrogantly consigned Israel to the theological waste bin.[4] The question was correct, the answer was gracious, the issue was timing, and the fulfillment is certain!

The disciples clearly understood from the Lord's post-resurrection teaching that the kingdom of God could not come without the restoration of Israel. The two were intertwined in the purposes of God. If Jesus were to reign as King over the earth, then He had to reign as King over Israel. As the nineteenth-century Church of England bishop Edward H. Bickersteth (1825-1906) insightfully wrote:

> The emphasis is on the words **at this time**. They [the disciples] had no manner of doubt, nor ought we to have, that the kingdom will one day be restored to Israel ... Our Lord's reply (ver.7), does not countenance the rash charge of carnal expectations, which has been too often levelled against the apostles for their question. He restrains, indeed, their eager gaze into futurity: "It is not for you to know the times or the seasons ... which the Father hath put in his own power" ... But his answer implies that when the fullness of the time was come, national supremacy should be again restored to Israel.[5]

One King, Two Thrones

The last the unbelieving world saw of Jesus the Messiah was as a condemned man nailed to a cross and crowned with thorns. His appearance

---

[4] See "Calvinism's Legacy" in Wilkinson, *Israel Betrayed, Volume 2*.

[5] Edward H. Bickersteth, *A Practical and Explanatory Commentary on the New Testament* (London: Virtue, 1864), p. 191.

was disfigured, and many despised Him. When the unbelieving world next sees Jesus, they will behold a glorified man descending from heaven to judge and rule the earth. The Lord's majestic appearance will strike such terror into their hearts that they will weep and wail on account of Him (Rev. 1:7). A name will be written on His robe and on His thigh that will reveal the glorious commendation and vindication of the Father: "King of kings and Lord of lords" (Rev. 19:11-16).

Following the death, resurrection, and ascension of Jesus, the gospel spread, the church grew, and the Jewish religious leaders continued to resist the Messianic claims that were being made by His followers. In Thessalonica, for example, Paul proved from the Old Testament that Jesus was indeed the Messiah. The Jewish leaders reacted angrily and formed a mob. Stirring up the city, they dragged a man by the name of Jason, along with some of his fellow believers, before the authorities. This was the charge that was brought against them: "These men who have turned the world upside down have come here also, and Jason has received them, and they are all acting against the decrees of Caesar, saying that there is another king, Jesus" (Acts 17:6-7).

The day will soon dawn when every Caesar will fall and God will put an end to the world's defiant decrees. It will be just as the heavenly hosts announced in the Revelation: "Then the seventh angel blew his trumpet, and there were loud voices in heaven, saying, 'The kingdom of the world has become the kingdom of our Lord and of His Messiah, and He shall reign forever and ever'" (Rev. 11:15). For this to be fulfilled, at least three things need to happen or be in place:

1. A literal, physical second coming to earth of the King who is to reign
2. A literal, physical throne on earth upon which He is to reign
3. A literal, physical kingdom on earth over which He is to reign

Otherwise, the angelic announcement of Revelation 11:15 was meaningless. In other words, there has to be a literal and physical reality to the announcement; its fulfillment has to be seen and recognized.

In Psalm 2, God gave the kings and rulers of this world—past, present, and future—a solemn warning:

> The kings of the earth set themselves, and the rulers take counsel together, against the LORD and against His Anointed . . . He who sits in the heavens laughs; the LORD holds them in derision. Then He will speak to them in His wrath, and terrify them in His fury, saying, "As for me, I have set my King on Zion, my holy hill." I will tell of the decree: The LORD said to me, "You are my Son; today I have begotten you. Ask of me, and I will make the nations your heritage [*nachălâh*], and the ends of the earth your possession" . . . Now therefore, O kings, be wise; be warned, O rulers of the earth. (Ps. 2:2-10)

The language here is earthly and political, not heavenly and spiritual. The decree was and is for the rulers *on earth*. Furthermore, in his letter to the Laodicean church, Jesus promised, "The one who conquers, I will grant him to sit with me on my throne, as I also conquered and sat down with my Father on His throne" (Rev. 3:21). Two separate thrones are clearly in view here: "my throne" and "His throne." These *cannot*, by any stretch of the imagination or rules of grammar, be one and the same. Right now, Jesus is seated at the right hand of the Father in heaven on *the Father's throne*.[6] At some point in the near future, He will return to earth to take up *His throne* in Jerusalem, fulfilling all of the prophecies that foretold His earthly, millennial reign. The angel Gabriel told Mary that God was going to give to His Son "the throne of His father David" and that He would "reign over the house of Jacob forever, and of His kingdom there will be no end" (Lk. 1:32-33). Isaiah famously prophesied that "of the increase of His government and of peace there will be no end, on the throne of David and over his kingdom, to establish it and to uphold it with justice and with righteousness from this time forth and forevermore" (Isa. 9:6-7). In the book of Hosea, we read that in the last days the people of Israel will turn back to God and seek their Messiah and King:

> For the children of Israel shall dwell many days without king or prince, without sacrifice or pillar, without ephod or household gods. Afterward the children of Israel shall return and seek the LORD their God, and David their king, and they shall come in fear to the LORD and to His goodness in the latter days. (Hos. 3:4-5)

---

[6] See Mt. 22:44; 26:64; Mk. 16:19; Acts 2:33-34; 7:55-56; Rom. 8:34; Eph. 1:20; Col. 3:1; Heb. 1:3; 8:1; 10:12; 12:2; 1 Pet. 3:22.

Clearly, prophecies like these have not yet been fulfilled, but they must. It goes without saying that David's throne was here on earth. At no time was it ever airlifted to heaven!

Announcements of this nature can only be understood *politically* and *geographically*, which is how the Jewish people in the days of Isaiah, Hosea, and Mary would have understood them. The Jewish expectation has always been that the Messiah will one day appear and reign, which explains the jubilation of the crowds on Palm Sunday. It also explains Simon Peter's offer to build a tabernacle for Jesus, Elijah, and Moses on the Mount of Transfiguration (Mk. 9:5). He believed that the kingdom of God was being ushered in. When Jesus taught His disciples how to pray, He included this petition: "Thy kingdom come, thy will be done, on earth as it is in heaven" (Mt. 6:10). Was the Lord thinking purely in salvational and spiritual terms about God's influence being exerted through believers during the church age? Surely there was and is so much more to it than that.

Conclusion

An underlying theme of this book has been the self-revelation of God. What the Lord has revealed about His character and His ways through His Word and His works is of paramount importance in understanding who He is and how He expects His people to relate to Him. "Who do you say that I am?" was the question Jesus asked His disciples. Many in Israel had their own ideas, but through the revelation of God the Father, Simon Peter was able to declare: "You are the Messiah, the Son of the living God!" (Mt. 16:16). That revelation was to be the rock on which Jesus would build His church (16:18).

In this chapter, we have focused on the revelation of Jesus' kingship. In closing, I would like to make the following proposition. If, to many in the church, Jesus is only "King of the Jews" during a Christmas nativity play or Good Friday remembrance service; if He is only "King of the Jews" in the question posed long ago by the Magi or in the Palm Sunday hosannas of the Jerusalem crowds or in the Roman inscription that was nailed to the cross; if He is only "King of the Jews" in a spiritual sense reigning through the church on a heavenly throne today and not in a literal sense reigning over Israel on an earthly throne "tomorrow," then who is this Jesus? He is not the Jesus of the Bible in the fullness of His self-revelation! The kingly titles we have considered in this chapter are not spiritual epithets merely intended to inspire devotion from the church. They are political titles grounded in earthly events prophesied millennia ago that, in the majority of cases, are still awaiting their fulfillment. They are tied to the fact that Israel in particular and the world in general represent the Lord's *nachălâh*—His earthly inheritance.

We close this final chapter with a poem that was written by Charles Deayton. Entitled *Five Words*, it was inspired by the ministry of John the Baptist, who simply pointed people to Jesus, the Lamb of God and King of Israel:

Five Words

1 Corinthians 14:19 – John 1:36

They heard John speak, and quickly they
Another pathway trod;
Five words with understanding giv'n –
Behold the Lamb of God!

A model servant here we find,
A messenger indeed,
His words rang true, as sent by God
His holy rights to plead.

He spake of Christ, and Christ alone,
It was his humble lot,
When pressed as to himself, he said
Just simply – *I am not.*

The sermon, eloquent in words,
May lack a message true –
Five words may, by the Spirit's pow'r,
Bring Jesus into view.

Ten thousand words in unknown tongue
Can never save a soul –
Five words may serve, when used by God,
To make a sinner whole.

This lesson let us take to heart,
If we would serve the Lord,
To give the message we are giv'n,
And simply speak His word.[7]

---

[7] Deayton, Charles. "'Five Words,' A Door of Hope and Other Poems (1963)." *My Brethren - Poetry - A Door of Hope*, Gordon Rainbow, retrieved from www.mybrethren.org/poetry/fram door.htm.

Israel: The Inheritance of God

Conclusion

> Remember me, O LORD, when you show favor to your people; help me when you save them, that I may look upon the prosperity of your chosen ones, that I may rejoice in the gladness of your nation, that I may glory with your inheritance [*nachălâh*]. (Ps. 106:4-5)
>
> I will recount the steadfast love [*chesed*] of the LORD, the praises of the LORD, according to all that the LORD has granted us, and the great goodness to the house of Israel that He has granted them according to His compassion [*racham*], according to the abundance of His steadfast love [*chesed*]. (Isa. 63:7)

In closing this book, I realize that I have barely scratched the surface of God's Word as far as His abundant love for Israel is concerned. It is a most extraordinary love, which has emanated and continues to emanate from the heart of an extraordinary God. Like the psalmist, I set out from the beginning to "ponder all your work, and meditate on your mighty deeds"; and with the psalmist, I can now draw the same conclusion: "Your way, O God, is holy. What god is great like our God? You are the God who works wonders; you have made known your might among the peoples" (Ps. 77:12-14).

In the book of Exodus, the Lord told Moses what He was planning to do in response to Pharaoh's refusal to let His people go:

> "Then I will lay my hand on Egypt and bring my hosts, my people the children of Israel, out of the land of Egypt by great acts of judgment. *The Egyptians shall know that I am the* LORD, when I stretch out my hand against Egypt and bring out the people of Israel from among them." (Ex. 7:4-5)

The Lord said the same to Moses after the Israelites had left Egypt and were encamped by the Red Sea with Pharaoh and his armies about to pursue them: "And I will harden Pharaoh's heart, and he will pursue them, and I will get glory over Pharaoh and all his host, and *the Egyptians shall know that I am the* LORD" (Ex. 14:4).

As noted throughout this book, the end or ultimate goal of all things is the glory of God. These things include the restoration and redemption of

Israel, and by "Israel" I mean the nation as we see it today in the Middle East, not some spiritualized reinterpretation of "Israel" that was conceived in the malevolent mind of the father of lies. Time and again in Scripture, we hear God declaring at moments of great crisis that He will be seen and glorified not only by His own people but also by the nations of the world. In one of the great restoration prophecies of the Bible, we read promises that we have had the privilege of seeing fulfilled in our own time, at least in part:

> "And you shall rejoice in the LORD; in the Holy One of Israel you shall glory. When the poor and needy seek water, and there is none, and their tongue is parched with thirst, I the LORD will answer them; I the God of Israel will not forsake them. I will open rivers on the bare heights, and fountains in the midst of the valleys. I will make the wilderness a pool of water, and the dry land springs of water. I will put in the wilderness the cedar, the acacia, the myrtle, and the olive. I will set in the desert the cypress, the plane and the pine together, *that they may see and know, may consider and understand together*, that the hand of the LORD has done this, the Holy One of Israel has created it." (Isa. 41:16-20)

Many in the church who look at Israel today have indeed considered and understood "that the hand of the Lord has done this." They have praised God for what He has done and are earnestly praying for the *spiritual* revival of the nation. Although no faithful believer will ever seek a reward for their advocacy of Israel, Scripture makes it clear that blessing is promised to those who seek the true peace and prosperity of God's people:

> Pray for the peace of Jerusalem! May they prosper who love you! (Ps. 122:6, RSV)

> Rejoice with Jerusalem, and be glad for her, all you who love her; rejoice with her in joy, all you who mourn over her ... that you may drink deeply with delight from her glorious abundance. (Isa. 66:10-11)

In 1939, American soil conservationist Walter Clay Lowdermilk visited Palestine, as it was then known. There he witnessed for himself the astonishing efforts that were being made by the Jewish people to reclaim the land, which had been rendered desolate by centuries of Arab/Muslim neglect. Lowdermilk wrote a glowing report:

> The Jews have proved themselves capable of this herculean task of reclaiming the long-neglected Holy Land. Since 1882 they have been struggling against

great odds … to restore it to a high level of fertility and civilization. With religious zeal and sacrificial martyrdom they have flung themselves into this cause of reconstruction and redemption … The way in which these changes are being wrought in the land is one of the most remarkable phenomena of our day. The Rev. Norman McLean, chaplain to King George VI, recently stated: "There is no experiment in human uplift, now to be seen on the face of the earth, that can compare to the work of the Zionists".[1]

High praise indeed from such distinguished gentlemen, but we know from Scripture that what Lowdermilk and McLean witnessed was only the beginning of what the Lord had planned and promised.

Today, the hearts of so many Jewish people remain derelict and in urgent need of renewal. Perhaps more than any other chapter in the Bible, Ezekiel 37 speaks of the great national revival that is to come when the Spirit of God will enter into His people. As the prophet gazed upon the valley that was full of dry bones, the Lord asked him, "Son of man, can these bones live?" (Ezek. 37:3). I trust, as we reach journey's end, that our own answer is firmly grounded in the words, ways, and wisdom of God and not in the faulty, fanciful, and fallacious theologies of fallible men. As Ezekiel watched the bones coming together, before they were clothed with sinews, flesh, and skin, God explained to the prophet what he was witnessing:

> "Son of man, these bones are *the whole house of Israel*. Behold, they say, 'Our bones are dried up, and our hope is lost; we are indeed cut off.' Therefore prophesy, and say to them, 'Thus says the Lord GOD: Behold, I will open your graves and raise you from your graves, O my people. And I will bring you into the land of Israel. And you shall know that I am the LORD, when I open your graves, and raise you from your graves, O my people. And I will put my Spirit within you, and you shall live, and I will place you in your own land. Then *you shall know that I am the LORD*; I have spoken, and I will do it, declares the LORD." (Ezek. 37:11-14)

Anyone who has visited Yad Vashem, The World Holocaust Remembrance Center in Jerusalem, will recall seeing part of verse 14 of Ezekiel's prophecy inscribed over the entrance: the promise of life in the midst of

---

[1] Walter Clay Lowdermilk, *Palestine: Land of Promise* (London: Victor Gollancz Ltd., 1944), p. 19.

death. The end of the verse, which is not shown at Yad Vashem, speaks of Israel knowing that God is the Lord through His miracle of restoration and resurrection. In the book of Ezekiel alone, God declares on sixty-two occasions that either His own people or the nations will know that He is the Lord by what He will have accomplished on Israel's behalf. This is heightened at the end of chapters 34-39, where we read:

> "And *they shall know that I am the LORD their God* with them, and that they, the house of Israel, are my people, declares the Lord GOD." (Ezek. 34:30)

> "As you rejoiced over the inheritance [*nachălâh*] of the house of Israel, because it was desolate, so I will deal with you; you shall be desolate, Mount Seir, and all Edom, all of it. Then *they will know that I am the LORD*." (Ezek. 35:15)

> "Then *the nations* that are left all around you *shall know that I am the LORD*; I have rebuilt the ruined places and replanted that which was desolate. I am the LORD; I have spoken, and I will do it . . . Like the flock for sacrifices, like the flock at Jerusalem during her appointed feasts, so shall the waste cities be filled with flocks of people. Then *they will know that I am the LORD*." (Ezek. 36:36-38)

> "My dwelling place shall be with them, and I will be their God, and they shall be my people. Then *the nations will know that I am the LORD* who sanctifies Israel, when my sanctuary is in their midst forevermore." (Ezek. 37:27-28)

> "So I will show my greatness and my holiness and make myself known in the eyes of many nations. Then *they will know that I am the LORD*." (Ezek. 38:23)

> "Then *they shall know that I am the LORD their God*, because I sent them into exile among the nations and then assembled them into their own land. I will leave none of them remaining among the nations anymore. And I will not hide my face anymore from them, when I pour out my Spirit upon the house of Israel, declares the Lord GOD." (Ezek. 39:28-29)

The Holy One of Israel did not end there. He had something yet more glorious to reveal to His people: visions of a new Temple that will be filled with His glory, together with instructions concerning a future, millennial division of the land "as an inheritance [*nachălâh*] among the tribes of Israel" (Ezek. 48:29). But even then, the Lord saved the best until the very last sentence, as we will read in a moment.

In chapter 12, we considered God's burning jealousy for Zion. When His beloved Son, Jesus, returns to Jerusalem in power and great glory, this idolatrous and divided city will be called "the faithful city" (Zech. 8:3). This is hard to imagine but easy to believe once we have humbly received into our hearts the glorious promises and self-revelation of Israel's Creator, Father, Husband, Shepherd, King, Messiah, Savior, and Redeemer. Remember what has been said throughout: Israel's importance is not confined to the nation but to the One who set the nation apart for Himself. Israel has failed, but God has triumphed. Israel was faithless, but God has remained faithful. Israel's love has been "like a morning cloud, like the dew that goes early away" (Hos. 6:4), but God's love has remained loyal and steadfast throughout. The Creator of the universe set His own name upon this people and blessed them. He also made everlasting promises to Israel, He issued His law through Israel, and from Israel He brought forth His Son to bring salvation to the world.

Israel's sin, and more specifically her rejection of Jesus, is what presently separates the nation from God. This is why *the nation*, in her unbelief, must pass through the tribulation judgments to come following the rapture of every individual Jew and Gentile who has turned to Jesus for salvation. Toward the end of this horrific time of Jacob's trouble, a remnant of Israel will finally call upon the name of Jesus/Yeshua, and He will deliver them. As the Lord declared through the Prophet Hosea, "I will return again to my place, until they acknowledge their guilt and seek my face, and in their distress [or 'affliction'] earnestly seek me" (Hos. 5:15).

Let us recall what the Lord told Solomon in a dream after the young king had dedicated the Temple: His name, His eyes, and His heart would be there "forever" / "perpetually" / "for all time" (1 Kgs. 9:3). When God concluded the prophecies that He had given to Ezekiel, He made one final announcement about Jerusalem, which must have thrilled and consoled the heart of the prophet and which I pray will thrill our own hearts as we anticipate its fulfillment: "And the name of the city from that time on shall be, The LORD Is There" (Ezek. 48:35). On that day the world will know once and for all that Almighty God, in and through the Person of His only begotten Son Jesus, will have taken rightful possession of His earthly inheritance—His earthly *nachălâh*.

God is not man, that He should lie, or a son of man, that He should change His mind. Has He said, and will He not do it? Or has He spoken, and will He not fulfill it? Behold, I received a command to bless: He has blessed, and I cannot revoke it . . . The LORD their God is with them, and the shout of a king is among them . . . For there is no enchantment against Jacob, no divination against Israel; now it shall be said of Jacob and Israel,

"What has God wrought!" (Num. 23:19-23)

Oh, the depth of the riches and wisdom and knowledge of God! How unsearchable are His judgments and how inscrutable His ways! "For who has known the mind of the LORD, or who has been His counselor?" "Or who has given a gift to Him that He might be repaid?" For from Him and through Him and to Him are all things.

To Him be glory forever. Amen. (Rom. 11:33-36)

Bibliography

Baron, David. *Israel in the Plan of God*. Grand Rapids, MI: Kregel Publications, 1983.

Bellett, John Gifford. *A Short Meditation on the Moral Glory of the Lord Jesus Christ*. 17th Ed. Kingston-on-Thames, England: Stow Hill Bible and Tract Depot, 1963.

Bickersteth, Edward. *The Restoration of the Jews to their own Land, in Connection with their Future Conversion and the Final Blessedness of our Earth*. 2nd Ed. London: R. B. Seeley and W. Burnside, 1841.

Bickersteth, Edward H. *A Practical and Explanatory Commentary on the New Testament*. London: Virtue, 1864.

Bonar, Andrew A. *Memoir and Remains of Robert Murray M'Cheyne*. Edinburgh: Banner of Truth Trust, 1978.

Bonar, Horatius. *When God's Children Suffer*. Grand Rapids, MI: Kregel Publications, 2017.

Brown, Michael L. "1385 ברך." VanGemeren, *The New International Dictionary*.

Cutting, George. *Christian Privileges*. London: W.H. Broom and Rouse, n.d.

Darby, John Nelson. "Examination of a few Passages of Scripture, the Force of which has been Questioned in the Discussion on the New Churches; with Remarks on Certain Principles alleged in Support of their Establishment (1850)." Kelly, *The Collected Writings*. Vol. 4.

_____. "Reflections upon the Prophetic Inquiry and the Views advanced in it (1829)." Kelly, *The Collected Writings*. Vol. 2.

Deck, James G. *Hymns and Sacred Poems*. 5th Ed. Winschoten, Netherlands: H.L. Heijkoop, n.d.

Ellern, Hermann and Bessi. *Herzl, Hechler, the Grand Duke of Baden and the German Emperor 1896-1904 / documents found by Hermann and Bessi Ellern, reproduced in facsimile*. Tel Aviv: Ellern's Bank Ltd., 1961.

Elon, Amos. *Herzl*. New York: Holt, Rinehart and Winston, 1975.

Feinberg, Charles L., ed. *Prophetic Truth Unfolding Today*. Westwood, NJ: Fleming H. Revell, 1968.

Fruchtenbaum, Arnold G. *Israelology: The Missing Link in Systematic Theology*. Tustin, CA: Ariel Ministries Press, 1993.

Grief, Howard. *The Legal Foundation and Borders of Israel under International Law: A Treatise on Jewish Sovereignty over the Land of Israel.* Jerusalem: Mazo, 2013.

Harris, R. Laird, Gleason L. Archer, and Bruce K. Waltke, eds. *Theological Wordbook of the Old Testament.* Chicago, IL: Moody Publishers, 1980.

Hechler, William Henry. *The Restoration of the Jews to Palestine.* London: 1884.

"Irenaeus: Against Heresies." Roberts and Donaldson, *Ante-Nicene Fathers.* Vol. 1.

Jamieson, Robert and Edward H. Bickersteth. *The Holy Bible: With a Devotional and Practical Commentary – Isaiah to Revelation.* London & New York: Virtue & Co., n.d.

Kelly, William, ed. *The Collected Writings of J. N. Darby.* Kingston-on-Thames, London: Stow Hill Bible & Tract Depot, n.d.

Lowdermilk, Walter Clay. *Palestine: Land of Promise.* London: Victor Gollancz Ltd., 1944.

Mackintosh, Charles Henry. *Notes on the Book of Numbers.* London: G. Morrish, 1869.

MacRae, Allan A. "Hath God Cast Away His People?" Feinberg, *Prophetic Truth Unfolding Today.*

Merkley, Paul C. *The Politics of Christian Zionism 1891-1948.* London: Frank Cass, 1998.

Oesterley, W.O.E. *The Psalms.* London: SPCK, 1953.

Patai, Raphael, ed. *The Complete Diaries of Theodor Herzl.* Vol. 1. London: Herzl Press & Thomas Yoseloff, 1960.

Pilgrim Portions: Meditations for the Day of Rest, Selected from the Writings, Hymns, Letters, etc., of J.N.D. London: G. Morrish, n.d.

Price, Randall. *Rose Guide to the Temple.* Torrance, CA: Rose Publishing, Inc., 2012.

_____, ed. *What Should We Think About Israel? Separating Fact from Fiction in the Middle East Conflict.* Eugene, OR: Harvest House Publishers, 2019.

"Rev. C. Simeon's Address to the Undergraduates of Cambridge, at their Meeting, October 31, 1836." Bickersteth, *The Restoration of the Jews.*

"Rev. W. H. Hechler to the Grand Duke Frederick of Baden. March 26, 1896." Ellern, *Herzl.*

Roberts, Alexander, and James Donaldson, eds. *Ante-Nicene Fathers.* Vol. 1. Peabody, MA: Hendrickson, 2012.

Robinson, Andrew D. *Israel Betrayed, Volume 1: The History of Replacement Theology.* San Antonio, TX: Ariel Ministries, 2018.

Ryle, J. C. *Are You Ready for the End of Time? Understanding Future Events from Prophetic Passages of the Bible.* Fearn, Scotland: Christian Focus Publications, 2001.

Scofield, C. I. *Prophecy Made Plain: Addresses on Prophecy.* London: Alfred Holness, n.d.

Spurgeon, Charles Haddon. *The Restoration and Conversion of the Jews: A Sermon Preached on Thursday Evening, June 16th, 1864 … at the Metropolitan Tabernacle, Newington, in Aid of the Funds of the British Society for the Propagation of the Gospel amongst the Jews.* Pasadena, TX: Pilgrim Publications, n.d.

_____. *Morning and Evening (October 12—Evening).* McLean, VA: MacDonald Publishing Company, 1973.

_____. *The Treasury of David.* 3 Vols. Peabody, MA: Hendrickson, 2005.

"The Mind of Christ Respecting the Jews." Bickersteth, *The Restoration of the Jews.*

Thomson, William McClure. *The Land and the Book; or, Biblical Illustrations drawn from the Manners and Customs, the Scenes and Scenery of the Holy Land.* London: T. Nelson and Sons, 1858.

VanGemeren, Willem A., ed. *The New International Dictionary of Old Testament Theology and Exegesis.* Vol. 1. Carlisle, UK: Paternoster Press, 1997.

Wilkinson, Paul R. *For Zion's Sake: Christian Zionism and the Role of John Nelson Darby.* Milton Keynes, UK: Paternoster, 2007.

_____. *Understanding Christian Zionism: Israel's Place in the Purposes of God.* Edited by Andrew D. Robinson. Bend, OR: Berean Call, 2013.

_____. *Israel Betrayed, Volume 2: The Rise of Christian Palestinianism.* San Antonio, TX: Ariel Ministries, 2018.

_____. "What Should We Think About Israel's 'Occupation'?" Price, *What Should We Think About Israel?*

Websites / Blogs

Behold Israel. "Israel Ranked 8th Most Powerful Country in the World Throughout 2019." Dec 2, 2019. https://beholdisrael.org/israel-ranked-8th-most-powerful-country-in-the-world-throughout-2019/.

Christ in Prophecy. "The Eastern Gate: Interview with Dr. James Fleming." Feb. 1, 2013. www.youtube.com/watch?v=qc8mlSGyNYg.

Jerusalem Post. "Zionism Is Not Racism: A Speech 40 Years Ago." Nov. 9, 2015. www.jpost.com/Israel-News/Politics-And-Diplomacy/Zionism-is-not-racism-A-speech-40-years-ago-432506.

Liphshiz, Cnaan. "Danish Bible Society's translation omits dozens of references to Israel." *Times of Israel.* Apr. 21, 2020. www.timesofisrael.com.

Medley, Samuel. "Awake, My Soul, To Joyful Lays." www.blueletterbible.org/hymns.

One For Israel. "Scott Schwartz (I Met Messiah)." www.oneforisrael.org/bible-based-teaching-from-israel/video/jewish-testimonies-i-met-messiah/scott-schwartz-how-i-met-messiah/.

Paul, Jonny. "Christian leader pivotal to Herzl's work recognized." *Jerusalem Post*, Feb. 2, 2011. www.jpost.com/international.

Smith, Chuck. "Numbers 21-28 (1979-82 Audio)." www.blueletterbible.org/audio_video.

The Times of Israel. "Rouhani urges Iranians to 'put all your curses on Zionists, US'." Mar. 18, 2019. www.timesofisrael.com/rouhani-urges-iranians-to-put-all-your-curses-on-zionists-us/.